Joint Force Harrier

Joint Force Harrier

COMMANDER ADE ORCHARD RN

with JAMES BARRINGTON

MICHAEL JOSEPH
an imprint of
PENGUIN BOOKS

Joint Force Harrier is a personal account of life in a
front-line squadron. The views expressed are those of
the author and do not necessarily represent the views
of the Royal Navy or Her Majesty's Government

MICHAEL JOSEPH

Published by the Penguin Group
Penguin Books Ltd, 80 Strand, London WC2R 0RL, England
Penguin Group (USA) Inc., 375 Hudson Street, New York, New York 10014, USA
Penguin Group (Canada), 90 Eglinton Avenue East, Suite 700, Toronto, Ontario, Canada M4P 2Y3
(a division of Pearson Penguin Canada Inc.)
Penguin Ireland, 25 St Stephen's Green, Dublin 2, Ireland (a division of Penguin Books Ltd)
Penguin Group (Australia), 250 Camberwell Road, Camberwell, Victoria 3124, Australia
(a division of Pearson Australia Group Pty Ltd)
Penguin Books India Pvt Ltd, 11 Community Centre, Panchsheel Park, New Delhi – 110 017, India
Penguin Group (NZ), 67 Apollo Drive, Rosedale, North Shore 0632, New Zealand
(a division of Pearson New Zealand Ltd)
Penguin Books (South Africa) (Pty) Ltd, 24 Sturdee Avenue, Rosebank, Johannesburg 2196, South Africa

Penguin Books Ltd, Registered Offices: 80 Strand, London WC2R 0RL, England

www.penguin.com

First published 2008

1

Printed in Great Britain by Clays Ltd, St Ives plc

A CIP catalogue record for this book is available from the British Library

HARDBACK
ISBN: 978–0–718–15399–1

TRADE PAPERBACK
ISBN: 978–0–718–15400–4

www.greenpenguin.co.uk

To the families, friends and loved ones of all those who fight for their country, for they are the ones who truly endure the fear and uncertainty of war

Commander Ade Orchard has received no payment for telling his story in *Joint Force Harrier*. All income that he would have been entitled to will, instead, be shared equally between the following two charities:

Combat Stress – The Ex-Services Mental Welfare Society
www.combatstress.org.uk

Royal Navy Historic Flight
www.royalnavyhistoricflight.org.uk

Learn more about the Royal Navy at
www.royalnavy.mod.uk

List of illustrations

18. The Navy's here.
19. It's not much, but for the four months of the det, this was home.
20. Burger King.
21. Here I'm enjoying a coffee with Hoggy, one of my more junior pilots.
22. A Russian-built Ilyushin Il-76.
23. A USAF C-130 Hercules.
24. The next big thing. A Predator UAV.
25. The United Nations Mi-26 Halo.
26. The squadron's engineers worked round the clock to keep the Harriers flying throughout the det.
27. The bomb dump.
28. The route to and from the bomb dump was well worn. Over the course of a four-month det we dropped over 100,000 lbs of ordnance.
29. 'Bombheads' – naval armourers – load a 540 lb dumb bomb on to the outboard pylon of a Harrier.
30. Pre-flight briefing.
31. The stencils sprayed on to the side of the jet give a pretty clear indication of the intensity of the operations flown by the squadron in Afghanistan.
32. The safety tags are removed from a 1000lb Paveway II laser-guided bomb before take-off.
33. Yours truly, just before climbing in to the cockpit.
34. With the jet chained to the ground, the squadron engineers run a high-power engine test.
35. The office – the instrument panel of the Harrier GR7.
36. The view from the pilot's seat, which clearly shows the position of the Head-up Display (HUD).

55. Santa's got a brand new sleigh.
56. When the scramble bell rings, the alert crews drop whatever they're doing and run to the jets.
57. On alert. A Harrier, armed, pre-flighted and ready to go, sits on the hangar, waiting for the scramble bell to ring.
58. Scramble. A GR7 gets airborne on another GCAS mission.
59. Wingman. A great portrait of one of the Harriers.
60. Flares fired from the Harrier's belly were our best defence against the threat from heat-seeking surface-to-air missiles.
61. A GR7 breaks right, high over the mountains.
62. A job well done. I spoke to the squadron on our last day in Afghanistan to acknowledge the success of the det.
63. Something to remember us by.

Acknowledgements

My sincere thanks to all the officers, men and women of 800 Naval Air Squadron whose belief, loyalty and professionalism allowed us to succeed and whose collective experiences form the bedrock of the book. To Carol, who accepted with ultimate grace and patience the impact creating this book had on the precious little free time a modern military career affords. To Nate who throughout the writing of this book thought that the manuscript was simply paper to draw on; I hope when you're old enough to understand and appreciate this book Afghanistan is closer to the peace it deserves. And finally to my dad, whose total pride and support along with my mother, throughout my career, helped make me who I am today. I wish you were here now to read it.

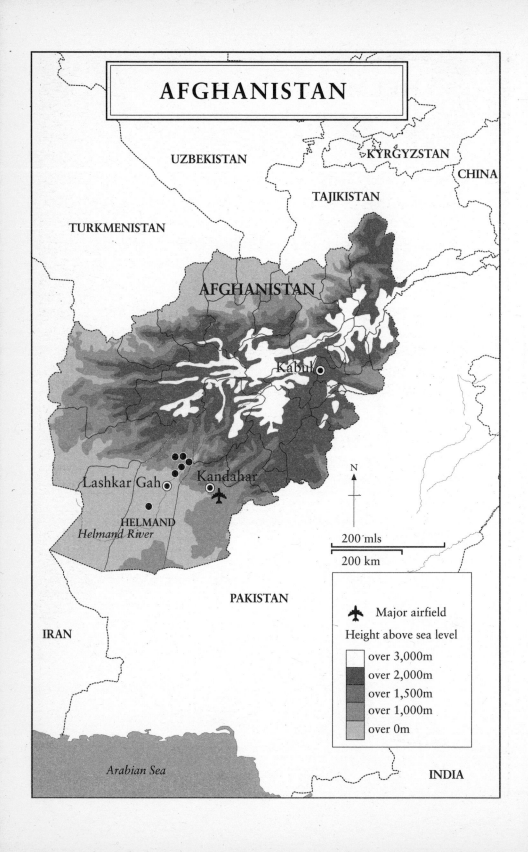

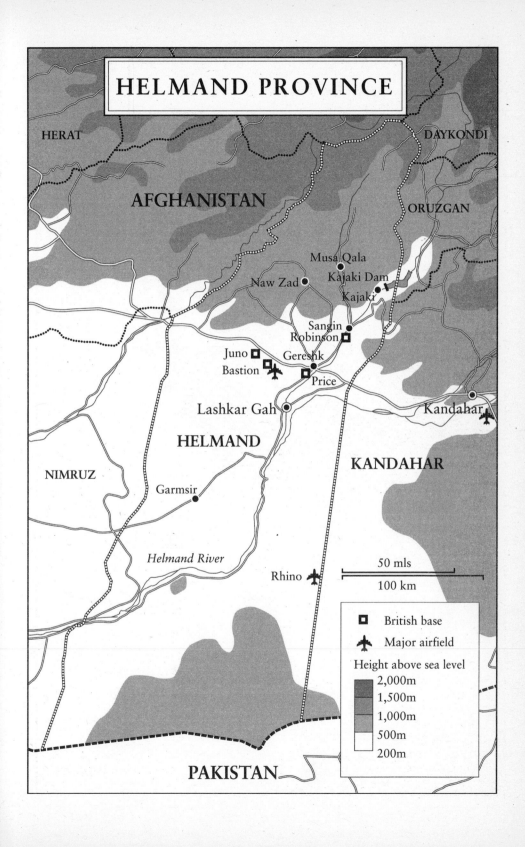

Prologue
Kandahar Province, Afghanistan

'Four Five, Four Six. Looks like your jinx is still working, boss,' Dunc Mason radioed.

'Don't you start,' I snapped. I was in charge, but all of my pilots seemed to be getting a lot more action than me. And they really enjoyed reminding me of it.

We'd been airborne for nearly an hour, cruising at 20,000 feet waiting for trade. The first part of the sortie had been very quiet and I guessed I would – yet again – be returning to Kandahar Airfield with the bombs still under my wings. But at that moment, as so often happened in Afghanistan, everything changed in a matter of seconds. A new voice cut through on the radio.

'Recoil Four Five, this is Crowbar. TIC Charlie declared. Position Eight Seven Charlie Quebec, keypad five.'

There were Troops in Contact – under fire – and we were the cavalry. 'Eight Seven Charlie Quebec, keypad five' told us how to find them – based on the normal latitude and longitude system that divides up the surface of the planet into oblongs. Each oblong was then divided into boxes, and each box given an alphanumeric code. Each of these then had a theoretical telephone keypad overlaid on it. 'Keypad five' put them right in the centre of the box.

'Recoil Four Five, roger,' I replied.

I turned the Harrier north and pushed the throttle

fully open with my left hand, checking that Dunc – my wing-man, Squadron Leader Duncan Mason – was still with me. As always, the adrenalin flowed as we increased speed. In these circumstances we never knew what we were going to find.

One of the first things we had to do was to sort out enough airspace for us to make our attack. With the Harrier pretty much flat out at over 500 knots, I quickly checked my map, then called Crowbar – the RAF Tactical Air Control authority at Camp Bastion.

'Crowbar, Recoil Four Five, requesting airspace Eight Seven Charlie Quebec two two zero to the deck and Eight Six Charlie Quebec, keypads three, six, nine.'

'Recoil Four Five, Crowbar, approved. Contact is Jaguar Zero One on Olive One Two.'

'Jaguar' was an American Joint Terminal Attack Controller (JTAC) and 'Olive One Two' the code for his designated radio frequency. I punched it into my radio.

Because communications quality with them was usually poor, I'd received the call from Crowbar on a non-secure radio, but as soon as we were heading in the right direction I switched to the secure frequency to talk to the troops on the ground.

We were approaching the designated position when I raised the JTAC.

'Jaguar Zero One, Recoil Four Five.'

'Recoil Four Five, Jaguar Zero One. Ready for fighter check-in.'

He needed to know what he had heading his way.

'Jaguar Zero One, Recoil Four Five. Flight of two UK Harriers. Playtime is ninety minutes. Recoil Four Five has thirty-eight rockets and two 540lb bombs, one impact and one airburst. Recoil Four Six has two 1,000lb laser-guided and GPS-guided bombs. All aborts will be in the clear.'

Over the secure radio we didn't need to use abort codes. He could simply tell us exactly what he wanted us to do.

'Estimate ninety seconds to overhead your position,' I finished, 'and we're approaching from the south.'

'Recoil Four Five, roger. Stand by for SITREP. We're a combined Afghan National Army and US patrol, and we've been out for three days. We're on the high ground east of the river and taking fire from the western side. The nearest other friendlies are two clicks downriver, and all friendlies are east of the river.'

'Recoil Four Five, copied.'

It was all vital information, part of the 'talk-on' – the passing of the targeting and attack data to us in a situation report by the JTAC. Our highest priority was to ensure we avoided causing any casualties to our own side, so finding out exactly where the 'blue', or friendly, forces were located was crucial. And as the patrol had been out in bandit country for three days we knew they were probably already low on ammunition.

'Roger,' came the reply. 'Look ahead for the river. To the east of it there's a small area of high ground with scattered vegetation, and a track leading across it. That's where we are. We're taking heavy machine-gun fire from the tree-line on the west bank, and we're pinned down. We can't go forward or back because there's no cover either side of our position. Until the bad guys are taken out, we're stuck here.'

And he didn't need to add 'and get here as quickly as you can and sort this out'. That was perfectly clear from the tone of his voice.

'Roger. Understand you're on the high ground east of the river, hostiles engaging you from the wood on the west side. Confirm.'

I knew that was exactly what he'd just told me, but when you're about to drop high-explosive heavy ordnance within metres of your own side, it's essential to know precisely where they are. Every member of the armed forces dreads being involved in a blue-on-blue incident and so we checked, double-checked and then checked again.

'Confirmed.'

'Roger, overhead now.'

As I broke into a hard turn, I looked down into the cockpit of the GR7. The altitude indicator seemed to swing on to its side as I was pushed deep into my ejection seat. Below me was a small river and on its east side, just as the JTAC had described, was an area of high ground. Directly facing it was a tract of trees and thick under-growth, and that was obviously where the insurgents had set up their ambush.

From the enemy's point of view, it must have looked like a pretty good spot. Although the coalition forces held the high ground, which should have given them a slight tactical advantage, the terrain and the position of the Taliban attackers meant that the coalition troops couldn't descend safely in any direction. They were effectively trapped on the hilltop, which was why they'd called for air support.

The situation was clear-cut and easy to resolve. We

knew both where the friendly forces were located and exactly where our targets – the Taliban – were holed up.

'Recoil Four Five, Jaguar Zero One. Type Two control, and we'll take the five-forty airburst.'

'Roger.'

As always, the JTAC on the ground made the decision. Essentially he's delivering the attack himself, and the Harrier and its pilot are simply extensions of his weapon system. For this attack, against a soft-skinned target like a gang of Taliban, he'd gone for the lowest-yield weapon we carried, apart from the CRV-7 rockets, and chosen the 540lb airburst bomb. The right choice, I thought.

But although the JTAC effectively owns the weapon, that does not preclude negotiation between him and the pilot, because it's conceivable that the aircrew might be aware of something that he isn't; civilians in the target area perhaps. Or the JTAC might have overestimated the distance between himself and the Taliban and be placing friendly forces in danger if the pilot attacks without checking all aspects of the target and terrain. I was satisfied that we knew exactly where the target was and that the friendly forces were over 800 yards clear of where the weapon would explode, so they were well outside the risk distance.

Dunc and I quickly carried out our checks. We cross-referred our ID of the target to ensure that the three of us – the JTAC and both pilots – were all looking at the same thing. Then we did the same thing with the weapon, double-checking the type, the fusing, the attack height and direction alongside details of the counter-measures programmes we'd have running during the attack to protect us from attack.

'Laser fires,' Dunc said.

'Roger.'

I pulled the control column further to the right, driving the Harrier into a hard 4G right-hand turn and glanced down to check my switch selection and target information. And I needed to confirm that Dunc's laser targeting pod was illuminating the correct spot. It was.

An optical sensor in the aircraft's nose-cone detected the reflection of the laser from the target and slewed a television camera towards it. Inside the cockpit, my screen displayed a clear video image of the target. Right in the centre of the screen were the cross-hairs, and right in the centre of these was the exact spot where the laser energy was pointing. Excellent.

'Four Six, Four Five. Good spot.'

With my left hand on the throttle, I began to set up the bomb release.

And then, in the instant that I looked up from the television display of the laser spot tracker, the massive white bulk of an Mi-24 helicopter suddenly filled my forward view, barely yards away.

I had less than a second to react. My Harrier was turning right, straight towards the UN transport helicopter — the wrong way to go. Immediately and instinctively I flick-rolled the Harrier's wings to the left and carved down and away from the big Russian chopper. That meant I lost sight of it, but I was right out of options.

'Jesus Christ,' I muttered, as the sudden change in direction tried to throw me all over the cockpit.

The Mi-24, NATO reporting name Halo, which had been a little above me and on a reciprocal heading, seemed to have come out of nowhere. And with a closing speed between us of well in excess of 400 knots, it was far too close for comfort.

'Watch out! There's a bloody helicopter right in here with us!' I radioed Dunc, who at that moment I couldn't see, watching my mirrors as the whale-like chopper chugged past me.

Focused on the attack, neither Dunc nor I had seen the thing approaching. But, in our defence, we *had* been busy.

It shouldn't have been anywhere *near* us. Not above a notified firefight area – all TICs were routinely notified to all airborne aircraft. And the Halo's crew should have then stayed well clear.

Whatever it had been doing there, the urgent evasive action I'd had to take had comprehensively cocked up my attack, and that irritated me because I knew that delays in delivering weapons could mean lives lost on the ground. All I could hope was that the coalition troops were well dug in and could hang on for a couple more minutes.

When I'd joined the Royal Navy, I'd expected to spend my career flying jet fighters off the deck of an aircraft carrier at sea. Bashing around over the dusty plains of Afghanistan dropping bombs on a bunch of heavily armed insurgents wasn't quite what I'd had in mind. But here I was. Having lost the opportunity to attack on the first pass, I had no option but to go round again. Still angry, I turned away from the target area to set myself up again for another attack. I rolled in again and began my bomb run.

I

'It's late,' I needled the RAF officer standing next to me.

'Your watch must be wrong,' he replied, glancing down at his own.

Any debate about the timing of the RAF's new Typhoon meant a jibe from a Royal Navy pilot was inevitable. The truth was, though, that for all the traditional rivalry between the Navy and the RAF, we were now working together much more closely than we ever had in the past.

It was a beautifully sunny day in the tiny Midlands county of Rutland. RAF Cottesmore was heaving with top brass from both services. The Chief of the Air Staff was rubbing shoulders with the First Sea Lord and the Commander-in-Chief Fleet, and there were too many two-, three- and four-star officers to count. Virtually all the members of the Navy and Air Force Boards seemed to be there. Then there were all the families, and finally the press, both general and specialist, because it was clearly going to be a big news day. *Jane's Defence Weekly*, *Air Forces Monthly* and most of the other military and aviation publications had sent reporters and photographers to witness the three separate but interrelated events.

The third of April 2006 was the day that 3 (F) Squadron RAF – the 'F' standing for 'fighter' – one of the Royal

Air Force units flying within the new Joint Force Harrier (JFH) construct, was being decommissioned. It was then to be immediately recommissioned as a Eurofighter Typhoon squadron. Those were the first two ceremonies of the day. The third and final event was where I came in: the recommissioning of 800 NAS as a purely Royal Navy squadron to fly the Harrier GR7, but still operating within JFH.

At that time 800 NAS was still smarting from the retirement of its long-serving Sea Harriers. The original idea of JFH had been to bring the Navy's Sea Harrier fighters and the RAF's ground-attack Harriers together under a single command. But then the decision was made to take the Sea Harrier out of service. With its demise the Fleet Air Arm lost its ability to provide air defence for the rest of the Navy.

Without the Sea Harrier, the Falkland Islands would probably still be flying the Argentine flag, and all of us in the Navy knew it. And if another hostile power suddenly decided to appropriate one of the other odd bits of territory Britain still has dotted about the globe, there wouldn't now be very much that the Royal Navy, at least, would be able to do to stop them. And we all knew that as well.

I don't think anyone in the Fleet Air Arm was happy when the axe fell on the Sea Harrier but, in the end, it really was the only sensible option.

The final version of the Sea Harrier, the FA2, was fitted with enhanced avionics, top-drawer radios and navigation kit, plus the ground-breaking Blue Vixen radar system, one of the best in the world and later used as a development base for the state-of-the-art radar installed in the new Typhoon. The Blue Vixen, linked to the brilliant Raytheon AIM-120 AMRAAM missile (also known as the 'Slammer'), created a fantastic weapons system that allowed the FA2 to excel in the long-range firefight. This was an environment where speed and manoeuvrability were much less important than target acquisition and a good long-distance missile. And in this situation the Blue Vixen and the AMRAAM proved an unbeatable combination. The Sea Harrier's excellent operational ceiling also helped. It could climb higher than the RAF's Tornado F3, for example, being able to get above 30,000 feet while carrying a full war load on the wings.

Towards the end of the Sea Harrier's career there was a fierce debate about whether or not it could hold Q – that is, act as the QRA (Quick Reaction Alert) fighters used to intercept unknown aircraft approaching the United Kingdom – for a short period of time, to relieve the Tornado F3 fleet. At that time the Tornado fleet was short of two squadrons' worth of the best-capability F3s, which had been loaned to Italy to plug the gap between their old Lockheed F-104 Starfighters and the Italian Air Force's own Typhoons.

The response from the RAF to this suggestion was a refusal, on the grounds that, because the Harrier wasn't supersonic, it didn't have the capability to do the job required. The Tornado *is* supersonic, and the RAF maintained that this meant it could reach the intercept point quicker than a subsonic Harrier, but this argument is somewhat simplistic and misleading. Nobody would dispute that, once in the air, the Tornado could go like a bat out of hell and reach any designated point faster than a Harrier, but the crucial phrase is 'once in the air'.

With its new navigation system, the Sea Harrier FA2 could get off the ground in about five minutes, but to get a Tornado airborne took significantly longer. In the extra time the Sea Harrier could travel about sixty miles, which, for an aircraft based at a Scottish airfield and responding to a Russian Bear or Badger bomber heading south towards the UK, might easily be a third of the distance to the intercept. So in most cases, from the time an alert was declared to the time the intercept would take place, there would actually have been little difference between the Harrier's and the Tornado's response times.

And there were other factors too. The Harrier, with a full weapon load, would be doing about Mach 0.85 at around 35,000 feet. The Tornado, carrying a similar load, would realistically be stuck about 10,000 feet lower and, even though it might be supersonic, it wouldn't be overtaking the Harrier very quickly. Partly for noise abatement but mainly to save fuel, the Tornado would be unlikely to travel all the way to the intercept at high supersonic speeds. And, finally, with its Blue Vixen and fully integrated AMRAAM system, the Sea Harrier actually had a better long-range weapon capability than the Tornado did at the time, particularly in its ability to engage targets at very high altitudes.

As a Sea Harrier pilot, I felt that allowing the FA2 to hold Q might have relieved some of the pressure on the Tornado F3 force, and been a sensible role for the jet to occupy as it approached the end of its service life. In defence of the UK, the always underestimated 'Shar' would, I suspect, have acquitted itself just fine. But the aircraft did have its limitations.

Even in its ultimate FA2 form, the Sea Harrier didn't have a tremendous range or endurance compared with more modern aircraft but, from a fleet defence point of view, it had been exactly what we needed. It was small, simple, robust, reliable and easy to maintain.

Its major disadvantage, though, turned out to be its engine. Operating in the hot air of the Middle East, or even the Mediterranean summer, it didn't have sufficient thrust to land vertically on the deck of a carrier if it was still carrying all of its weapons. And dumping unused Slammers – each one costing the British taxpayer just under £200,000 – into the sea before being able to land was neither an attractive nor an acceptable option. In short, the Sea Harrier was an evolutionary dead end. But the Navy, to its credit, had the good sense to recognize this. Money allocated to the aircraft's development was diverted and enabled the service to buy into the Joint Force Harrier programme and share the RAF's ground-attack Harrier GR7s. And in retrospect this *was* a good decision.

If the Royal Navy *hadn't* taken this route, the retirement of the FA2 wouldn't have merely marked the end of an era, but could also have spelt the end of naval fixed-wing aviation itself. If the Royal Navy had decided to persevere with the Sea Harrier FA2, in 2006 the aircraft would probably still have reached the end of its operational life, and there would have been no replacement on the horizon.

Instead the Fleet Air Arm now had access to a proven machine that had played a crucial role in nearly every war of recent years. And that, sadly, couldn't be said for the old FA2, although it wasn't for want of trying.

We'd pushed very hard to get involved in the 1991 Gulf War with our Sea Harriers. That year my squadron was on the *Ark Royal* in the eastern Mediterranean, basically acting as the Cyprus guard ship. We were able to demonstrate that we could reach the areas to the west of Baghdad from the carrier's position, though that would have meant overflying Israel, which might not have been the smartest of ideas. But in fact we never got involved, and with hindsight I believe this was probably the right decision.

I think the real question here is: what would the Sea Harrier have been able to do if we *had* got involved? The answer is: not a lot. The FA2 was a fighter aircraft, and the reality is that after the first two or three days it would have had almost nothing to do, because what was left of the Iraqi Air Force stayed firmly on the ground. There were very few pure fighter tasks, only CAP – Combat Air Patrol – around the carriers, and even that would have been problematic for the Sea Harrier.

This was because the carrier zones were so far from mainland Iraq that the FA2, with its very limited endurance, would have had to spend a lot of its time getting fuel in the tanker stacks, and not very long on task. The F-15Cs, in contrast, which carried out the majority of the air-defence tasks during this period, could manage about ninety minutes on task before they needed to refuel. The bottom line was that the UK's contribution to the

1991 Gulf War simply didn't require the Sea Harrier's participation.

But during Operation TELIC, the 2003 invasion of Iraq, the RAF's Harrier GR7s played an important and valuable role. And I know that because I was flying one of them.

And I can say categorically that for all my time flying Harriers – nearly twenty years now – while I felt a sense of achievement returning from deployments to Bosnia, it was coming back from Operation TELIC in 2003 as one of the first two RN pilots to migrate over to the RAF as the JFH concept took root that was truly a defining moment in my flying career. I suddenly realized that with the right gear – and even then I believed that the Harrier GR7 *was* the right gear – your effectiveness on the battle-field was just immense.

The reality is that, as a fighter pilot, you're unlikely to ever find out how good the combination of you, your aircraft and your weapons really is. The last time any British fighter actually shot down an enemy aircraft was over the Falklands. You can practise and train, and do as well as you can in exercise scenarios, but you never *actually* know whether you are good enough at your job. And that's because, unless there's another major conflict, you will simply never face an armed enemy aircraft in air combat. But when you're employed in air-to-ground operations you're fulfilling your primary tasking all the time. You know immediately if you've delivered the weapon cor-rectly and accurately. That gives you a kind of immediate and unarguable feedback that simply doesn't exist in the world of modern air-to-air combat.

In the Balkans campaign in the mid-1990s, FA2s were used to attack Serb positions with 1,000lb bombs, but there were severe problems with aiming these. Operational constraints meant that the bombs had to be dropped from high level, around 10,000 feet, but the sighting system was designed for fairly low-level releases, so the pilots had to try to compensate for this inadequacy in their attacks.

The result was at best crude and the bombing very inaccurate and not particularly effective. The Harrier GR7, in contrast, was designed from the first for Close Air Support operations. Its primary weapons are bombs of various sizes, CRV-7 rockets and the Brimstone and Maverick anti-armour tactical air-to-ground missiles. And that was the aircraft that 800 NAS was now going to be flying.

With the recommissioning of the squadron in April 2006, the focus of Fleet Air Arm fixed-wing aviation changed dramatically, through the simple expedient of now possessing the right aircraft to do the job required in today's theatre. With the GR7, we were no longer in the business of fleet air defence. Instead we were going to have to learn a new discipline – Close Air Support and ground attack.

And we needed to get up to speed quickly. Because, while both services enjoyed the ceremony, at Cottesmore that day in April, I was only too aware that the Harriers were needed to support British troops fighting in Afghanistan, and that we were scheduled to deploy there in under six months.

But before we went we would be indulging in more traditional pursuits. Within a fortnight we'd be embarking aboard HMS *Illustrious* in the Mediterranean.

2

We took off from RAF Cottesmore just after 10am on 13 April 2006, flying as two three-ship formations, split by forty minutes, and routeing down across France. An Air Group normally deploys to its parent aircraft carrier in a civilized and agreeable manner off the south coast of England, usually just off St Catherine's Point, which is nice and close to the Royal Naval Air Stations at Yeovilton and Culdrose in the event of any problems with either aircraft or ship. It was different for us, because the joining point for the squadron was further away. In fact it was nearly 2,000 miles further away, because the *Illustrious* was already in the Mediterranean, steaming just off Crete and heading east towards the Suez Canal.

Each formation was accompanied by an RAF Vickers VC10 tanker that stayed with them as far as Sardinia and then turned for home after giving each jet a last top-up. Averaging about 360 knots with the tanker trail, the transit took nearly five hours. And at the end of it one of my pilots, Lieutenant Brian Semple, known in the squadron as 'Bernard' and fresh out of the training squadron, successfully recovered on board a ship for the first time in his life. And the challenge of that was not to be underestimated. It was not just his first carrier landing, it was the first time he'd ever deployed as part of a Naval Air Squadron.

'It's strange, boss,' he told me in the briefing room afterwards, 'but when we were out there in the low wait I was watching you, focusing on your aircraft, but also watching the ship steaming along. And then the sun glinted off the rank tabs on your shoulder – those three thick gold bars – and it suddenly dawned on me that I'd finally made it to a Navy squadron.'

That might seem a strange remark, but I knew exactly what he meant. Although Bernard was a Royal Navy lieutenant, he had never really been *in* the Royal Navy. He was one of the first-ever straight-through GR7 Harrier pilots, so apart from his brief few months at Britannia Royal Naval College at Dartmouth, his flying grading at Yeovilton in Somerset and the odd visit and hold-over, he'd never really spent any time in the Navy itself. All the rest of his military career up to that point had been spent entirely within the RAF's pilot training system, just wearing a different colour uniform. So, for him, being a Royal Navy pilot in a Royal Navy squadron on a Royal Navy ship was in every way a new experience. And he wasn't the only member of the squadron discovering for the first time what life was like on board a warship.

Implicit in the Joint Force Harrier concept is the ability to mix Royal Navy and Royal Air Force personnel within the same squadron, and one of our first 'tame crabs' was Squadron Leader Dunc Mason, a former Red Arrow pilot and all-round good egg.

Dunc was a big, well-built guy and kept very fit. He was always quite jovial and gregarious, and had a great sense of humour – which, as he often pointed out, he really needed if he was going to be forced to continue working with the Royal Navy.

He was posted at pretty short notice to the fledgling Naval Strike Wing – which at the time consisted only of 800 NAS – from 1 (F) Squadron RAF as one of the flight commanders, and deployed to the carrier just ten days later. He'd served for three years on 3 (F) Squadron, flying Harriers from 1997 to 2000, but hadn't previously 'enjoyed' landing an aircraft on a carrier at sea.

But at least he didn't have to fly out to the ship in a GR7: instead he embarked like a gentleman up the gangway when the *Illustrious* docked in northern Crete. When I saw him for a drink in the wardroom bar a few days later, he explained what a delightful experience that had been.

'I carted all my kit on to the boat . . .'

'In the Royal Navy, Dunc,' I interrupted, 'a boat is something you either row or sail, or a submarine. This is a *ship*.'

His smile said he knew what I was up to.

'Anyway, I was told to follow someone who had some idea where the hell he was going, because it's ridiculously easy to get lost on this thing. There's a maze of compartments, rooms, cabins, galleys, gulches, corridors, staircases, even a bloody great hangar. None of the spaces have any windows, so you've no idea where you are in the ship, and there's not even a signpost pointing the way to the officers' mess . . .'

'That'll be the wardroom,' I said.

When he said he returned to his own room, I was about to say 'cabin' but instead took another sip of my beer and let him continue: 'It was a surprisingly spacious seven foot square and was going to be my home for the next two months. Luckily I hadn't brought a cat with me, because there was sod-all room to swing one.'

Shooting a mock-defiant look at me, he pressed on: 'The bed – I refuse to call it a bunk – was easily two or three centimetres wider than the width of my shoulders, so that was pretty much like sleeping on a plank, and it's even got straps, for God's sake, so I can lash myself into it in a rough sea. That's really encouraging. And I didn't discover the icing on the cake until we sailed off into the Mediterranean.'

He paused and sank a significant proportion of his beer.

'Which was what?' I asked.

'My room is conveniently located right next to the rudder. This primitive steering device is in constant motion and sounds like a distressed whale. It takes some getting used to.'

'Some people,' I pointed out, 'find the noise comforting.'

'They must be completely bloody demented,' he laughed.

'It's life on board ship,' I said. 'You'll get used to it. So how was your first flight?'

When Harriers are launched from a ship everything is calculated down to the tiniest detail, much more so than when operating from a land base. And that means from the take-off run required in the heat of the Mediterranean or, as would become much more crucial later in the deployment, of the Indian Ocean, to the amount of fuel required on recovery to guarantee that the engine has enough performance to keep the aircraft in the hover while the pilot manoeuvres over the designated landing spot on deck.

'The planning was interesting. You're taller than me, just, so how the hell do you manage in that bloody room?'

Dunc had a point. Planning, briefing and post-mission debriefing is conducted in a large – by Navy standards – space near the stern of the ship, apparently purposefully designed with numerous hanging metal boxes and other accoutrements fitted with razor-sharp corners on which to slash your head open. So anyone standing over five feet three – which was pretty much everyone – ended up walking around there with a constant stooping gait to avoid head injuries.

'And the take-off?' I asked.

A huge grin creased Dunc's face. 'Now *that*,' he said, 'is really something else. It was exhilarating!'

The first few sorties we'd planned for our new pilots were fairly simple, designed to allow them to settle into the routine of operating from a carrier. The focus was on getting them to the right bit of the sky at the right time and letting them practise instrument flying in case of poor weather on return to the ship after a mission. But the big event of the first sortie, and in fact of every sortie, was undoubtedly the landing, and I knew Dunc had had an 'interesting' first landing on board.

Compared with landing, the take-off is incredibly easy. You simply line up the Harrier where the marshaller tells you, ensure that all your pre-take-off checks are complete and you've got all the switches and controls in the right place, then give a thumbs-up to the marshaller and wait for the Flight Deck Officer to give the signal to launch.

'That was a bit disappointing, actually,' Dunc said. 'In all the Hollywood films this always looks quite dramatic, with a snappy salute and a sort of lunge towards the sharp end of the boat with a kind of pointy outstretched arm. Not on this ship. The FDO took a quick look round, made sure the traffic light thingy was green and then, with typical British reserve, raised a very small green flag to just above shoulder height like a bored railway platform attendant.'

The moment you're clear to launch, you park the throttle firmly in the top left-hand corner of the cockpit, keeping your feet forced down hard on the brakes to run the jet up to its highest possible power setting before accelerating down the deck. As you imagine your feet going off the end of the ramp, you rotate the nozzles downwards to provide lift, until the forward speed of the Harrier has increased enough for the lift generated by the wings to keep the aircraft in the air. You carry out post-take-off checks and make sure there are no problems with the aircraft before popping up the gear and flaps, and gradually move the nozzles to the fully aft position.

Most pilots never tire of launching off ski jump at the front end of a CVS – the military designation enjoyed by the British *Invincible* class carriers. The feeling as you accelerate down the deck towards the ramp and then smash up into the sky is simply breathtaking.

The build-up to the launch was also interesting for pilots unused to operating on board ship. Much more time than normal is allowed for the pilot to get to the aircraft, to do a walk-round inspection and then get strapped in. Given the sea's constantly moving surface, extra time is needed for the alignment of the navigation kit and other systems. On top of that, normally only half of the external inspection can be carried out because the tails of the aircraft often hang precariously out over the side of the flight deck. The pilots have plenty of time to sit in the cockpit with the canopy open and watch the naval hardware being energetically manoeuvred, all with the accompaniment of the constant hum of the four Olympus gas-turbine engines of the carrier throbbing away far beneath them. Aircraft engines are only started when directed by the FDO and, from that point on, all actions are initiated only with permission from the deck marshallers, or 'chock-heads' as they are affectionately known.

Some of the chains that tie the aircraft down to the deck will be removed and then power and flaps checks can be carried out. This done, the rest of the chains are released and the pilot taxies against power, following the marshallers' exact directions. Their job is extremely skilful, as they manoeuvre the aircraft within inches of one another, giving encouraging nods to the pilots while marshalling them past other aircraft or close to the side of the deck.

I looked round the wardroom, waiting for the squadron's Qualified Flight Instructor, Lieutenant Commander Neil Bing, known as 'Bing Bong', to appear. The QFI had, I hoped, a message for me, and for Dunc.

Dunc seemed to have run out of steam, so I prodded him by asking: 'And how was your first landing?'

'Ah, yes, well, the landing. That really focuses the mind. I know what the sequence is *supposed* to be.' Dunc stood slightly back from the bar and began checking off the points on his fingers.

The sequence sounds simple enough. You fly the Harrier downwind at 600 feet, then turn base leg towards the ship, selecting the short take-off and landing flap and staying level around the turn. Then you move the nozzles to sixty degrees and start descending towards the deck, continuing the turn to roll out so that the aircraft is pointing slightly towards the ship, at an angle of about ten degrees. You work out where to take the hover stop with the nozzles, depending on the wind, but ideally at about a third of a mile out. Then you adjust your forward speed to come alongside the ship, about one wingspan out from the side of the deck and at about ninety feet up. That height puts Flyco – the Flying Control Position on the port side of the bridge – on the horizon.

'I did all that, no problem,' Dunc said, taking another mouthful of beer as he described his approach. 'Then I looked for the deck marshaller, who ran out in his bright yellow coat and pointed at the spot he wanted me to land on.'

The carrier has several Harrier landing spots, from number two near the bow to number six at the stern.

'At first he clearly didn't think I was exactly on the spot, and gesticulated wildly to let me know that he thought I was a buffoon who should definitely have done better through training. When I was positioned more to his liking he then ran off, very sensibly.'

Dunc was recounting all this light-heartedly, but

performing a vertical landing on a moving deck is extremely demanding for any pilot. Throughout the deceleration it's vital to monitor the engine very closely to make sure that the aircraft has the performance to hover and won't just sink into the sea as the forward speed washes off.

And the really tricky bit is what comes next. Once established in a steady hover alongside the ship, the pilot has to transition across the deck exactly level and stop crisply on the centreline. Then he has to check his references to ensure that he isn't drifting forwards or backwards, and then take a little power off to lower himself smoothly but firmly on to the deck. As the wheels touch the steel he slams the throttle shut, puts the nozzles aft and taxies forward under the marshaller's directions to be positioned, probably with the aircraft's nose hanging over the side of the ship.

Dunc took up the story again. 'I was unlucky enough to be the first pilot to launch from this boat since the squadron reformed with the GR7s. So this meant that, as it was the first sortie with a new aircraft, and with a crab driving it as well, there was an audience watching from one of the upper decks – I believe you call these people "goofers".'

I couldn't tell whether he was showing off his grasp of the lingo or just taking the piss. Probably the latter.

'Anyway,' he continued, 'my first attempt at landing on the ship went reasonably well to start with, right up to the point where I was supposed to "transition across the deck exactly level". I looked down and could see that the chock-head was indicating number four spot for me. Not perfectly, but reasonably steadily, I positioned myself on the centreline, checked the fore and aft references and took off a little power to start the aircraft descending towards the deck.'

He was now in his stride, enjoying telling the tale and talking fast as he recalled the intensity of his first deck landing.

'This seemed to take longer than I was expecting. I took a bit more power off. But I found this new rate of descent a bit alarming, so I put the power back on again. And as I was doing this the aircraft hit the deck. Then I remembered that at this point I was *supposed* to have slammed the throttle shut. Too late. With the power still on I bounced back up into the air. Not considered good form on any landing especially when you're bouncing left, towards the edge of the flight deck.

'Oh Christ, I thought, I'm going off the side on my first landing attempt. I chopped the throttle back to idle and dropped back on to the deck, hitting with the left outrigger first, and several feet further left than I'd intended. It was such a heavy impact that I thought the outrigger was going to break and then the aircraft would roll over the side.

'But luckily the old girl held together and I was able to taxi forward. I noticed the hordes of goofers watching, and probably laughing, as I taxied towards my parking spot. As I shut down and waited for the other aircraft to land behind me, I thought about what had just happened and about all those people watching, and I comforted myself with the thought that perhaps it was one of those landings that felt a lot worse than it looked. This cosy feeling lasted right up until the moment when I climbed out of the aircraft, where the chock-head was waiting for me. "Fucking hell, sir," he said, "that was *shit*!"'

I smiled at Dunc as Neil Bing finally appeared beside us, his face serious.

'Boss,' he said, nodding briefly to me, then turning to face Dunc. 'I've just come back from the hangar, and it isn't good news. We all know the Harrier's a really tough aircraft, but that landing of yours, Dunc, was so heavy it's bent the main wing spar. It's a non-flyer, pretty much a write-off, and we're going to have to divert back to Cyprus immediately to have it lifted off by crane and wait there for a replacement cab to be flown out from the UK. That means we probably won't be able to get to Oman in time for Exercise MAGIC CARPET. The captain isn't happy about any of that, and the CAG's out looking for blood. Yours, to be exact.'

I'd never actually seen anyone literally turn white before, but the blood simply drained from Dunc's face when Neil mentioned the Air Group Commander. He could see what was left of his career in the Royal Air Force vanish straight down the pan.

'Really?' he croaked.

But I couldn't keep a straight face any longer. 'No,' I said, 'not really. The aircraft's fine. Just try and do a bit better next time, eh?'

'You bastard!' he spluttered, realizing it was all a wind-up, then checked himself: 'Sir . . .'

The strength of our relationship with Dunc was evidence of how well the new joint squadron was gelling. The Royal

Navy and the Royal Air Force are two of the best-trained, most highly committed and supremely professional armed forces anywhere, but they have rarely seen eye to eye on anything, from the Loyal Toast and passing the port to the use of a razor.

More seriously, as far as harmony within a joint unit was concerned, there are important differences in the way the Royal Navy and the RAF train the people who work on their aircraft.

It's a fact that RAF aircraft engineers are initially trained to a higher standard than our Royal Navy aircraft maintainers – though it's also generally accepted that this is not necessarily a good thing – because of the different ways the two services work. Naval maintainers are taken through basic training and then sent to a squadron to learn their trade on the job. The RAF feed their engineers through a much more comprehensive training programme so that when they arrive on a squadron they are already fully trained and can be put straight into a primary job.

Neither philosophy is right or wrong – they're just different – but the discrepancies between them had proved to be the source of some friction within the joint squadron before 800's recommissioning. My Navy maintainers had been growing just a little tired of being repeatedly told that they weren't as good as their RAF counterparts. In fact several of them had told me they were really looking forward to getting back into a 'proper' dark blue unit again.

My own impression was that almost all the Navy guys in 3 Squadron who were anticipating going to 800 NAS were desperate for it to happen because they had been working within the RAF system for so long, some of them for nearly four years. Most of them agreed that enough really was enough. As one of the chief petty officers told me: 'If I'd wanted to work for this length of time *with* the RAF, I'd have *joined* the bloody RAF.'

Inter-service rivalry is often seen as a good thing, on the basis that it makes you support your own side all the more. But I knew very well that a lot of effort could be wasted if Royal Navy maintainers became too determined to prove to their RAF counterparts that they could do the job just as well as them, when their *actual* job was to make sure that the aircraft were properly and correctly maintained and get them into the air.

And it wasn't just the maintainers. One evening shortly before we recommissioned I was in the bar of the officers' mess at Cottesmore with some of my pilots. We were talking about the forthcoming changes when one of my pilots remarked, succinctly and somewhat irreverently: 'It'll be a great relief when we finally get back to the Royal Navy and its traditions, instead of the RAF and its habits.'

But even after 800 NAS had formed, there were still RAF personnel involved with the squadron. Of the twenty-six excellent Air Force engineers who remained with us in our unit for the first six months, about half told me they would have been very happy to stay on longer because they really enjoyed what they did and liked working with the Navy.

But we knew we had to guard against just becoming a small and insular Navy unit. People just had to accept that despite the apparent separation into light and dark blue, and whatever the views of the personnel of both services, all Harrier pilots were now a part of a joint force – Joint Force Harrier. For some, that was a slightly bitter pill to swallow. There were those who still believed that the services should be separate, that the Royal Navy and the Royal Air Force should continue to operate largely independently.

But the reality is that the RAF is extremely good at what it does, which is getting aeroplanes into the air and then operating them to the very limits of both the aircraft's and the pilot's ability. And although some of the 800 NAS personnel may have been relieved to be working in a naval environment again, there was absolutely no doubt that we had all learnt an enormous amount during our time in 3 Squadron. After all, we in the Navy hadn't been involved in any form of land-based expeditionary operations for about half a century – since the Suez crisis – so we had a hell of a lot of catching up to do.

Indeed, without that solid grounding and invaluable experience behind us, I would have been a lot less happy about our forthcoming detachment to Afghanistan.

This was particularly important to me because there was another factor in this situation. Some time before we flew out to Kandahar I'd had some long chats with fellow Navy officers and the message had been clear: our performance would be very closely scrutinized. To be fair, any unit deploying to the frontline for the first time is under the spotlight. But the concerns I shared with every other squadron boss in a similar position were compounded in my own mind because we were the sole Navy component of JFH.

At a squadron level, people were less concerned about this. They were just eager to do a good job. And I didn't share the pressure I'd put on myself. In any case, in the end it was simple: 800 NAS had a difficult and dangerous job to do, and I could see the most effective way to validate both Joint Force Harrier and the squadron itself. Since actions speak louder than words, the best justification for the squadron's existence was for us to do a proper professional job of whatever task we were given.

Even so, the warnings I'd been given irritated me. I was very much aware that I was the commanding officer of a brand-new squadron and that in less than six months we would be flying out of Britain to operate in one of the most hostile environments on the planet. Afghanistan was exactly the kind of operational theatre where any shortcomings in our training and equipment, as well as in our personal abilities and commitment, would become very clear very quickly.

In this most difficult of environments the slightest mistake or error could result in the loss of an aircraft or, infinitely worse, the loss of a life, either of a member of the squadron or one of the troops we were supporting on the ground. That was the major concern for me.

And all I could do was ensure we did everything possible to prepare the squadron for the baptism of fire to come.

3

Since its inception in April 1933, 800 Naval Air Squadron has flown some fifteen different aircraft types in a wide variety of roles. These include dive-bombing the German cruiser *Königsberg* at Bergen flying Blackburn Skuas; carrying out reconnaissance sorties during the Korean War using Supermarine Seafires, and, latterly, low-level strikes with Blackburn Buccaneers. In the Falklands War, flying Sea Harriers from HMS *Hermes*, the squadron was back doing air-to-air combat, and this is the discipline that has occupied 800 NAS for most of its history.

Air-to-air – with all the images of Top Gun and dog-fighting that it conjures up – is arguably the *crème de la crème* of military aviation, but with the demise of the Sea Harrier that role could no longer be filled by our aircraft. Instead the squadron had descended, literally and figuratively, to the opposite extreme, and become a bunch of mud-movers, as ground-attack specialists are somewhat disparagingly known.

That, at least, was one opinion, held mainly by those who were still in a state of mild shock that the squadron was no longer engaged in fighter missions. But the reality was that the unit had been given a different job of work, and that job was ground attack.

In fact the Fleet Air Arm has a proud, if little known, lineage in this discipline, especially in Aden and Korea and, most significantly, Suez, which was entirely a land war. In that conflict RAF bombers operated from Cyprus and Malta, and Royal Navy Hawker Sea Hawks – an aircraft designed for both air-to-air and ground attack – carried out many sorties from the three British carriers *Albion*, *Bulwark* and *Eagle*.

During the Pacific Campaign in the Second World War, Royal Navy aircraft were flown from a variety of airfields, so operating from Kandahar would not be a novel experience for the service in that respect. Besides, during Operation TELIC in Iraq, Harriers – both US Marine Corps and British aircraft – operated from land bases as well as from carriers. But the Afghanistan 'det' would be the first time Royal Navy aircraft had ever been stationed in a landlocked country to conduct a dedicated ground-attack campaign, based essentially within a war zone itself.

This was the first time in thirty-five years that any of 800's pilots had been given ground attack as a primary mission. And the about-face in terms of tasking required a whole new outlook.

Fighter pilots are trained to think in three dimensions, to keep an accurate air picture running in their head of exactly who's behind, in front, above and below them, and many are very disparaging about the mud-movers. I've heard comments like: 'Their necks are fused.' 'They can't look up and they can only think in two dimensions.' 'They can only see what's right in front of them.' 'They're the kings of tunnel vision.'

Nothing could be further from the truth. Air-to-ground combat is complex and challenging, and can be quite brutal, and that's what some air defenders still find difficult to grasp. Some of the Sea Harrier pilots, in learning to fly a new aircraft, struggled a bit because, while they might have been able to maintain a good 3D picture and work out in their head what was going on forty miles from their present position, they found it a considerable challenge to operate with the pinpoint precision necessary for ground attack.

They needed to grasp the fact – and quickly – that the soldier on the ground, the man we mud-movers were there to support, had an engagement range of around fifty to a couple of hundred yards, because that was what his weapons were optimized for. He wouldn't give a toss about what was happening forty miles away, or even four. A pilot could be the best 3D picture builder in the world, but in ground attack the only thing that mattered was whether or not he could deliver a rocket accurately within perhaps seventy-five yards of his own friendly troops, or a bomb within 500 yards.

And in Oman, taking part in Exercise MAGIC CARPET, we were reminded that even the most reliable of weapons can sometimes develop faults that produce unexpected results. The squadron accepted an invitation to drop weapons on the Ramlat As Sahmah range in Oman and, with a single exception, they all landed precisely where they were supposed to. The odd one out was a Paveway 2,000lb laser-guided bomb that failed in flight and ceased responding to directional guidance. Far from impacting the target, it drifted well off course, ending up almost on the edge of the range boundary, and the outcome could have been disastrous. It was a sharp reminder to us that smart munitions are only smart when they work as advertised. We all knew very well that if a big 2,000lb high-explosive bomb went awry in Afghanistan it could be catastrophic.

When the squadron returned home to Cottesmore from '*Lusty*' our entire focus shifted to preparing for Afghanistan. With the concerns raised by senior Royal Navy officers very much at the forefront of my mind, I was determined that my squadron would be ready in all respects for the task ahead. But our preparations sometimes took an unexpected turn.

'Bit of a bloody cheek, this, isn't it?' I heard one of my pilots remark.

In getting us ready to do battle with the Taliban, the powers that be decided we needed to go camping to prove that 800 NAS could operate while living in tents. This ignored two facts. First, many of our pilots and maintainers had already worked in Afghanistan as part of the RAF squadrons in which they had essentially served their apprenticeships in JFH. Second, at Kandahar we would be operating from a large, well-equipped airfield where the only tents we would find would be the rubberized hangars used for aircraft maintenance.

I had mixed feelings about this training exercise myself. When 800 Naval Air Squadron was recommissioned it was a brand-new military unit with no history of having operated in such conditions. The counter-argument to this was that the day before 800 NAS was called into existence it had been – to most intents and purposes –

3 Squadron RAF, a fully operational front-line squadron with entirely adequate experience of all aspects of Harrier operations.

On balance, I think it was probably right to insist the squadron have a combat-ready work-up before going away on front-line real-world operations less than a month later. When a new squadron is formed it doesn't automatically have the experience and skills to go off to war immediately, and he clearly wanted to make sure he was signing off on a unit that was fit and competent in all respects.

The irritation felt by some members of the squadron was that the squadron was due to deploy to Afghanistan for a four-month stint – four months that included Christmas 2006 – and, three weeks before the personnel left for a very active war zone, the RAF top brass had decided it would be a good idea if they spent a few days living in tents in the middle of nowhere.

But at least it was going to be a whole-station exercise, what's known as Sector Level Training, in which everybody is involved, and that made us feel slightly better about it. Or, rather, that was the original plan. As the exercise date approached, it began to look as if the only people who would be 'playing' were going to be the members of 800 NAS. One of the RAF squadrons was already in theatre and the other, because of the pressure on the whole Harrier force, wasn't available. My efforts to explain their absence from the fun to the guys in the squadron were met with the usual scepticism. It began to look as if we were being placed under the microscope by the RAF, and some of the squadron members had their noses put out of joint about that.

In the end the exercise was de-scoped slightly. It was conducted on the base itself, RAF Cottesmore, rather than halfway up some mountain in Wales or somewhere equally bleak and remote, and fortunately it lasted just a week and a half. The squadron moved into a city of tents and began running an extensive series of training exercises that involved practising classic field operations of the sort that used to be carried out in Germany. And while the exercise scenarios bore no resemblance whatsoever to the conditions we were about to encounter in Afghanistan the important point about such activities is that they allow the command to test people in a slightly austere and inhospitable environment under a certain amount of time pressure, and with some sleep deprivation thrown into the mix, to see how effectively their decision-making processes function in those circumstances.

On the last day of the exercise it sounded as if the Third World War had broken out on the airfield. The Directing Staff simulated that the deployed operating base occupied by the squadron was being attacked and they had arranged a huge firefight. The number of blanks fired that day must have numbered in the thousands. All around me people were loading full magazines of blanks and firing their weapons at anything that moved and most things that didn't.

Great for relieving any pent up frustration, if not particularly useful for anything else except scaring the birds. That said, the constant clatter of semi-automatic weapons again served to focus our minds on the realities of the forthcoming deployment. It was just days now until we'd arrive in theatre.

4

The sun streaming through the aircraft windows woke those few among us who had, against all the odds, managed to snatch some sleep during the long flight out to Kabul.

Just after six in the morning, Afghanistan time, the doors of the old RAF TriStar opened and we stepped down on to the cracked concrete and into a beautiful, warm sunny morning beneath crystal-clear skies. But we weren't going to be on the ground long. Ushered into a handling area, we were processed like walking pieces of baggage. The structure was a big rubberized hangar filled with long, cheap pine tables, presided over by an aggressive Army logistics sergeant who barked out orders in a 'don't mess with me, sonny' tone of voice. To almost everybody's surprise, the sergeant was a woman, though you had to get pretty damn close to her to tell for sure.

In fairness, the place was packed full of people, many of whom had never been to Afghanistan before and had little clear idea about where they were supposed to go or what they should be doing. With that sort of chaos, it probably needed someone like her at the helm.

As we waited to board the Hercules for the last leg of our journey, I sat in a corner of the handling area, surrounded by squadron personnel, most of them lying snoring on camp beds, and inevitably began thinking about the pre-mission briefings and the task facing us. And, of course, my mind drifted to those who might be looking out for our failures rather than for our successes.

In truth, the comments my fellow Royal Navy officers had relayed to me were a matter of very real concern. I had every faith in my personnel, and was quite sure that each man and woman in the squadron had trained thoroughly and would do his or her very best to ensure that everything ran as smoothly as possible. But, for all that, there was no denying that it would be the first time many of them had operated in Afghanistan, or indeed in any war zone.

I'd tried to brief them as comprehensively as I could on what they could expect to find, and I'd ensured that they had attended all the required lectures and collected the correct kit. That was the easy part. Yet I was still worried that something would happen at Kandahar that would catch us off-guard. Some event, or even a chain of events, that would negate all our careful planning and training at a stroke.

The squadron motto was 'Never Unprepared' but suppose we didn't come up to scratch? Naturally the re-sponsibility would be mine: when you wear a commanding officer's hat that's where the buck stops. I knew I would have to be extra vigilant about absolutely everything that happened, good and bad, so that I could take any remedial action as quickly as possible.

Just as the TriStar had been when it left Brize Norton, the trooping flight Hercules to Kandahar was pretty full. As well as the 800 NAS personnel, the passengers included some of the people we would be working with in theatre and protecting, so there were quite a lot of Royal Marines sitting and standing in the back of the aircraft. About sixty per cent of United Kingdom troops deployed to Afghanistan during this period – October 2006 to January 2007 – weren't Army but Royal Navy and Royal Marines, the latter from 3 Commando Brigade.

Comfort was never the strong point of the ubiquitous C-130 Hercules. There's a long-standing joke in the military that its manufacturer, Lockheed, solved the noise problem by keeping it all inside the aircraft, and within five minutes of getting airborne I knew exactly why the story had started. The noise inside the hold was deafening, and vibration from the four turbo props throbbed through the aircraft. The seats were metal-framed webbing seats that offered about the same level of comfort as a plank of wood. It made your average charter flight seem like the lap of luxury.

As the big transport passed top of climb and settled down at its cruising level, I think everyone breathed a sigh of relief. Yes, we knew that the aircraft had excellent self-protection systems and that the pilots had done the trip dozens of times before, but it was still good to know that the aircraft was now out of range of any SAMs the Taliban were likely to have.

I'd recognized one of my fellow passengers immediately. Major Nick Williamson had been on the Advanced Course with me at the Staff College at Shrivenham in Wiltshire, and as soon as the Hercules levelled out I decided to go and have a word with him. I looked round, checking that everyone in the squadron was OK, then unbuckled my seat belt and walked to the back of the aircraft, where I'd seen Nick standing.

'Oh, hi, Ade,' he said. 'What're you doing here?'

'This lot' – I pointed at the ranks of people reading, talking or trying to sleep in the webbing seats, many of whom looked frighteningly young to me – 'are most of 800 NAS. We're relieving IV (AC) Squadron at Kandahar' – the 'AC' stood for Army Cooperation – 'it's our first time in theatre as a squadron, and we'll be out there for the next four months, including Christmas.'

'You drew the short straw, obviously.'

I nodded. 'I suppose we did. So what's your story?'

'I'm OIC designate of Z Company, 45 Commando – an aggressive manoeuvre group.'

'Sounds like fun,' I offered.

Nick grinned at me. 'That may not be *exactly* the right word,' he said. 'We're going to be doing regional engagement stuff, trying to track down the Taliban in their home territory, plus the usual convoy support and other proactive tasks. It's probably going to be fairly bloody.'

A white-faced marine got up from a seat just in front of us and squeezed past.

'He must be bloody desperate,' Nick said, as the man vanished behind a hanging tarpaulin. The Hercules's sanitary facilities are pretty basic. Just behind where we were standing was a lavatory bowl connected to a stainless-steel pipe, the output from which led God knows where. There was no cubicle or door, just a tarpaulin screening the bowl.

As we chatted, the aircraft's manoeuvres repeatedly caused the tarpaulin to swing to one side or the other, revealing an embarrassed squatting trouser-less figure, with each appearance greeted by hoots and whistles from his mates. It was better than crouching at the edge of the ramp and crapping into space, but that's the best you could say about it.

For obvious reasons we moved away slightly to stand right at the back of the aircraft by the raised ramp where there are two dispatcher doors, one either side, and both fitted with windows that gave us a good view of the ground thousands of feet below.

As we chatted there was a sudden loud thud that sent a huge shudder through the airframe and a double flash of light either side of the aircraft that we could both see clearly through the window.

'What the fuck was that?' said Nick, grabbing at a handhold and staring, transfixed, out of the window.

For the briefest of instants I was certain that we'd been hit by a missile, or at the very least had suffered a near-miss. But the Hercules seemed unaffected, flying straight and level and, despite the clearly agitated passengers in the hold, none of the aircrew seemed in any way concerned.

Moments later I realized what had happened. One of the aircrew had been testing the IR decoy flares in preparation for the aircraft's arrival in Kandahar, which was then a much more dangerous place than Kabul.

Deep in conversation, Nick and I had missed the warning from the crew. And so missed the opportunity to spread the word to our people. Instead, the whole episode just scared the crap out of everyone.

Nick was particularly irritated. He was quite happy at the prospect of facing the Taliban on their own ground, but the idea of being blown out of the sky before he even got to Kandahar didn't appeal at all.

But it served as another reminder that we were already in the middle of a war zone – and heading for one of the most active parts of that zone. It was very much a 'buckle up, Dorothy, we're not in Kansas any longer' moment.

Back in my seat, I glanced around at the squadron personnel, some of whom I'd known for years, others whose faces were comparatively new to me, and wondered exactly what would be waiting for us on the ground at Kandahar.

Before we landed, everyone suited up with their body armour. Like the take-off, the descent was tactical, which meant quite violent. The idea is that, in order to confound potential attacks, the pilot tries not to present a stable picture of the aircraft at any stage of its approach. So he mixed steep descents with hard turns until he finally plopped it down on the runway.

For squadron personnel used to operating from British airfields, our first sight of Kandahar through the windows of the C-130 was something of a revelation. On both the runway and the taxiway we immediately noticed that the place was covered in rocks and stones – not a friendly environment in which to operate aircraft with powerful jet engines. The problem was that the sweepers were fighting a losing battle. The condition of the taxiways and hard standings was so bad that for every stone they swept up, another got knocked out of the concrete. At the same time the airfield was so busy that trying to attend to the problem was difficult.

The runway had been fully resurfaced, but all of the taxiways were in very bad condition, the concrete crumbling and breaking up. This was at least partially because of the big transport aircraft that parked on them. Kandahar has a single main runway and an outer taxiway but, because the runway had been rebuilt by the Russians during their long but ultimately unsuccessful occupation of the country, it also had short linking taxiways running from the runway itself to the perimeter taxiway in a kind of herringbone pattern. These were designed as high-speed offshoots, to allow landing aircraft to clear the runway as quickly as possible to allow other fighters or bombers to land or take off behind them.

The offshoots made convenient parking slots for heavy transport aeroplanes like the C-17 Globemaster III, mainly because these aircraft were so big that few of the hard standings could accommodate them easily and manoeuvring such massive machines in relatively confined spaces could create problems. The standard procedure was to park the C-17s facing the runway, then use reverse thrust to back the aircraft out of their parking slots on to the perimeter taxiway, before moving round to the take-off position. It was the reverse thrust that seemed to do most of the damage to the surface.

Even as our Hercules taxied in, heading for the tactical hide, a section of hard standing surrounded by the ubiquitous international containers, the cargo hold was already warming up, and when the ramp dropped, a flood of heat rushed in through the rear of the aircraft and hit us in the face. This blast furnace of air was the classic welcome to the hot, dusty desert, that and the crystal-clear sky, marred

45

somewhat by thick black smoke belching from the engines of an ex-Russian transport aircraft taking off from the runway close to where our Hercules was parked.

At last 800 NAS had arrived in theatre, and instantly created another 'first', being the first Royal Navy fixed-wing squadron to deploy to landlocked southern Afghanistan, as well as being the first RN squadron to operate the Harrier GR7, the ground-attack variant of the AV-8B Harrier II, the legendary Harrier Jump Jet, from an airfield inside a war zone.

We climbed out of the Hercules to find a group of guys from IV (AC) Squadron RAF waiting for us on the hard standing, all very pleased to see us because we were there to replace them and that meant they were going to get home in time for Christmas. They had several vehicles available, and helped our personnel transport their stuff to the accommodation area and get settled in.

Wing Commander Ian Duguid, the Officer Commanding IV (AC) Squadron, was there to meet me. 'Squid', as he was known, reminded me of a terrier, but he was easy to get on with and told everything like it was. About anything to do with warfare he was very businesslike and efficient. We jumped into his jeep and he drove me to the opposite end of the airfield, where the Harrier detachment was accommodated. And on the way we did a little tour of the airfield to help me get my bearings.

It was quite a sight. Every kind of aircraft seemed to be there. Rows and rows and rows of helicopters, combat choppers like the Apache and lots of Chinook transport and troop carriers, dozens of C-130s and the enormous C-17 transport aircraft, and aeroplanes like the floppy-winged Russian Ilyushin Il-76s and Antonov An-24s that usually seemed to be flown by mercenaries. Simply scores of them.

None of the Russian aircraft looked as though they were very airworthy, but this was partly a design feature. British- and American-built planes tend to be quite rigid, but Russian ones just sag because that's the way they're built, with wings that seem to droop down as if they're tired. Antonovs, in particular, sag so much that they look as if they're broken even before you get in them.

There were little pockets of activity all over the helicopter area, in among this huge diversity of aircraft types, most of it centred around Rubb hangars. Technically known as 'tension membrane relocatable structures', these are semi-permanent rubberized fabric hangars of various sizes that are quick and easy to erect and dismantle. Each of them had a little ecosystem inside, with lighting, plug-in heating and other services, and at night it was easy to tell which ones were working because of the glow coming from inside. Inside them everyone was busy with the enormous amount of maintenance that needed to be done to the helicopters, which flew almost non-stop.

All the aircraft, in fact, flew much more than they were ever expected or intended to, so there was a constant stream of take-offs and landings. The place was noisy and dusty, with the ever-present background rumble of the heavy machinery employed in building roads, hard standings and other structures. Water trucks trundled around the airfield spraying water in a steady but fairly futile effort to keep the dust down.

One of the hangars caught my eye because it was so derelict.

'Can't anyone do something to repair that one?' I asked Squid. 'Or maybe bulldoze it? It's obviously not used any more.'

I pointed at the horrible, rusted structure with rotting pieces of corrugated iron hanging from the roof. Daylight streamed through the dozens of holes in the roof where panels were missing. I guessed that the OC would just confirm that it was scheduled for demolition. But his reply was most unexpected.

'You won't believe it, but that's one of the busiest hangars on the airfield,' he said.

'Really? Who uses it?'

'If I tell you that, I might have to shoot you afterwards.'

At the accommodation area I wanted to check that everyone was settling in, but as I climbed out of Squid's jeep I immediately became aware of a pervasive and very unpleasant smell. And I wasn't the only one who'd noticed it.

'What the fuck's that smell?' somebody called out.

'I think it's stale shit.'

'What does stale shit smell like, then?' another voice asked.

'Just like this, you wanker.'

'It's Poo Pond,' Squid explained, as we stood beside the accommodation block, trying not to breathe too deeply. 'The problem is that Kandahar Airfield was never intended to be used as living accommodation for the sort of numbers that are here, and one result of that is Poo Pond. In fact the name's wrong. It's actually a sodding

48

great *lake* full of piss and shit. It's just over there' – he pointed to the south-west – 'and it's basically the end of the sewage disposal system for the entire airfield, which is entirely inadequate for the task.'

'Wonderful,' I said. 'I suppose you get used to the smell?'

'I haven't,' he replied with a grin. 'It still closes up my sinuses every time I smell it. But there is some good news.'

'Which is?'

'You're not the closest to it: the Romanians are. Incidentally, rumour has it there was a $100 bet that nobody would be prepared to swim across it. Apparently three guys tried it – two Romanians and, predictably enough, one member of the Parachute Regiment. The para won, of course. Nobody would go near him for weeks.'

The accommodation was typical of military establishments everywhere – rows of long pre-fab huts divided into rooms, each capable of holding between two and four beds – and by now the squadron personnel were sorting out where they were going to sleep and stow their gear. Some of the comments I overheard suggested not everyone was entirely happy with what was available.

'Bit of a shithole, this.'

'Could be worse, mate. It could be a leaky bloody tent like we had back at Cottesmore. At least this is a solid roof over your head.'

'Yeah, well I'll take a leaky tent and people firing blank ammunition over this place, the smell of shit and the murderous bloody Taliban any time, thank you very much.'

*

'Right,' Squid said to me, 'once you've got your kit stowed and you've sorted yourself out, let's kick the tyres and light the fires. We'll get into the air and do a familiarization flight. See if we can find any trade for you to sink your teeth into.'

5

The Ops building at Kandahar was about two miles from the flight line, and as the two of us drove round the airfield it soon became clear that in some ways the drive there was almost more dangerous than the subsequent flight. We weren't allowed to travel on the runway, of course, or the taxiways, unless we were responding to a Ground Close Air Support (GCAS) scramble call, because Kandahar is a *very* active airfield, with stuff going on all the time. So we had to drive all the way through the camp on an unmade track that snaked over rough ground, very bumpy and dusty when the weather was dry, and which Squid told me turned into a quagmire on those rare occasions when it rained.

The track was bad enough but, to make matters worse, there were significant traffic hazards. Huge transporters would appear round corners without warning, easily big enough to swat our South Korean-built Ssangyong 4x4s right off the road, and there were dozens of other vehicles, ditches, bumps, potholes, obstructions, pedestrians and all sorts of other crap on it.

'Jesus, is it always like this?' I said, as yet another lorry appeared round a corner on our side and Squid took early avoiding action.

He shook his head. 'No, it's fairly quiet at the moment. Some days it's a *lot* worse.'

About the only good thing was that the track had been cleared of mines, but it was clearly going to be a nerve-racking ten or fifteen minutes in a 4x4 every morning before we even got to the dispersal area.

'The routine here's simple enough,' Squid said, leading the way into Ops. 'As soon as we arrive, we all get a full briefing to update us on what's happening, even the pilots who aren't scheduled to fly immediately. The situation here is really fluid and can change very quickly. If it all goes to the wire, we need to be in a position where every-body can get airborne, knowing the situation on the ground, and do whatever's required of them, without any delays.'

'Makes sense.'

'So everyone gets an Intel brief, an Ops brief and a Ground Liaison brief. And if you're the incoming Duty Officer, you'll then take over the desk and be given a handover, which explains where the aircraft are, what the serviceability is, what tasking had been given and what was going on in theatre.'

As well as these general briefings, the pilots collected their individual briefing packs prepared by the Squadron Intelligence Officer – or Squinto – and looked through what they were doing that day.

Assisted by the Operations Officers, the Squinto pulled together the tasking that came in from the command sys-tem, which was on a seventy-two-hour forward-planning cycle, so he always knew roughly what was coming up three days ahead. Twenty-four hours in advance, the Squinto and his team extracted the detailed tasking instructions from the computer, and put these into the briefing packs. They also loaded the basic reference points for each specific sortie into the mission planning system computers that the pilots would use to prepare their own detailed mission plans. These plans eventually ended up in the 'data bricks' we plugged into the Harriers before we started the engines.

As part of the main brief, the Squinto provided the intelligence update, an ops update and a briefing on the situation on the ground. In effect this was the most important part of the entire process, because we were there to provide a service to the troops on the ground, and, if we didn't understand what was happening down below us, we were a potential liability.

'Right,' Squid said. 'Once you've done all that, you sit down at the mission planning computer, locate the file the Squinto has prepared, and open it up. You'll find a big digital map of Afghanistan and all the relevant locations, with the basic mission and the reference points already entered. Then you can add anything else you feel is necessary for the mission.'

As we completed the full briefing and self-briefing process, he asked: 'Ready to go?'

'I'm ready,' I told him.

We walked through the main accommodation building, into the crew room, where some of the off-duty personnel were sitting watching TV and reading, past the main engineering admin area and into the survival equipment section. There we both collected the combat survival waistcoat that held our personal weapon. For this, the Navy's now standardized on the Walther PPK 7.65mm semi-automatic pistol rather than the old Browning 9mm. Because of the possibility of Taliban attacks against

Kandahar, we all either carried, or had rapid access to, our personal weapons at all times while on the base.

'Right,' Squid said. 'The last thing we do before leaving Ops is the out-brief.'

This took about five minutes, and was essentially a last-minute check by the authorizing officer that the pilots were ready in all respects for their sortie before they climbed into their aircraft. He checked that we'd done everything, and had collected everything we needed for the sortie. These checks also confirmed that we had our pistols, along with a wad of money so that we could try to barter our way out of a situation on the ground. Few of us had any illusions about how successful that might be.

We also carried a small, tear-proof sheet, colloquially known as a 'blood chit' or a 'goolie chit'. This second name was a hangover from Royal Flying Corps operations in the First World War in India and Mesopotamia, where local tribesmen routinely handed over captured aircrew to their women, who almost invariably sliced off their testicles as a first step in the negotiations.

The Afghan women had exactly the same reputation, but the chit was intended to avert this painful and brutal surgery. It stated, in English and all the major languages of the region, that we meant the people of Afghanistan no harm and that they would be handsomely rewarded if they could help the bearer reach the nearest coalition troops. It might have had some influence with the Afghans – money talks, after all – but it's not likely that any of these aids would have been much help to any of us if we'd fallen into the hands of the Taliban.

*

54

We walked out to the dispersal to get kitted up. Like a lot of the other aircraft at Kandahar, the Harriers lived in little fabric 'pods' which offered some protection from the wind, provided shade during the day and could be heated, though not very effectively, at night. In the dark I discovered these could look slightly eerie, a bit other-worldly, as I looked down the line and saw the noses of the aircraft poking out of these dimly illuminated saucer-shaped pods.

Even though the Safety Equipment (SE) ratings had already prepared our equipment and laid it out, getting kitted up was a laborious process because of everything we had to wear and carry. Squid and I pulled on the g-suit – a pair of tight-fitting over-trousers made of a kind of webbing mesh and incorporating air bladders – over our flying overalls. The g-suit, sometimes known as 'speed jeans', was plugged into the aircraft system. It automatically squeezed our thighs as the aircraft pulled high levels of g-force, to help stop the blood draining to the extremities and potentially causing a blackout or g-loc – a g-induced loss of consciousness.

Over the top of the g-suit we pulled on the cold-weather flying jacket, followed by the combat survival waistcoat, which carried everything we might need on the ground – food, water, flares, spare ammunition, survival kit, medicine and so on. This was a very bulky bit of kit, so the SE rating had to help us get it on and fitted properly.

The final layer was the life jacket, which went on top of everything else. This over-jacket carries the personal equipment connector and also incorporates a life vest.

We'd be unlikely to end up in the water if we ejected over Afghanistan, unless we were directly over the Kajaki Dam in Helmand Province when we bailed out. Even so, we would still inflate the vest if we did have to eject, as it would provide a good solid support round the neck, which could be important to avoid injury when we hit the rugged terrain below.

The last items we grabbed were a set of gyro-stabilized binoculars and our flying helmets and gloves.

One thing we'd noticed, back at the warehouse at Cottesmore, was that criticism by forces personnel, and inevitably the media, of the quality of some of the military equipment issued for use in Afghanistan and Iraq had prompted a massive over-swing to correct some of the deficiencies. As a result, a lot of the gear we were supplied with for this detachment was the best that the commercial manufacturers can produce. In the harsh light in theatre, for instance, brilliant high-impact sunglasses, complete with three sets of filters for snow, sand or sun, were particularly welcome. We were even issued with elasticated over-covers to turn our standard green camouflage-pattern rucksacks – very high-grade pieces of kit made by Gore-Tex – into desert-coloured ones. Throughout history, the British armed forces have consistently demon-strated an ability to make do with some less than perfect equipment. This time, it was a great relief to have access to such high-grade gear.

Fully booted and spurred, we stopped at the engineers' desk to look at the logbook for our respective aircraft and check for any notified faults or outstanding issues. We checked with particular care which weapons the book said were fitted to the aeroplane and how they were set up, and then signed out the aircraft.

That done, Squid and I strode out to our Harriers carrying our helmets. Already crowding the jets was a rating responsible for the weapons, plus the plane captain, the man in charge of the aircraft itself and an avionics technician. While we'd been inside getting kitted up, they had all been in and around the Harriers, preparing them for the mission. Powered by external generators, the jets' navigation systems were already aligning. I greeted the ground crew and climbed up the ladder to do my initial checks.

The first thing was to make sure the aircraft was safe to walk around, and that meant making sure that the master armaments safety switch was off, as this renders all of the weapon stations unpowered and inert. This switch is crucial, controlling not just weapon release but other systems, including the fuel tanks. The flares and self-defence systems are independently controlled.

Next I checked that the ejection seat was safe. This used to be done with steel pins that had to be manually inserted and removed. But in the GR7 there's now an oblong handle on the panel on the right-hand front of the seat that can be pulled backwards from the seat-locked position, where it says 'safe' and is painted green, to the 'live' position, where a distinctive red and white diagonal pattern is displayed.

Happy that the seat was secure, I put the helmet and the other gear on the cushion, did a quick sweep round the cockpit to make sure that all other switches were correctly set, then checked that both sets of igniters were working. Leaning in, I pressed the ignition button on the throttle, then glanced round to see the plane captain nodding. All of us could hear the igniters clicking away inside the engine.

I jumped down spent about ten minutes carrying out the external checks before finally climbing the ladder again to settle into the cockpit.

Strapping in was always a challenge, because we had so much gear on that we pretty much filled the cockpit. Each time we needed one of the maintainers to help secure the seat belts as we couldn't reach all of them without assistance. Especially at night, with very restricted visibility, we got used to doing everything by feel. Harrier pilots generally find most of their controls by feel, simply because most of the side panels are invisible without severe contortions.

Harnessed and ready to go, the safety cover was removed from the cockpit's delicate glass head-up display (HUD). I carried out a sweep from left to right around the various panels and controls.

On the right-hand front panel were the fuel system controls, behind those the radios and, right at the back, the slot for the data brick that carried all our mission details, and which I had prepared back at Ops as part of my pre-flight planning. The brick was a block of electronics, something like a removable hard disk, that I slotted in. Once this was in place, the mission was downloaded into the Harrier's computer. I programmed each of my weapons to do whatever I needed it to do, such as setting the impact angle for the bombs. On that first sortie my aircraft was carrying two 1,000lb laser-guided bombs, while Squid had two 540lb bombs and a couple of pods of CRV-7s.

The Harrier GR7 can be fitted with a variety of ordnance. The smallest is the CRV-7 rocket. Each pod contains a total of nineteen of these, and two pods will normally be carried. These are very flexible weapons, permitting anything from a single rocket to be fired to all thirty-eight of them in one go.

In terms of yield, next up is the 'five-forty' bomb, which comes in two guises. It can be configured to explode either on contact with the target or in an airburst above the target. The airburst configuration includes a basic radar altimeter, or radalt, that triggers the weapon when it reaches a specific pre-set height above the ground. In this mode the five-forty is normally used against soft-skinned targets like people and vehicles, when it's set to detonate at about twenty to thirty feet above the ground. Used in this way, the weapon has a lethal radius of some 200 yards. Outside that range, the blast would certainly smart a bit, and a piece of shrapnel could kill or maim, but most people would survive, so its effects are relatively limited.

The Maverick air-to-surface missile, weighing about 600lb, is one of the Harrier's primary weapons against moving targets. It's a subsonic rocket of fairly old design, but it's very good at what it does, and is equipped with either infrared or TV guidance systems.

The heaviest weapons carried by the Harriers in Afghanistan are the 1,000lb bombs. And these can be hugely destructive. Dropped through a hangar roof to detonate inside, the shockwave from one of these monsters would blow all the walls out, leaving nothing much more than a crater twenty feet deep and thirty across. Thousand-pounders can be 'dumb' – completely unguided, though nowadays they are rarely used in this way because of their inherent inaccuracy – or laser-guided. They can be laser-guided in isolation or laser-guided with GPS, and are spectacularly flexible and very accurate weapons. We can 'lase' the target without knowing its geographical coordinates, just by aiming a targeting pod at the objective or, with the latest version of the Harrier, the GR9 – which is a genuine digital aircraft – the pilot can create a set of coordinates from his own targeting system. The system transfers the GPS coordinates into the bomb and, when the weapon is released, it will automatically be guided to impact the GPS coordinate point. However, if it subsequently detects laser energy it will alter its flight path to follow the laser beam, ensuring pinpoint accuracy and flexibility after release.

The 1,000-pounder is the biggest weapon we use in Afghanistan. The Americans also use 2,000lb 'stores' there, but a bomb of this size is often too big to use – a sledgehammer to crack a nut. Bearing in mind the usual nature of the targets, it's rarely called for.

I set up the radios – the front one for talking to the JTAC and other control units, and the back for internal communication with my wing-man Squid; the airborne TACAN system that would tell me where my wing-man was in relation to my own aircraft; and dialled the last two digits of my callsign into the IFF (Identification Friend

60

or Foe) transponder. 'Recoil Four Two' was ready to go.

As I glanced across at Squid's aircraft I was suddenly very conscious of his much greater experience in theatre. I knew the aircraft I was flying as well as any pilot, but what was waiting for me – and for all my pilots – beyond the blast walls and razor wire of Kandahar Airfield was entirely new to us. I just hoped that we'd have a few days to get accustomed to the area, to finding landmarks and reporting points, and to RT, radio-telephony, procedures, before we got too involved with our primary tasking – taking on the Taliban.

That, it turned out, was a vain hope indeed.

6

Squid and I climbed up to medium altitude – each of us levelling at a different height for de-confliction purposes – as quickly as possible. Throughout our time in Afghanistan we were always very much aware that the climb to 10,000 feet was the most dangerous part of the flight, so we'd be watching the three rear-view mirrors around the frame of the canopy for any signs of missile attack.

Once established at altitude, I took a few seconds to look down at Afghanistan's stark, unfamiliar beauty. Almost as far as the horizon, the ground below me was a sea of reddish sand dunes, sculpted by the wind into shapes that looked remarkably like frozen waves. In the far distance a few steep-sided hills rose abruptly from the dunes, but for the most part the terrain was flat and largely featureless. A river snaked through the dunes off to my right, and I could clearly see a multitude of vehicle tracks that joined and crossed the river where it was shallow. Near the ford were dozens of sheep or goats, a number of people and a small cluster of tents erected close to the river bank.

Peculiarly, on the opposite side of the water the terrain was more grey and white than red. It was as if the river was a kind of demarcation line between two different soil types of different colours. And on the grey side there were again people wandering about and a few tents, but no animals as far as I could see.

As we cruised west, all the jet's systems were online. The relatively delicate heads on the targeting pods – easily damaged if hit by a stray stone on the ground – were uncaged.

The air-to-air TACAN counted down the range as I closed in on Squid's aircraft and, as soon as we were both visual, we joined up as a pair. Flying well above the threat envelope of any weapons likely to be in the hands of the Taliban, and with all our checks completed, Squid advised the air traffic controller back at Kandahar that we were 'going tactical'. Then he checked in with the Command and Control (C2) authority at Camp Bastion, the main British military base in Afghanistan, located near Lashkar Gah in Helmand.

'Trumpcard, this is Recoil Four One.'

'Recoil Four One, Trumpcard, roger. Traffic information for you. Bone One Two is working the block two seven zero to two nine zero. Whistler Eight Nine is working Perch Modified.'

'Bone' was a B-1 bomber callsign, 'Whistler' a fuel tanker and 'Perch Modified' one of the tanker tracks in the area. There were almost always tankers in the air over Afghanistan, simply because of the intensity of the air activity, and tanker tracks all over the place. The tracks' locations were repeatedly changed to keep the aircraft safe from possible surface-to-air missile attacks, and these locations were biased to the areas where it was anticipated that most of the trade would be coming from.

The callsign we used for the Harriers for most of this detachment was 'Recoil', followed by a number beginning with 'Four'. So the first sortie of the day would involve

'Recoil Four One' and 'Recoil Four Two', as listed on the daily Air Tasking Order (ATO) issued by the Combined Air Operations Centre (CAOC), followed by 'Recoil Four Three' and 'Recoil Four Four', and so on. 'Recoil Four Seven' and 'Recoil Four Eight' were always the two night-flying aircraft. Another callsign we were allocated was 'Junta Zero One', but this was purely for test flights, and at various times we also used the callsigns 'Devil' and 'Mamba'. Predictably enough, the American F-15 jockeys have always used 'Dude'.

There are various ways of indicating a target or other object of interest, but the way we did it in Afghanistan was to use keypoint descriptors – appropriate names given to shapes on the ground – and the first thing Squid did was show me how this worked. We flew to the Panjwayi district, to the west of Kandahar Airfield. This was the heartland of the Taliban, the very area where the radical group originally formed.

'OK,' Squid said on the radio, 'we're more or less directly over Panjwayi now. Look down and to your right. There's a large field with a smaller field directly beyond it. See them?'

It took a few moments, but then I saw what he was indicating. 'Got them,' I said.

'Right. Look above the small field, and there's an even smaller enclosure. Now look on either side of the big field. What does the whole shape remind you of?'

It took me few seconds to identify the entire shape, but then it was obvious. The conjoined set of fields formed a shape like a big fat body, smaller head, two arms sticking out, almost a carrot nose formed from a jagged tree, and a small square field above it that looked like a top hat.

'A snowman,' I said. 'A classic child's snowman.'

'Excellent,' Squid said. 'That's what we call it.'

So instead of the FAC – the forward air controller – trying to direct a Harrier pilot to a specific location through a maze of small fields and trenches and compounds or whatever, he could just say, 'Can you see the Snowman? Right, go two clicks east-north-east,' and the pilot would know exactly where he meant. It was a quick, unambiguous and very effective method of indicating a target or position.

This might seem a strange method of reporting locations and contacts, but it allowed both new and experienced pilots to get familiar with their theatre of operations very quickly. Although there are other ways of doing the same thing – various classified methods – using keypoint descriptors was probably the easiest.

We had barely started following Squid's route when our plans were thrown out of the window.

'Recoil Four One, Trumpcard. TIC Charlie declared at Garmsir.'

'Recoil Four One, roger. En route,' Squid acknowledged.

We turned the two Harriers south and gathered speed. I could feel the acceleration pressing my body back in the seat as I advanced the throttle to the stops.

On the way to Garmsir we learnt the rest of the story. Most actions involving coalition troops in Afghanistan take place when patrol members come under fire somewhere and call in air support if they find themselves outnumbered or for some other reason are unable to handle the contact themselves.

I thought about what we could do to help. Both our Harriers were armed with bombs – Squid's with two five-forties and mine with a pair of 1,000lb Paveways. His aircraft was also carrying rocket pods and mine was fitted with a laser targeting pod under the fuselage.

'Widow Zero Two, this is Recoil Four One.' The 'Widow' callsign indicated that we were talking to a British JTAC.

'Recoil Four One, Widow Zero Two. Ready for fighter check-in.'

'Widow Zero Two, Recoil Four One. We're two UK Harriers. Playtime is fifty minutes. Recoil Four One has thirty-eight rockets and two five-forties, one impact and one airburst. Recoil Four Two has two 1,000lb laser-guided and GPS-guided bombs. All aborts will be in the clear. Estimate one minute to your overhead, and approaching from the north.'

'Recoil Four One, roger. Stand by for SITREP. We're a British TACP on JTAC Hill, and taking heavy fire from a compound about 500 yards down to the south. No other friendlies known to be in the area apart from the normal coalition checkpoints near the district centre.'

JTAC Hill was on the outskirts of Garmsir District Centre, on which there was a near-permanent Tactical Air Control Party (TACP) consisting of four men – the JTAC himself, two signallers and a trooper – and they had come under heavy fire from a group of Taliban close to the end of one of the roads below the hill.

The TACP's job was to call in 'fast air' in support of

troops on the ground, because that area had been the scene of countless clashes between coalition forces and the Taliban. Indeed the area below JTAC Hill looked very much like the Somme in the First World War, pock-marked with numerous craters testifying to the intensity of the coalition's bombing. JTAC Hill was such a well-established location in the area that it was both a regular visual reporting point – it was one of the keypoint descriptors we used from the air – and also a normal waypoint in our navigation kit. So Squid had no problem at all in identifying the patrol's location and pointing it out to me, and I could see it clearly enough through the onboard optics.

'Roger, Widow Zero Two.'

'Recoil Four One, Widow Zero Two. We called up an Apache to try to suppress the enemy fire, but he's just been engaged by an RPG so he's had to haul off. It was a real near-miss: it passed within about thirty yards of his tail rotor. He's now moved to the western side of the river, out of range, and he's unable to continue the attack.'

The Boeing AH-64 Apache attack helicopter is designed to be tough enough to withstand the half-inch rounds fired from a heavy machine-gun, but a rocket-propelled grenade, or RPG, is altogether a far more serious weapon. A direct hit from one of those, anywhere on the airframe or on the rotors, would almost certainly cause the loss of the Apache and its crew. It was no wonder that the helicopter had sensibly withdrawn to wait for the cavalry – which was us.

A further complication was that, although the JTAC had established the location of one group of Taliban, there was a strong possibility that other groups were lying in wait elsewhere in the immediate area, hoping either to bring down the Apache with another RPG or just to kill the members of the TACP.

'Recoil Four One, Widow Zero Two. Type Two control, and we'll take one of the five-forties.'

'Roger, Recoil Four One.'

Every conflict has extremely detailed Rules of Engagement, and Afghanistan was no exception. Our two Harriers were carrying very different weapons, and the JTAC had decided, quite correctly, that the most appropriate one for the target we were facing was hanging under the wing of Squid's aircraft. My Harrier's weapons – 1,000lb bombs – were simply too big, on grounds of collateral damage and proportionality.

When he calls in 'fast air' a JTAC offers one of three different kinds of control. Type One is something of a hangover from the Cold War, a classic run-in from an Initial Point, where the JTAC can see both the target and the attacking aircraft and will clear the aircraft in as soon as he's certain that the pilot has seen and identified the correct target.

Type Two means that the JTAC can see the target from the ground – not difficult in the present circumstances as the Taliban were just a few hundred yards away from him on the other side of the river – but can't necessarily see the responding aircraft either because they are too high, as we were in this case, or are approaching from a direction where he lacks a clear line of sight. For Type Two control, the JTAC needs confirmation from the pilot that he can see and has properly identified the target, and he will only call him in and clear him to drop when he is satisfied.

Type Three control means that the JTAC can see neither the target nor the attacking aircraft – there can be a number of reasons for this – and all he is able to do is tell the pilot that there's a target out there, and place the onus on the aircrew to find, identify and engage it.

As we overflew the target area for the first time, our immediate problem was to identify the specific compound where the Taliban gunmen were hiding out. I looked down from the cockpit as I pulled the Harrier into a turn. JTAC Hill was clearly visible, but there were a number of compounds that could have been where the insurgents were hiding out. One of the problems with picking out areas occupied by hostile forces from the air is that we can neither see nor hear firing that is perfectly evident to the troops on the ground. An additional problem in Afghanistan is that there are usually very few ground features clear and distinctive enough to use as markers.

Then I had an idea. The Apache had been *attacked* by an RPG. The pilot was going to remember *exactly* where the weapon had been fired at him. I thumbed the RT button.

'Squid,' I called over the back radio, 'why not get the Apache to fire a laser at the target for us?'

'Good idea.'

'Widow Zero Two, Recoil Four One. We're having problems identifying the target. Can you call the Apache pilot and ask him to lase it for us?'

'Roger. Stand by.'

Moments later the Apache moved closer to the target, though still doing his best to keep out of range of any

Taliban armed with RPGs, and illuminated the target compound for us. We both tracked his laser and that enabled us to identify the appropriate spot in the correct compound, which confirmed the exact position of the target. But Squid couldn't enter the location into his kit because the laser spot doesn't automatically produce a designation for the aircraft systems.

'Ade, Squid. I'm happy with the location now. I'll open out to the west for the attack run.'

'Roger that. I'll lase the target for you.'

Although Squid could probably have identified the target for himself as he ran in over the compounds, now that the Apache had designated it, I knew if I marked it for him with my laser it would make his job a lot easier. This is what's normally termed a cooperative attack: two aircraft working together to achieve the aim.

'Widow Zero Two, Recoil Four One. Estimate two minutes.'

In those two minutes both of us had a lot to do. Squid had to start his aircraft heading in the right direction, which at that stage meant away from the target, before turning round to start the attack run. Each of us would read through a brief checklist of actions on our knee board, beginning with confirming which of the two 540lb bombs the JTAC has selected, either the airburst or the impact weapon.

On the back radio we chatted between the cockpits – what's known as Crew Resource Management – to ensure that the pilot carrying out the attack had correctly selected the airburst weapon. We cross-referred the target location again, just as a final confirmation, to ensure that we were both confident that we'd selected the right target. Then I said: 'Call one minute and then I'll lase the target for you.'

Coming inbound from three or four miles away, Squid accelerated. His Harrier needed to be flying at above 300 knots for the bomb to arm as it came off the aircraft.

Shortly afterwards Squid called: 'One minute.'

I set up a wagon-wheel round the target, timing the positioning of my Harrier so that, as Squid ran in, I was approaching the target on a more or less parallel track, but higher so that there was no danger of confliction. That meant I would be firing the laser from the same piece of the sky that he was approaching from – the ideal solution and one that would give him the best possible opportunity to detect the reflected laser energy.

I hauled my aeroplane round and unmasked my laser so that I could see the target. Once I was happy I was tracking it, I called: 'Laser fires.'

Squid pushed the nose of the Harrier down into a thirty to forty degree dive and began trying to acquire the target.

A few seconds later he located the reflected laser energy.

'Good spot,' he confirmed.

He'd identified the laser spot and was tracking it. With the target acquired and tracking started, the aircraft systems automatically updated the targeting solution. Now Squid could commit to an automatic attack.

I concentrated on keeping my laser properly locked on to the compound that was our target. I could tell that my aircraft was detecting the laser because the indicator on the targeting pod was showing this clearly.

Then, on the front radio, Squid told the JTAC he was inbound.

'Widow Zero Two, Recoil Four One, sixty seconds.'

'Call wings level with direction.'

Squid replied: 'Recoil Four One, wings level from the west, in hot.' He was running in, the weapon prepared, and he was ready to carry out the attack.

The JTAC responded: 'Clear hot.'

I knew Squid would be dropping the weapon automatically, so at about this moment he pressed the small, red weapon-release button – the WRB or 'pickle button' – on his control column. But this didn't drop the weapon. Instead, it authorized the computer to do so at the optimum moment. Then Squid flew along the track that represents the ideal approach to the target, as accurately as possible following the azimuth steering line displayed in the head-up display. As Squid bore down on the target, the jet's computers calculated the bombs ballistic release point.

I watched as Squid streaked straight over the target compound. The five-forty he was carrying was unguided – dumb – but the energy from my laser was hitting the compound and bouncing back up to his aircraft to provide him with a very accurate firing solution. Then the bomb dropped from beneath his wing, bobbling a little before settling into a steep ballistic dive towards the ground. It speared straight into the target, eliminating – or, to put it more crudely but far more accurately, killing – the enemy gunmen in an ugly cloud of billowing brown dirt.

'Recoil Four One, Widow Zero Two. Direct hit, thank you, and the firing's stopped.'

'Roger that. If you're happy, we'll RTB.'

'Four One, Zero Two, that's affirmative.'

Squid changed radio boxes. 'Ade, Squid, let's call it a day and head for home.'

'Roger.'

So, within half an hour of getting airborne on my first sortie in Afghanistan, I was already providing laser tracking for a weapon to be delivered into the first target of the day. It was a real eye-opener, but entirely typical of the intensity of operations we would encounter over the weeks that followed.

What was also typical, though I didn't know it then, was that I was going to land at Kandahar carrying precisely the same ordnance as when I had taken off. I also didn't know then what a source of personal irritation this habit would later become.

Squid, by contrast, had finished his last sortie before heading home by clearing his wing.

7

Given its understandably low priority, the living accommodation at Kandahar was pretty basic. The Nissen-type huts had shared rooms, but the sleeping quarters were single-sex. After all, not every young girl wants to wake up first thing in the morning to the unedifying sight of a hairy-arsed sailor pulling on his underpants.

Essentially, though, it was dual-sex accommodation, but some of our personnel didn't realize this on the first day in theatre. The washing and ablution areas were combined. Even though there were individual shower cubicles, immediately outside them was a communal area. The idea was that people would hang their clothes and towel outside, step into the cubicle and shower, reach out and grab their towel and clothes when they'd finished, then leave the cubicle fully dressed.

Unfortunately, nobody told the squadron members this when we arrived at Kandahar. That evening the team sorted out their accommodation and settled in, and one of the marines decided it was a good opportunity to wash off the dust of the journey. He grabbed a towel and wandered off, whistling, to the ablution block at the end of the sleeping quarters.

He showered, emerged from the cubicle and began to dry himself, more or less oblivious to his surroundings. The squadron's accommodation block had a large number of female operations assistants, and two of these girls just walked in, to be confronted by the sight of a naked man bent over in front of them drying his legs.

To their credit, they didn't bat an eyelid, but just walked across to the sinks which were next to the showers and started doing whatever they had come in to do. The marine continued drying all his various bits and pieces, then turned round in complete shock as he heard the unmistakable sound of two women talking together and giggling.

He didn't bat an eyelid either.

'Sorry, ladies,' he said without too much concern, then, 'Good evening,' and carried on sorting himself out.

Our handover lasted for two very busy days. The most important thing for the squadron members was to find out where they were sleeping, where they could stow their gear, where they could eat and where the loos were. After that we were able to start the handover proper.

The squadron formed a part of 904 Expeditionary Air Wing, an administrative construct for Afghanistan, as part of Operation HERRICK, the codename of all the British operations in that country.

The allocated two days turned out to be barely long enough, for Harrier operations didn't stop just because our new squadron had arrived. So, as well as finding out where weapons, tools, spare parts and all the other odds and ends were stored, and checking the maintenance history of the aircraft they were assuming responsibility for, our ground staff still had to keep the Harriers properly maintained and get them prepped, armed and into the air, assisted by the outgoing RAF engineers.

It was no easier for my pilots. They were of course familiar with the aircraft they were flying, but the whole area was new to them and they had to learn the reference points and the procedures very quickly, and in the unforgiving environment of an active battle zone. We had arrived at a time when operations were proceeding at a very high tempo, and almost all of my pilots dropped weapons on their first sorties in theatre, which probably wasn't what most of them had expected. And life inside the wire, it turned out, wasn't much less intense.

The relative silence in the Ops building was suddenly shattered by the atonic screeching of a siren.

'What the hell's that?'

'Missile attack! Hit the deck and grab your armour!'

It was 29 September, our second day in theatre. As I pulled on my helmet I glanced through the windows to the Harrier dispersal. My immediate concern was the squadron engineers maintaining the Harriers, which were totally exposed. Kandahar has a dedicated radar system specifically designed to detect incoming rockets or mortars, and this was the first time we'd heard it in action.

Outside, the maintainers reacted instantly, hitting the deck and dragging on their body armour. Inside Ops we all did exactly the same.

Most of the weapons used by the Taliban were Russian-built BM-12 107mm unguided free-flight rockets. These weighed 42lb, were thirty-three inches long, carried 3lb of explosives in their warheads and had a range of about three and a half miles. They were intended to be fired from a launcher in salvoes of up to a dozen to maximize the chances of hitting something, and could realistically only be used against a large static target like an opposing army or a centre of population. Or, of course, an airfield.

These weapons had a flight time of about thirty seconds, and the procedure on hearing the attack warning was simple enough. You threw yourself to the ground with your body armour on, because the best place to be, offering the least chance of being hit, was flat on the ground. Once the first salvo had landed, you scrambled up and got to the nearest air-raid shelter as quickly as possible because that provided an additional layer of protection should another salvo be launched.

We all waited, and seconds later a salvo of rockets landed about 100 yards from the maintenance site, with three deafening explosions, but fortunately on the other side of the blast wall.

'Holy shit,' said one of the chief petty officers, standing up and looking out of the window. 'They were fucking close.'

If the Taliban had elevated the launchers by even as much as a degree or two, the rockets could have landed on the other side of the blast wall, among the Harriers and the men working on them – with disastrous results.

'Is that it?' someone asked, as we looked around cautiously.

'I don't know,' I said, then raised my voice. 'Right, everybody get to the shelter, just in case there's a second salvo on its way.'

Everybody got up and scrambled to the nearest shelter. After a few minutes, when the all-clear had sounded, we emerged and looked around cautiously. I walked over to the dispersal to check that all the maintainers were un-injured and that our aircraft had suffered no damage in the attack. As far as I could tell, although a fair amount of shrapnel from the exploding warheads had flown over the wall and landed on the aircraft pad itself, none of it seemed to have hit either the men or the machines.

It's drummed into everyone who flies or works on aeroplanes that FOD, foreign object damage, is a major but usually avoidable problem for modern aircraft, and particularly for those with jet engines, which can suck small solid objects into their huge intakes with a poten-tially disastrous result. And the pan was littered with small bits of twisted, smoking metal from the exploding warheads.

'Everything OK, chief?' I asked as I looked around the pan.

'Yes, no problem, sir. Once that stuff's cooled down, we'll get it shifted. I don't think any of it hit the cabs.'

Out of the corner of my eye I saw a few of the junior ratings bending down to start picking up the bits of shrapnel, reacting instinctively to clear the area of FOD. What they didn't realize was that the fragments were still red hot because the rocket warhead had exploded only a few minutes earlier. Almost immediately there were howls of pain as they dropped the twisted lumps of metal, clutching at their burnt fingers and hands.

The chief petty officer was less than sympathetic.

'You muppets!' he shouted. 'Use your bloody heads. That stuff's just been blown out of a fucking rocket's warhead, so it's bound to be a bit warm, isn't it? Leave it for twenty minutes.'

78

'Right, chief,' I said. 'I can see you've got everything under control.'

Although that attack caused no damage – apart from leaving a few of the junior men with minor burns and some embarrassment – it was an immediate wake-up call for us all. After that, nobody in the squadron had the slightest doubt that we were all at risk of life and limb, even though everybody except the pilots would be spending the entire detachment behind the blast walls.

Kandahar is a big airbase with a 12,000-foot runway – that's over two miles long – and you would have to be pretty unlucky to be close to one of the rockets when they hit, because they're not particularly accurate.

But, after that first attack, knowing this didn't make me sleep any easier. My main concern, just as it would be for any CO, was to make sure I brought all my people back. I wasn't *expecting* any of my aircrew to be shot down, although I always knew that this could happen. I thought that they were well enough trained, and flying a sufficiently good aircraft, to be able to fly and fight their way out of most situations. But if I were to lose one of my pilots in theatre in their aeroplane, whether as a result of mechanical failure or enemy action, I thought I could accept it because we all knew the risks, and flying a combat aircraft in a war zone was the job we had all signed up to do.

Even before we'd arrived in theatre, one of my biggest fears was that somebody could be killed or maimed by a rocket attack on the base. That, somehow, would have been more difficult to reconcile. My very worst nightmare was one of my squadron members being killed or getting their legs blown off by a 107mm rocket as they walked back from the gym to the accommodation block.

The following day one of our SE maintainers approached me in Ops.

'We were attacked yesterday,' she said.

'I know we were.'

'With rockets,' she added.

'Yes, I was there. You do remember the briefings we had back in the UK before we came out? They told us we would be likely to experience rocket attacks almost daily.'

'I know. It's just that hearing those rockets land made it all so much more real, if you know what I mean. It's one thing for some officer to stand up in front of us and say that we would be attacked by rocket and mortars, but actually hearing the things explode all around you, and having to run for the shelters, that really brings it home to you.'

I knew exactly what she meant. For her, and probably for many of the personnel who were out in Afghanistan for the very first time, the attack had been an instructive experience. Because of it, they knew that the briefers hadn't been lying to them. What they'd been told was real, and I felt the more that young woman and everyone else was able to talk about it, and acknowledge that we were all in the same boat, the less of a drama it was for them.

Squid's squadron would be glad to see the back of it all. Despite the intense level of operations they'd been involved in, the IV (AC) Squadron personnel did an excellent handover, doing everything they possibly could to ensure that we settled in as quickly as possible. Everything was in the right place, and the RAF guys all knew exactly what they were doing. It was one of the most seamless, easy and satisfactory handovers I've ever experienced.

'Good luck,' Squid said, shaking my hand, then turned to walk away towards the waiting Hercules.

'Have a good Christmas,' I called after him.

At that he stopped and turned back to look at me, a grin spreading slowly across his face. 'I'll bet my Christmas will be better than yours.'

'I should bloody well hope so,' I told him as I waved him off.

One of the first things we did after we arrived at Kandahar was request permission from the First Sea Lord to fly the battle ensign from the flagpole, on the reasonable grounds that, the lack of some kind of a warship notwithstanding, the detachment was involved in front-line offensive operations in Afghanistan.

But the squadron personnel decided that wasn't enough. We were members of a Royal Navy squadron and therefore, they decided, we really ought to be provided with an aircraft carrier, or something similar, to operate from. As Afghanistan is landlocked, we couldn't get a real vessel anywhere near the airfield, so they looked around to see what else they could do.

Everywhere on the airfield were things called Johnson barriers. They were preformed concrete slabs measuring about twelve feet by ten, with a kind of dumb-bell shape at the base to allow the barriers to slot together to form blast walls. Quite a number of these had been erected around the engineers' compound, to provide a safe working environment for them.

A sort of tradition had grown up in the Harrier det that every squadron would select one of the barriers and paint a design or a pattern on it for the period that the squadron was there. In 800 Squadron there was one guy who was an excellent artist, and he'd done a really good design, but they decided they wanted to do more than that.

The first step was to modify the air-raid shelter that was right outside the engineers' accommodation. They created a decked area at its base so that they could sit out or play ping-pong when it was quiet. On top of the shelter they built a sun deck that provided a good vantage point in the evening to watch the sun go down behind Three Mile Mountain.

One of the enduring mysteries about Three Mile Mountain was that it was actually four miles away. It was perhaps three miles distant from the extreme western edge of the airfield boundary, but from the living quarters on the east side it was at least four. Possibly there had originally been a datum of some sort on the western side of the airfield, or maybe the distance had simply been measured incorrectly. But, whatever the reason, nobody really knew, or frankly cared, and Three Mile Mountain became a standing joke on the base.

The air-raid shelter sun deck became a good place to sit out and watch the world go by. But the engineers decided that instead of being a sun deck, it should become a poop deck, so they set about turning the shelter beneath it into an aircraft carrier.

1. The late, lamented Sea Harrier FA2. With the early retirement of the radar-equipped, missile-armed SHAR, the Fleet Air Arm was, for the time being at least, out of the air-defence business. From now on we were mudmovers – ground-attack specialists.

By Admiral Sir James Burnell-Nugent,
Knight Commander of the Most
Honourable Order of the Bath and
Commander of the Most Excellent Order of
the British Empire, Vice Admiral of the
United Kingdom, Admiral in Her Majesty's
Fleet and Commander in Chief of Her
Majesty's Ships and Vessels employed and
to be employed in the Fleet.

800 NAVAL AIR SQUADRON

RE-COMMISSIONING ORDER

Whereas 800 Naval Air Squadron is to be re-commissioned at RAF COTTESMORE on 31ˢᵗ March 2006, or as soon afterwards as circumstances permit, you are to proceed forthwith to prepare for Service.

On re-commissioning you will be under my full Command. You are to bring to my immediate notice, through Commander (Operations), anything which gives you cause for dissatisfaction with the Squadron or any other matters of importance, in particular those relating to the welfare of your personnel.

May God's blessing be upon the Squadron hereby entrusted to your Command, and may your endeavours to uphold the high traditions of the Royal Navy in the service of Her Majesty The Queen be crowned with success and happiness.

Given under my hand this 14ᵗʰ day of March 2006.

James Burnell-Nugent.

Admiral Sir James Burnell-Nugent KCB CBE

To: Commander A P Orchard Royal Navy

2. 800 Squadron returns. The re-commissioning order from CINCFLEET.

3. 800 Naval Air Squadron re-commissions at RAF Cottesmore in Rutland. It was a joint Navy and RAF affair. And on the same day, 3 Squadron RAF converted to the new Eurofighter Typhoon.

4. The re-commissioning cake listing the squadron's long list of battle honours: Norway, Mediterranean, Malta Convoys, Bismarck, Diego Suarez, North Atlantic, Battle of France, Aegean, Burma, Korea and the Falklands.

5. My new office.

6. The new 800 NAS livery adorns the side of a Harrier GR7 fuselage.

7. HMS *Illustrious* at sea.

8. Take-off is optional, landing is obligatory. Moments before touchdown, a Harrier, held airborne on four columns of thrust from its powerful Rolls Royce Pegasus engine, recovers vertically aboard HMS *Illustrious* off Oman.

9. 800 NAS in its element – a GR7 on the deck of HMS *Illustrious*, with HMS *Gloucester* riding shotgun alongside.

10. Red Sea Rig. 800 NAS, in our trademark red cummerbunds, pose on deck. Time aboard the carrier provoked an outburst of beard-growing.

11. With the jet resting on jacks, 800 NAS engineers begin work on an engine change inside HMS *Illustrious*'s hangar.

12. Ready for take-off.

13. Armed with a pair of live 1,000 lb laser-guided bombs, a GR7 accelerates down the flight deck.

14. Lift-off. A GR7 captured at the moment it takes to the air. By almost throwing the jet off the bow of the ship, the ramp (or ski jump) enables the Harrier to take off carrying heavier loads.

15. The jet climbs away *en route* to the Omani bombing ranges – our last chance to train with live ammunition before deploying to Afghanistan.

16. Members of the squadron check and pack their new kit before leaving for Afghanistan.

17. Disembarking from the RAF Tristar at Kabul, we got our first glimpse of Afghanistan's rugged landscape.

18. The Navy's here. The White Ensign flies alongside the RAF flag over Kandahar Airfield (KAF) – a clear reminder of how, as Joint Force Harrier, the two services were working together.

19. It's not much, but for the four months of the det, this was home.

20. Burger King. Self-contained within a standard international shipping container, it was simply flown in, in the back of a C-17.

21. It wasn't all bad. The Americans made sure that Kandahar airfield had all the amenities. Here I'm enjoying a coffee with Hoggy, one of my more junior pilots.

Scenes from KAF.

Clockwise from top left:

22. A Russian-built Ilyushin Il-76

23. A USAF C-130 Hercules

24. The next big thing. A Predator UAV - Unmanned Air Vehicles have really come of age over Afghanistan.

25. The United Nations Mi-26 Halo

They found some wood from various places and created a ski jump at one end. The whole top of the shelter then became the flight deck, which they marked out just like the deck of a CVS, albeit rather smaller than the real thing. Directly in front of the shelter was another one of the Johnson barriers, in exactly the right position to become the 'sea'. So they painted the concrete to make it look as though the 'ship' was ploughing through the waves. And thus HMS *Kandahar* was born, or rather launched.

'What the bloody hell is that supposed to be?' asked Dunc Mason when he walked round the corner and saw the 'aircraft carrier' in front of him.

Neil Bing, who always joked with Dunc about 'crabs' – the Navy's nickname for the RAF – was standing looking at the structure. He immediately explained.

'That,' he said proudly, 'is HMS *Kandahar*. A proper Navy carrier for a proper Navy squadron. Just a shame we have to have a bunch of crabs with us here at all!'

'You need us crabs,' Dunc replied amicably, 'because we're the only pilots round here who know what they're doing flying Harriers.'

The two of them walked away, still sniping good-naturedly at each other.

And our Naval presence was noted in Ops as well. On the back of the door that separated the Harrier squadron room from the C-130 Ops room was a sign that read: 'Do not enter – here be dragons.' Within a couple of days of our arrival at Kandahar somebody from the Hercules squadron had amended it to read: 'Do not enter – here be *sea* dragons.'

*

I sat under a brightly coloured umbrella outside one of KAF's – Kandahar Airfield's – many coffee shops. I was amazed at the facilities that had grown up so fast in this barren corner of the Afghan desert. In those early days I made every effort to get to know my way around to try to figure out how it all worked. Most services provided on Kandahar Airfield were firmly under the control of a major American contractor, but there were a few independent outlets. One of these was the Green Beans Coffee House, which soon became my home away from home. The café worked on a debit-card basis whereby you bought, say, $50 of credit and then each purchase was deducted from the balance on your card until you topped up your credit. You find Green Beans throughout the war zones, because they deploy with the American troops. Their relaxed and welcoming atmosphere is down largely to the staff, who, in Afghanistan, were mainly Indian and lovely guys to talk to, not only unfailingly polite but cheerful too.

For our main meals we had a choice of three dining facilities, or DIFACs, with food available in all of them 24/7. The British one served good old British fare – like chicken tikka masala – but traditionalists weren't hard done by, for puddings at least, with old favourites like treacle sponge, spotted dick and jam roly-poly on the menu.

In contrast, everything at the American DIFAC was frozen, prepared somewhere else or, more often, had come out of a packet. The food was full of preservatives, colourings and flavour enhancers, and the main courses all came with the mandatory 'Freedom Fries'. Dessert was usually Häagen-Dazs ice cream, piled high.

The Romanian DIFAC, so called because it was where most of the Romanians ate, was actually run by the Americans.

Each was a good place to socialize but we'd pick and choose between them. On a Thursday evening we might go for the Americans' seafood special with its huge Alaskan snow-crab claws. Traditional meals like this and meat loaf or steak with all the trimmings reminded their people of home. The American DIFAC was also big on theme nights like Halloween, which kept the troops happy.

I drained my drink and got up to leave. Behind me I heard the buzzsaw sound of a C-130 taxiing out to the runway, the latest in a never-ending stream of aircraft movements.

As I returned to the squadron buildings, the scramble bell rang. We had inherited an excellent specimen, just like those used in the Second World War to get the Spitfires and Hurricanes into the air, and for exactly the same reason – in both cases, time really was of the essence. When the GCAS system called for air support, it meant *now*, not in half an hour or an hour, or whenever the pilots felt like it. So it was the old Battle of Britain motto 'Ring the bell, run like hell!' brought right up to date.

A GCAS scramble was the ultimate test of the whole squadron. It demonstrated whether or not all of our personnel, from the aircrew to every last engineer and naval airman in the team, had done their job properly. In those hectic minutes after the scramble had been called, we pilots had to have absolute confidence that the aircraft were ready, had been fitted with the right weapons and would start, so that we could get airborne within a certain time and carry out a successful mission.

Every time it was as adrenalin-filled as you wanted it to be, just like in those old war movies. The moment the call came into the Ops room, always on a special phone, everybody stopped whatever they were doing and waited while the closest officer or senior rating ran to answer it. Meanwhile one of the staff rang the scramble bell to let the ground engineers in the dispersal know a scramble was on.

All kitted up and ready to go, the duty pilots got to the dispersal as quickly as possible from wherever they were on the base. The ground engineers rushed down to the pan area, so that by the time the pilots climbed in, the GR7s were fully prepped, with all systems switched on.

On every scramble we achieved the minimum required time to get the Harriers airborne. Each team member was aware that every second's delay in the scramble meant another second's delay in getting to the target area. And that extra second could be all it took for one of the troops in contact with the Taliban to die.

I watched from Ops and saw some squadron personnel – including a few that I had never expected to see running – covering the ground at a startling rate. The pilots started their engines. Capable of churning out around 24,000lb of thrust, the Rolls Royce Pegasus engine makes a noise of biblical proportions. It's an amazing sight too, creating a huge cloud of black smoke when it fires up. The exhaust gases emitted from the engine's back nozzles are at between 700 and 800 degrees Celsius; even the front nozzles expel air at 300–400 degrees. The heat rippled through the air around the aircraft in a fierce haze. Then it was chocks away and the two jets rolled towards the runway.

A few minutes later the distinctive scream of the Pegasus engines running at full chat echoed around the airfield as the pair of 800 squadron jets powered down the runway, one behind the other.

The two Harriers stayed low and fast, gathering speed, then pulled up, climbing like rockets as they completed their individual tactical departures.

I watched them reach top of climb and swing round to the west, towards Helmand Province, and mentally wished them happy hunting and a safe return.

8

'How's it going, Andy?' I asked as I walked into the briefing room.

'Fine, boss, we're all ready.'

Andy Baverstock, the Squinto and hard-core Royal Navy history buff, was preparing to give the aircrew a general overview of the situation in Afghanistan.

I'd known Andy for years, first meeting him in the nineties on the *Ark Royal* and then again out in Bosnia. He was originally a photographer who'd come up through the ranks to take a commission, and I'd always known he was excellent at his job. He was forever smiling and had a very positive outlook on life, but perhaps his most distinguishing feature, apart from his ginger hair and slight pot belly, was his 'red wine teeth'. Whenever he drank red wine, his teeth turned dark red, almost purple, almost immediately. Of course, we never saw this interesting phenomenon out in Afghanistan, because the det was 'dry'.

The Royal Navy has only fairly recently started employing dedicated intelligence officers to cope with the ever-increasing amounts of data available to front-line squadrons. Previously we had a small number of photographic interpretation specialists, or PIs, but they have now vanished.

Today's intelligence officers need to have a much broader skill base than just interpreting photographic data

– though this can be an extremely difficult discipline to master – and need to be able to process the entire battle-field picture. Every day the Squinto gave us the general intelligence briefing, plus every sortie had its own dedicated and much more detailed briefing, and he was able to put into context what was happening out in the field. He was essentially everything from a *News at Ten*-style announcer, providing general information about what was going on in our violent little corner of Afghanistan, right down to delivering classified information about the threats it was believed we would be likely to encounter in a specific location.

'Right,' Andy said, 'I'm going to start with a bit of background, for those of you who don't know too much about the history of this region. Ask questions whenever you want – don't wait until the end.

'Afghanistan is arguably one of the most war-torn nations on earth. Now at first sight this is somewhat peculiar for a country that has virtually no natural re-sources to fight over. Officially, its exports include natural gas, fruits, nuts, hand-woven carpets, wool, cotton, animal hides and skins, precious and semi-precious stones. According to government sources, these currently amount to a little over $450 million annually, an extraordinarily low figure from a population of just under 32 million.'

'That's ridiculous,' somebody called out. 'That's only about $15 per person per year.'

'Fourteen actually,' Andy said, 'but the future for the country is brighter than you might think. Some recent geological reports suggest that Afghanistan has significant reserves of natural gas and petroleum, and huge quantities of iron ore, gold, copper, coal and various minerals. The government is already beginning to exploit the country's copper reserves, and these could earn over one billion dollars annually for some thirty years. There's a lot of potential here, which is probably one reason why the Taliban are so determined to regain control.'

'What about the drugs?' the same officer asked.

Andy nodded. 'As you probably all know, that's Afghanistan's "hidden" export. Opium accounts for between thirty and fifty per cent of the nation's gross domestic product. The country is the world's principal source of the drug, producing about ninety per cent of all opium, most of which is processed into heroin and then sold illegally in Europe, Russia and America.

'Now, to understand the present-day situation in Afghanistan, it helps to know a little bit about the country's history.'

Andy explained that battles had been fought for centuries on Afghanistan's high plains and mountain passes. The nation could trace its history back to around 2000 BC, when Aryan invaders swept across the country. They were followed by Persian, Median, Greek, Mauryan, Bactrian, Indo-Greek, Scythian, Kushan, Parthian, White Hun and Göktürk armies. Even Alexander the Great turned up there.

'They kicked the crap out of us a few times, as well,' came a voice from the back of the room.

'Quite right. In the past two centuries British forces have entered Afghanistan three times – in 1839, in 1843 and finally in 1919 – with a marked lack of success on each occasion.'

The reason for this almost unbroken succession of invaders, Andy explained, was simply the location of the country. Afghanistan sits virtually at the crossroads of south, west and central Asia, and this accident of geography means its territory has been crossed and re-crossed countless times over the past three millennia by both migrating peoples and invading armies.

This confused and fluid history has resulted in a wild diversity of people from a host of different tribes and nations, who are now known generically as 'Afghans' or 'Afghanis'. They occupy a land whose boundaries weren't even finalized until the nineteenth century, and whose name – Afghanistan – referred to only one section of the Peshawar Valley until about the same time, and only became internationally accepted as the official name of the country in 1923.

This melting pot of nationalities is reflected in the number of languages still spoken in Afghanistan today, said Andy. The three official tongues are Dari, Farsi and Pashto, which are spoken by about ninety per cent of the population, but there are at least thirty other languages in use. These range alphabetically from Aimaq, spoken by about half a million people in central and north-west Afghanistan, to Wotapuri-Katarqalai, spoken by some 2,000. The least-used language is probably Mogholi, which has fewer than 200 remaining speakers who live only in the villages of Kundur and Karez-i-Mulla, near Herat.

'The result of all this is that there's really no such person as an Afghan in the way that you can describe somebody as being a Frenchman or a German,' Andy went on. 'Instead you have numerous different tribes who happen to live in Afghanistan. Roughly speaking, about forty per cent of Afghans are Pashtun, but these are subdivided into several tribal groups, the biggest of which are the Durrani and Ghilzai. The next largest ethnic group are the Tajiks, about twenty-five per cent of the population, then the Hazaras, representing some twenty per cent. Then there are the Uzbeks, Turkmen, Qizilbash and dozens of others. It probably won't surprise you to learn that most of these tribes don't get on with each other, and the country's been in an almost constant state of civil unrest for centuries.

'As far as the government's concerned, for most of the twentieth century Afghanistan was headed by a monarchy that later began experimenting with democratic ideas, but in the 1970s two successive coups resulted in the creation of a communist state. In 1978 Russian forces arrived in Afghanistan to help support the government, and stayed until 1989, when they were finally forced to withdraw, having suffered a series of humiliating defeats at the hands of the Mujahidin guerrillas.'

Like others before them, Andy explained, the Russians discovered that the people of the high mountains were almost impossible to defeat, because the terrain wouldn't permit conventional military operations, and always favoured the guerrilla-style tactics for which the Afghans seemed to have a particular aptitude.

Once their common enemy had been vanquished, the different tribes that had banded together to battle the Soviet invaders once again split into factions and resumed fighting one another in a continuation of the civil war that they had been engaged in for decades. From this chaos, an extreme Islamic breakaway group known as the Taliban – the word means 'students' – arose in Kandahar Province and began attacking just about everyone else, and achieved considerable success.

Composed of former Mujahidin and religious scholars, but with a preponderance of Pakistani members, the Taliban were armed, equipped and, to a large extent, directed by the ISI, the Directorate of Inter-Services Intelligence, Pakistan's principal intelligence organization. The idea behind the Taliban was clear – through the movement, Pakistan hoped to impose a measure of direction and control over its lawless and politically chaotic neighbour.

By the end of 2000 the Taliban controlled about ninety-five per cent of Afghanistan. Their only opposition was the Northern Alliance, based in the extreme north-east of the country, but that group was, somewhat bizarrely, still acknowledged by the United Nations as the Afghan government.

'Now,' Andy went on, 'we come right up to date. The reason that America decided to launch attacks on Afghanistan was because it was known that the alleged architect of the 9/11 terror attacks on New York, Osama bin Laden, had been involved with the Taliban since about 1997, and it was believed that this renegade Saudi had taken refuge in the country. Requests made to the Taliban by the Americans to hand him over were ignored. The initial attacks on the mountain strongholds of the Taliban were followed by a peaceful invasion of the country by a coalition of nations acting as a peacekeeping force in Afghanistan operating with the authority of the United Nations and at the request of the Afghan government

93

headed by Hamid Karzai in Kabul. Britain is a part of that coalition, and, as you know, we've been supplying ground troops, pilots and aircraft to what's now become the International Security Assistance Force, or ISAF.

'And we've already discovered, just like the Russians did, that the Afghan fighters are no pushover. Although the Taliban are comparatively lightly armed, they're a formidable and implacably determined enemy.

'To put that into perspective, the IV (AC) Squadron guys who've just left were involved in the fiercest fighting ISAF has seen out here so far, and most of it centred on 3 Para. According to figures from the MoD, 3 Para fired 450,000 machine-gun and rifle rounds, and launched 7,500 mortars and 4,000 light artillery rounds against the Taliban, and they were only in theatre for *six months*.'

'Bloody hell.'

'Exactly. That's the highest tempo of operations any British forces have experienced since Korea. Compared with this, Iraq was a walk in the park. And, so you know what you're all facing here, in their last month in theatre IV (AC) Squadron dropped about 30,000lb – that's fifteen tons – of ordnance on the Taliban.'

'So ground forces are fighting *pitched battles* with the Taliban?' The surprise in the question was evident.

'Sometimes they do, but that's not their intention. Usually the troops are sent out to secure a specific objective – a strategic location or a village where the Taliban are known to be established – and that's usually where the fiercest fighting takes place, because the insurgents don't give up ground easily.

'One of the tactics being used here,' Andy went on, 'is what's known as the "platoon house" concept. The idea is that ISAF forces establish a presence in an area known to be under Taliban control or influence. They establish a secure base – that's the platoon house – and then start mounting aggressive patrols in the area, designed to flush out the insurgents and at the same time establish good relations with the locals. It's a combination of hearts-and-minds and mailed fist, I suppose.'

'Does that work?'

'Yes and no. There have been a few cases where it seems to have gone quite well, and others where the platoon house has ended up being virtually besieged by the Taliban, under fire almost every day. But you've got to remember that we're not here to take and hold ground as if this were an old-style invasion. The coalition doesn't have the boots on the ground here to do that, and in any case an occupation would be totally counter-productive. Instead the key is to protect vital strategic points and aid all-important reconstruction. There have been reverses, of course, but we're playing a long game.

'Anything to add, boss?' Andy turned to me and asked.

'No, thanks, Andy.' I stood up and faced the squadron members. 'I think we've all learnt a lot from that. All I'd like to say is that we've arrived in theatre at a time when the level of fighting is at its highest ever, and when coalition troops on the ground are at their most vulnerable. That means they're most dependent on our support, so it's vital that every time we're scrambled, and every time we're called to a TIC we get there as quickly as possible and deliver our weapons with speed and accuracy. Quite literally, the lives of our troops depend entirely upon our proficiency and ability.'

'So no pressure, then?' Wedge called out from his seat at the back of the room, and most of the pilots laughed.

I grinned. 'No, no pressure, Wedge. Just get up there and do your stuff like you normally do.'

Wedge – Lieutenant Ed Philips – was pretty much as wide as he was tall, hence his nickname, and I did sometimes wonder how he managed to fit in a Harrier's cockpit, which is not the most spacious 'office' in the world. He wasn't fat, just solid, and a real Fleet Air Arm buff. He read naval history constantly and knew everything there was to know about the Royal Navy, especially about the Fleet Air Arm.

It was Andy's joke that if you cut him in half you'd find the words 'Royal Navy' running through his body like the writing inside a stick of rock, but if you did the same for Wedge, it would read 'Fleet Air Arm'.

The importance of a rapid response was emphasized a few days later. We were augmented by two pilots from the Harrier Training Squadron, Lieutenant Commander Dave Lindsay and Squadron Leader Chris Rogers. They stayed with us for the first two weeks as night flyers while we started night-flying and got fully up to speed, then they went home.

The squadron worked a ten-day cycle, which meant that every ten days we stood down from the Air Tasking Order and reverted to holding a two-hour GCAS alert for two aeroplanes. That day gave the engineers the opportunity to shift their routine from working days to working nights and vice versa, and gave them a twenty-four-hour acclimatization period to make the change.

Chris and Dave were teamed up as a pair. On the first maintenance day in theatre they were the duty GCAS pilots and were in the gym getting a bit of exercise on the running machines. The GCAS 120 meant that, in the event of a scramble, they had two hours to get back to Ops, dress, get briefed and get the aircraft airborne. The engineers had the same two hours to ready a couple of the aircraft to fly.

But, on this occasion, when they were paged they were told it wasn't a regular GCAS 120 scramble, and they needed to get airborne as soon as possible. They went from being on a treadmill in the gym to getting airborne, wheels in the well, in exactly twenty-seven minutes. That was extremely impressive because normally, from the bell going on a GCAS scramble to getting airborne, it took us about fifteen minutes, well inside the thirty-minute response time that we were allocated.

It only really worked because these guys shared a room, had flown together for ages and were able to brief each other on the run as they went from the gym and through the dressing and briefing process. So it took them just twelve minutes longer than normal and that time was mostly taken up running from the gym to Ops and getting dressed.

Twenty-seven minutes was a *really* fast response time in the circumstances, and they handled the delivery of their weapons as professionally as anyone would expect.

But for the guys on the ground, the troops being

engaged by Taliban heavy machine-guns and RPGs, every second before the Harriers arrived on station must have seemed like an eternity. That was the message I was always pushing to the aircrew, and that was what we were always so aware of. Time wasted meant lives lost, and I knew that the Harriers' arrival at a TIC frequently meant the difference between life and death to the troops on the ground.

But it wasn't always about *killing* the bad guys. Sometimes it was just a question of scaring them shitless.

As well as carrying out attacks on Taliban warriors in support of ISAF troops, the Harrier det was also tasked with what might be termed intimidation tactics, employing a low-level show of force, a low, fast run that never included the delivery of any weapons. This approach was a vital part of our arsenal in a war that was almost defined by the central importance of proportionality.

Our intention was to show the Taliban – and the Afghan locals, for that matter – that the coalition forces were in the area and were there to stay, and to demonstrate one of the weapons available to them in the form of the Harrier, which is quite an impressive, and certainly a very noisy, aircraft. We would fly very low and very fast, creating a lot of noise that would hopefully give them pause for thought.

The thinking was that if we could convince the Taliban and their sympathizers that we possessed overwhelming military strength, they might decide not to attack *us*, and then we wouldn't have to shoot or bomb *them*.

*

As Wedge and Flatters – Lieutenant Tim Flatman – arrived back in the squadron buildings after landing, they filled me in on what had happened. They had been out supporting Widow Eight Four, one of the British JTACs, on the ground, laying down some noise in an attempt to make the Taliban keep their heads down, and Flatters had conducted a low-level show of force.

'I ran out about ten miles,' he explained back at Kandahar after he'd landed. 'I did my usual checks, including making sure my Walther was snug in its holster, just in case it all turned to rat shit and I had to jump out. Then I turned back in towards the target area, dropped down to low level and started the run-in.'

Contrary to both popular belief and the images so dear to Hollywood, the world does not rush past in a blur when you're flying an aircraft fast at low level. We actually have plenty of time to see what's around us and pick out details. We can see rugs and washing hanging on lines, kids running around, the locals doing whatever they're up to, and almost count the number of animals – which in that area were mainly goats. We'd see horses and carts going up and down the *wadis*, or dry river beds, which were almost always the flattest ground and so made for the smoothest progress. Real life continued everywhere in Afghanistan, despite the presence of the coalition forces and the depredations of the Taliban.

Time, on these sorties, often seemed to slow down as our level of concentration rose. And we were supremely conscious that the slightest nudge of the control column would turn the aircraft into a spectacular fireball on the ground from which we wouldn't have the slightest chance of escape. And that *really* concentrated the mind.

Our biggest enemy in doing these low-level runs was the ground itself, or rather any obstacles on it that we hadn't seen, closely followed by the possibility of the Taliban taking potshots at us.

Bringing down, or even hitting, a high-speed, low-level aircraft would be difficult with the sort of weapons we knew the Taliban carried. They were mostly armed with Kalashnikov AK-47 assault rifles and RPG launchers, and heavy machine-guns that they used when ambushing coalition troops, but it was known that they also had access to Stinger surface-to-air missiles and possibly other types of SAM.

We knew that even small-arms fire posed a real threat to us. Although it was unlikely, one lucky bullet *could* bring down a jet if it hit the right place.

The Harrier GR7 is fitted with the highly capable Marconi Zeus ECM system, though this is optimized against radar threats, of which there were very few in Afghanistan. Zeus has a radar warning receiver – the RWR, or 'RAW' – that is able to identify over 1,000 different radar signals and automatically activate a jammer to counter any of them.

Of more immediate use in the Afghan theatre, we also carried a missile approach warning system, or MAW, linked to chaff dispensers that fired thin strips of reflective metal foil automatically whenever a missile was detected. The idea was that this cloud of foil would break a radar lock on our jets by presenting what appeared to be a juicier target. The aircraft were also fitted with a variety of expendables, primarily flares of various types, which were effective against heat-seeking missiles. Whenever carrying out an attack run we made sure all our self-defence systems were online, set to automatic mode and working properly, and that the appropriate expendables programme was running.

On our way in to the area, running at high speed and already at very low level, we were always totally aware of what was happening on the ground in front of us. We tried wherever possible to avoid overflying villages, but sometimes it was unavoidable.

'The ride was pretty bloody bumpy,' Flatters continued. 'The Harrier was bouncing about all over the place with the turbulence. I pulled it up another fifty feet and eased off the throttle a tad, just to give myself a bit of a safety margin, but it was still really uncomfortable. Mind you, there's nothing quite like barrelling along at 400 knots in a jet 100 feet above the ground,' he added with a smile.

'I had to pass close to a small village on the way in, and the moment I cleared the edge of it I saw a single figure standing there right in front of me holding a long, dark object, and I knew immediately what it was. Oh, fuck, I thought. Wrong place, wrong time. That's a Talib with a Stinger.

'I jinked sideways and slammed the throttle fully open, the g-suit barely coping with the sudden change of direction. Then I dropped back down again, maybe seventy feet, to try to get below the missile's acquisition envelope, and checked again that the self-defence systems were online and, I hoped, working properly.

'That took me right over the top of the man I'd seen, and as soon as I looked down at him I realized I was completely wrong. He was just a goatherd holding a staff, and all I'd managed to do was frighten him and terrify his animals. And cock up my approach to the target area. That wasn't my finest hour.

'Anyway, I turned back on track and a minute or so later steamed in over the Taliban positions, and I was pretty bloody pleased with the result, bearing in mind the problems I'd had on the approach. That sense of satisfaction lasted about fifteen seconds.'

As soon as he'd completed the run, Widow Eight Four came up on the radio.

'We've just heard the Taliban commander say that's the worst show of force he's ever seen!'

To add insult to injury, it turned out that it wasn't even a joke made by the JTAC: it's what the unimpressed Taliban had actually been heard to say. Apparently the report made its way quickly up the line and was later reputedly mentioned by the US General at the CAOC in his weekly brief.

9

The squadron arrived in Afghanistan in September, at the end of the summer, and very quickly got used to the fact that in the early morning it was *really* cold. Like most desert environments – and deserts almost always have the greatest diurnal temperature difference – in Afghanistan the temperature would swing from well below freezing to very hot indeed in a matter of hours as the sun rose into the sky. In the winter a daily temperature difference of thirty to thirty-five degrees Celsius was not unusual, though in the summer it would be slightly less, perhaps only twenty or twenty-five.

It was routine for the squadron personnel to wake up to a freezing day, perhaps with an air temperature of minus one or two, or even less, and be sweltering in thirty-plus by early afternoon. Getting up and driving to work in the morning would require heavy jackets or parkas, but by lunchtime shorts were more appropriate wear.

The squadron was billeted closer to Poo Pond – the open cesspit that struggled to cope with the number of people based at Kandahar – than any of us liked, and the unmistakable odour of decaying piss and shit was always there as an unwelcome reminder of the environment when we stepped outside our quarters. Taking a deep breath as you walked out of the building to greet the new day was not to be recommended.

Thank God, then, for the sanitized and air-conditioned Ops building, at the other end of the airfield. This was where, apart from planning and briefing all the squadron's sorties, I tried to keep on top of the admin. As I read through the reports, they made for startling reading.

During that first, very busy, period of about six weeks we were usually flying four pairs of aircraft every day, or twenty-four-hour period, to be exact. Usually this would be three daylight sorties and one during the night, and during this period at least one of those missions each day would drop one, and often more than one, weapon. And in addition to our regular sorties, every two or three days we would get involved in a GCAS scramble, and that would normally result in the delivery of additional munitions.

At the end of October 2006, our first month at KAF, we'd flown over 503 hours and dropped more than 32,000lb of ordnance. That's over 1,000lb every day and more than IV (AC) had dropped in support of coalition troops during their whole det. It was an impressive total but one that I personally, as Dunc Mason pointed out with delight and increasing frequency, had barely contributed to. It certainly wasn't deliberate. And I felt sure my luck would change.

It's also worth adding that a considerable number of the incidents we'd been involved in had resulted in our engaging the enemy with CRV-7 rockets and I had, at least, managed to fire a few of those. But they weighed very little and made up a tiny percentage of the total weight of ordnance. If we maintained a similar level of delivery throughout our entire four-month detachment to Kandahar, the squadron was going to get through over 100,000lb of bombs and rockets.

This was a stark contrast to the other theatre in which I had been involved previously. Back in 2003, when I was in Iraq as part of TELIC, we did deliver munitions at a fairly high rate during the combat phase, which itself only lasted a few weeks, but since the end of that year the rate has dropped steadily and at present the Tornados there are only releasing about one weapon every twelve to eighteen *months*.

The reason for this difference is simple enough. In Afghanistan we were fighting what is essentially an all-out war against the Taliban, who are desperate to regain their former power and position at any cost, a war that has grown steadily more intense since 2004 and which peaked in its intensity in the autumn of 2006. In Iraq the situation is far more like a low-intensity civil war, with the principal weapons being IEDs, and with suicide bombers used to ambush either coalition troops or members of rival factions and religious groups as they jockey for position. There are few battles in that theatre of the kind that have become so familiar to us in Afghanistan.

When assessing the expenditure of munitions, it's important to remember the incredible accuracy of the laser-guided weapons we were using. If that figure of 100,000lb of munitions is compared with the type of bombs used during the Second World War, it becomes apparent that to achieve the same results with those unguided weapons we would probably have needed something like ten times that weight of bombs – around a million pounds. And, of course, this would have caused enormous collateral damage. It's regrettable that bombs of any type have to be used, but at least modern munitions ensure that the target, and only the target, is hit. And, overall, probably half the attacks we carried out during our detachment used CRV-7s, a very low-yield weapon.

In modern warfare the yield of most weapons has been decreasing as their accuracy has improved simply because, if the bomb can be delivered precisely on target, a high yield is actually counter-productive because of the collateral damage it causes. Unguided bombs were essentially the ground-attack version of a shotgun. You dropped a large number of them in the hope that one would hit the intended target, much as a hunter would fire a shell containing fifty or so pellets at a flying bird, expecting to hit it with just a handful of them.

Every bomb dropped generated more paperwork, and as squadron boss I seemed to have rather more of it to do than anyone else. But I refused to sit in my office hunched over a desk *all* afternoon. I rubbed my eyes, grabbed my jacket and set out for the Boardwalk to clear my head with some fresh air and then coffee. As I walked the air was filled with the thumping beat of the rotor from the UN's resident Mi-24 Halo. Moments later the distinctive white form of the big Russian-made chopper accelerated across the horizon.

'The Boardwalk' was what the Americans called a refreshment area a couple of hundred yards square that had a Pizza Hut, a Subway, a Burger King and a Tim Hortons, the Canadian coffee shop. It's important in a war zone to make life as comfortable as possible, and the Boardwalk gave everyone confined to the base a choice of where to eat and drink apart from the DIFACs.

Some people changed into civilian clothing when they were off duty, feeling this distanced them from the reality of where they were and what they were doing. It was slightly odd, the first few times I walked into the crew room, to see a couple of my pilots sitting there in civvies watching the TV in the corner, while everyone around them was in uniform and hard at work.

The impression of strangeness was confirmed suddenly by the sound of the attack siren. When the wailing started we always reacted the same way, grabbing our body armour and helmet and diving on to the ground, then running for the air-raid shelters once the first salvo had landed.

The conversations in the shelters were usually ridiculous. We were just shooting the breeze and waiting either for the second salvo to land or for confirmation that there was only one, so we could all get back to bed, work or whatever. People talked about everything from football matches to the operations being carried out, to the snoring of the blokes they had been billeted with – most squadron personnel were sleeping four to a room because the accommodation was at best compact.

Somebody in the squadron dreamt up a game they called Rocket O'Clock. With more than a nod to Spot the Ball, this involved an enlarged picture of the airfield pasted on a board with a transparent grid superimposed on it, letters along one edge and numbers on another. Every day participants paid $1 and put a cross where they thought the next rocket was going to land.

The problem dawned on everyone fairly quickly – as time passed and the board began to fill up, sooner or later the only square left would be the accommodation block. And if a rocket did land there, the winner would certainly be able to collect his half-share of the roughly $100 'pot' (half was given to charity), but posthumously. This didn't seem like a good idea to anyone, so after a few weeks we stopped tempting fate and abandoned it.

In truth, the RAF Regiment had really got to work on the threat from rockets. Although the airfield was subjected to attacks for the whole time we were in theatre – and probably still is – the accuracy of the attacks got worse and worse as time went on, because the Taliban insurgents were pushed further and further away from the perimeter. And for that the Royal Air Force Regiment was entirely responsible.

Anyone who has read anything about the Afghanistan campaign will be familiar with the major forces taking part: 3 Para, the Royal Marines and others. But the RAF Regiment guys were the real unsung heroes during our det.

Before they arrived to take over the force protection of the airfield, the task seemed to have been approached less proactively. A swift and violent retaliation to Taliban attacks was always guaranteed, but there were fewer patrols outside the wire. And it was these that made it more difficult for the Taliban to set up their rocket batteries within range.

Most of the rocket attacks came from the sector that

lay to the north-east of the airfield, with just a handful from the south. The reason for this was clear to us: Highway One, the main road that runs from one end of the country to the other, passed right through that area, allowing attackers an easy route both in and out.

But all that changed as soon as the RAF Regiment took over. Their policy was completely different to that of their predecessors. They identified where the attacks were coming from and began mounting aggressive patrols outside the wire in those areas, and succeeded in pushing their safe perimeter so far out that the Taliban were having to fire their rockets from extreme range, with very little chance of even hitting the airfield itself, let alone any specific targets on it.

The guys from the RAF Regiment achieved their success not only by their patrolling, which often located rocket batteries before the Taliban had a chance to fire them – the rockets were normally fired by remote control – but also by having excellent sniper teams.

There's a misunderstanding about snipers. Most people seem to think that their job is just to go out into the badlands and kill people, but the primary role of a sniper team is usually reconnaissance and intelligence-gathering. In Afghanistan, in particular, they were watching for significant changes in the pattern of life in the villages and hamlets, because that was often the first clue that the Taliban might have moved in. They observed their targets through telescopic sights, but the fact that the sight was attached to a long-range sniper rifle was almost coincidental – it didn't automatically mean they were tasked with killing the people they were observing.

At Kandahar the snipers went out into the area and dug themselves in for days at a time, initially just watching the activity around them, acting as surveillance teams, and radioing their reports back to the regiment on the airfield. Only when they'd observed all they needed to would they then pick off the individual Taliban as they were setting up their rocket batteries, well before they were able to fire their missiles. And, even then, killing the men setting up or firing the weapons was only a part of it, because these were believed to be usually very low-ranking insurgents, given the most dangerous jobs. Whenever possible, the snipers preferred to target the people who gave the orders or directed the preparation of the weapons.

Once this operation got under way the numbers of rocket attacks on the airfield dropped sharply, and eventually almost stopped. It was an excellent demonstration of proactive force protection and, once the RAF Regiment took over, most of us at Kandahar slept a lot better knowing they were out there.

Counter-battery fire was, without doubt, one of the most impressive aspects of the RAF Regiment's considerable repertoire of skills. As the name suggests, the tactic is return fire directed at a rocket battery or gun that is firing into the defended area. I saw it used several times, but one occasion in particular sticks in my mind. The base was again the target of a rocket attack, but while the rockets were *still in the air* an RAF Regiment mortar team responded, firing their rounds at the location they'd calculated the rockets had been launched from.

When a reconnaissance party went out to check the

site the following day, they found the launchers exactly where they'd expected. They also found that one of the mortar rounds had landed within two feet of one of the launchers, and the other two at distances of about twelve feet and twenty feet. If any Taliban had been at the site when the mortar bombs landed, they would certainly have been killed. There were no bodies at the site, which was not surprising, as the Taliban invariably removed their dead and injured comrades, and we also knew that most rocket attacks were initiated by timing circuits.

This remarkable speed of response and staggering accuracy was down to the high-tech gear they used. The RAF Regiment mortar teams identified the location of the battery that fired the missiles, and a high-speed computer then calculated the trajectory required by their weapon to return fire.

Although the rocket attacks by the Taliban didn't usually cause serious damage, sometimes the effect of their impact could be devastating.

Fairly early on in the coalition's presence in Afghanistan, in October 2005, two Harriers were lost. One was totally destroyed and the second was eventually, after a couple of years, restored to flying condition. Both aircraft were damaged by a single rocket fired from outside Kandahar Airfield when they were parked in the dispersal.

These rockets are short-range, simple, basic, cheap – on Afghanistan's black market they can be picked up for about $100 each – and very inaccurate. Despite all that, about $100 was sufficient expenditure to write off one Harrier – an aircraft that had cost around £11 million, or over $20 million, to buy – and put a second one out of action for a couple of years.

In terms of overall strength, it meant that a single $100 rocket could have a disproportionate effect on the Harrier force and highlighted one of the main challenges of forward basing, especially the forward basing of aircraft in or near the battle zone. The need for a ring of steel to properly protect an airfield is immense, especially when it's faced with weapons like the Russian BM-12 rockets, which, despite all their limitations, have a range of over three miles. To sanitize a buffer zone three miles wide round an airfield would be almost impossible, particularly in Afghanistan, as Kandahar Airfield is very close to the town itself. It wouldn't have been churlish to complain. And, in any case, life was an awful lot more dangerous outside the wire, where it certainly wasn't just British forces who were taking a hammering.

10

The Graveyard actually *was* a graveyard, a reference point located next to the Snowman. When a group of Canadian troops became involved in a massive firefight I was pulled off task to divert there with my wingman. But when we reached the overhead we were instructed not to engage the target – which we could clearly see – because the ground forces were about to put down some suppression artillery. Instead we were told to hold above a certain height, for our own safety, which prevented us doing what we had planned and expected to do: to correctly identify the exact target and then surgically attack the bunch of Taliban who were doing the damage to the Canadian troops.

What followed was eye-watering. The Canadian forces fired a total of seventy-four 155mm shells into a fairly small area occupied by the group of Taliban they were in contact with.

That certainly wasn't suppression. It was closer to Second World War carpet bombing. The Canadians were taking no chances.

We had also been tasked with covering the movement of the Canadian troops as they passed through a particular choke point – a place where there's simply no alternative route – to their closest Forward Operating Base, or FOB. This choke point was just north of Highway One, which runs all the way through Afghanistan. From above, as shells rained down, we watched the whole thing. At the same time as the Canadian artillery hammered the enemy positions, they were also pulling back the troops who had been under fire from the Taliban.

This part of the operation looked almost comic from the air. Half a dozen of their LAV 3 eight-wheeled armoured vehicles raced down the road – which the Canadians were actually still building – dust streaming out behind them. They stopped at intervals to check that the road was still clear in front, then raced off again. Once they reached the location of the troops they stopped, loaded the men inside and dashed back up the road.

All the time this was going on we were watching the almost constant explosions of the 155mm shells – silent puffs of grey-brown dust from our vantage point, but lethal detonations on the ground – in and around the vicinity of the target area. It was an awesome display of firepower, but we had no concerns about collateral damage because the civilian population were long gone. It meant that if anyone was in the Graveyard they were by definition bad guys. And, as long as the Graveyard was home only to the Taliban, it would remain one of the most heavily shelled locations anywhere near Kandahar.

Two thousand and six had been a bad year for the Canadians. In July, accompanied by Afghan troops, they had entered Panjwayi as part of Operation ZAHARA, a campaign intended to clear the area of pockets of Taliban resistance. Heavy fighting began almost immediately in and around the mud-walled compounds occupied by the insurgents, who clearly had not the slightest intention of surrendering control of the area. But the coalition troops prevailed and, after what became known as the First Battle of Panjwayi, they managed to gain control of the area, killing or driving out the Taliban warriors amid heavy and almost continuous fighting.

But once the coalition troops left the area, large numbers of Taliban fighters moved back in and re-established themselves as the dominant presence in the district, and it soon became clear that ISAF troops would have to repeat the operation.

In September the Canadians launched Operation MEDUSA in a final attempt to root out all the Taliban fighters. It was a harsh, brutal campaign that led directly to the far more bloody Second Battle of Panjwayi.

On the first day of MEDUSA the Canadians managed to surround the Taliban positions. They called in air strikes and employed heavy artillery to assault the insurgents, and sustained no casualties themselves. But all that changed on the second day, when four Canadian soldiers were killed in two actions, three during an assault on a Taliban stronghold and the fourth in a bomb attack. The third day was no better: one soldier was killed and over thirty injured when an American A-10 Warthog strafed the Canadians' position in a blue-on-blue incident, after air support had been requested.

During the remainder of the campaign the Canadians faced daily ambushes, mortar attacks and gun battles from some 2,000 heavily armed Taliban warriors, who were well dug in – they had prepared trenches and seemed intent on fighting a First World War-style battle of attrition – and determined to resist to the last man. The Canadians finally managed to drive them out, although the Taliban continued to offer sporadic resistance, both in gun battles and direct contact, as well as sending out suicide bombers and preparing deadly IEDs.

Earlier in the year there had been several contacts between their troops and the Taliban, one of which had resulted in the death of Captain Nichola Goddard, the first female Canadian soldier to lose her life in front-line combat. She was acting as a forward observer, spotting the fall of artillery shells, in an action that also resulted in the wounding of three Afghan soldiers, the deaths of eighteen Taliban and the capture of thirty-five.

We were all acutely conscious of the dangers faced by the soldiers and marines on the ground. By the beginning of September 2006, coalition deaths in Afghanistan totalled 466, of which 329 were American, reflecting the very high proportion of US troops employed in ISAF. In comparison, only 39 British troops had been killed but that number was rising steadily. And so repatriations happened more often than any of us expected. Or hoped.

Whenever there's a repatriation scheduled, a brief email message is sent round to all the computers linked to the Kandahar intranet that states just the name of the dead soldier or marine and that the ceremony will take place that evening. There's no need to give the time, because it's always the same. The C-17 that will transport the body back to the UK always leaves Kandahar Airfield in the dark for self-protection reasons, and its departure is also timed so as to slot into the arrival and departure schedules back at RAF Brize Norton.

The first time I saw a repatriation message I didn't know quite what to expect at the ceremony, but I was determined that it would be a full, proper turnout by all the squadron personnel. I instructed that everyone who wasn't working was to be there, though even without my order everybody would have attended, simply because it's part of the military ethos. Personnel in the armed forces invariably honour their dead. We will always want to say a final farewell to our friends and comrades in arms.

Every nation was represented. They all turned out, every single time. Even if people were off duty, they would always put on their uniforms and attend the ceremony. It was never a case of 'I might just take a look'. At every repatriation everyone who could possibly make it was there. And unfortunately there were quite a number of these ceremonies, for troops of all nations.

The first of the many we attended was for Marine Gary Wright, who had been killed by an IED worn by a suicide bomber when it was detonated next to his patrol vehicle at Lashkar Gah on 19 October 2006.

The ceremony took place, as always, in front of the hangars. When I turned up with the squadron personnel, we initially thought we were in the wrong place because it was utterly quiet. The only sound we could hear was a faint hissing from the auxiliary power unit on the C-17 that was already parked there, tail ramp down and with the internal lights on but at a fairly low setting.

Then, as we walked round the corner of the hangar, everyone drew a sharp breath, because already there were probably close to 1,000 people there. They were formed up in ranks about 200 yards long, twenty or so lines of dark figures, two massive columns of people either side of the approach to the back of the C-17. And everybody present was totally silent. No commands, no talking, not even the slightest whispering, just the faint sound of movement as more and more people joined the huge crowd and silently took their places.

As my squadron personnel joined the ranks, I glanced around. There was a dais just to the right of the back of the C-17, where the padre was waiting, ready to say his piece. And on the ground 300 yards directly behind the C-17's tail, between the two massed ranks of personnel, was a single blue glow stick.

More and more people arrived, still in complete silence, until there were at least 2,000 men and women, standing and watching and waiting, alone with their thoughts.

Then there was a single sharp tap, which meant that the vehicle carrying the body was on its way. In one awesome moment every one of these officers, men and women came silently to attention, again without a single word spoken or command given. Beyond the airfield, by then in almost complete darkness, the looming shape of Three Mile Mountain was barely visible against the evening sky. Gradually the noise of an engine became audible and all of us could see and now hear a medical service Land Rover, with just its parking lights on, driving very slowly and sedately around the taxiway, heading towards the back of the waiting aircraft.

The vehicle drove between the two ranks of silent watchers and stopped directly over the glow stick. Shadowy figures climbed out of the Land Rover and slowly, with infinite care and absolute respect, they lifted out the coffin containing the body of their fallen comrade.

The CO of 3 Commando Brigade arrived in his own vehicle and walked beside the bearers as they carried the body slowly past the silent crowds towards the back of the C-17. They stopped at the bottom of the ramp and lowered the coffin gently on to a trestle.

Lieutenant Colonel Duncan Dewar RM ascended the dais and spoke quietly in the absolute silence of the early evening, his voice carrying easily.

'Marine Wright was an outstanding young Royal Marine whose determination and professional ability led to his selection as a member of our highly specialized Recce Troop. Extremely popular, with a good sense of humour, he was very highly thought of by everyone who worked with him. He was an excellent Marine who died doing the job he loved and will be missed by all his friends in 45 Commando. Our thoughts are very much with his family at this difficult time.'

Next the padre climbed on to the dais and spoke briefly about the man, his eulogy the more moving for its brevity and sincerity.

The bearer party then lifted the coffin again and marched slowly up the ramp into the aircraft. At the very moment that they lowered the coffin to the floor of the hold, all the interior lights snapped out and the back of the C-17 was plunged into complete darkness. And from the assembled mass of people came a sound like the exhalation of a single massive breath. The ramp was raised and at that point all of us in the watching crowd dismissed and returned to our duties.

For me, as for the other squadron members, it was an incredibly moving – and almost surreal – experience, and a defining moment in our time in Afghanistan. The squadron had been in theatre only about three weeks and most people were still on a bit of a high from the intensity of the operations we were carrying out. But that repatriation, more than anything else we'd seen or heard up to that time, was a reminder that we were fighting a war, whatever some choose to call it, against an enemy that would give no quarter. And the silent show of respect given to the dead man by his comrades was simply awe-inspiring.

If ever there was a way to die in combat and go back home, that was it. There was no more respect that you could have shown somebody than that ceremony, and the incredibly moving moment when the lights went out at the rear of the C-17.

The ceremony was filmed so that the family of Marine Wright could see the kind of send-off he'd been given. I hoped, though I knew nothing could ever compensate for his loss, that his family would get a sense of the pride, respect and dignity shown to their loved one by that short ceremony.

Watching the repatriation was a forceful reminder of my own responsibilities. The very last thing I wanted to do was to have to take Duncan Dewar's place on that dais and tell a couple of thousand people how good one of my men or women had been, and how much I regretted the fact that they were now dead. For me, that would be a failure of the very worst and bitterest kind.

But the pace of operations was ramping up still further. We were flying 24/7, apart from the single maintenance period every tenth day, and even then we were still responsible for providing two GCAS 120 alert aircraft. Nor was there any let-up in the quantity of munitions being delivered – in fact we seemed to be dropping *more*, if anything.

It wouldn't be long before I was given further cause to dwell on the risks faced by my own squadron personnel.

Still dressed in flightsuits, the two pilots walked in to the Ops building. They both looked like they'd seen a ghost.

'And what's the matter with you two?' I asked. Bernard and Mouldy – Lieutenant Commander Phil Mould – glanced at each other, then put down their gear and grabbed cold drinks.

'Well,' Bernard began, rubbing a hand over his chin. 'I suppose it was my cock-up, so I'll explain it. I took off as Devil Five Five with Mouldy here' – he pointed to the Senior Pilot, who'd sat down opposite me – 'as Five Six. We were tasked with supporting the Slayers – the Canadian JTACs – based in Panjwayi.'

They had been flying around for about an hour, he said, checking for any activity in the normal areas, when they were re-tasked to go to the Sangin Valley in support of Mastiff Zero Four. 'Mastiff' could have been either a British armoured personnel carrier's callsign or one used by an American JTAC, but in this case it was immediately clear that it was the second.

The two pilots checked in to find that the people on the ground were a small team of US troops who were in a really hard contact with the Taliban. They'd already taken casualties and were waiting for a Quick Reaction Force casevac helicopter to come out to them from Bastion. Their other big problem was that they were in ammunition state black, meaning they'd pretty much run out – a mute testimony to the intensity of the firefight taking place below.

Mouldy and Bernard worked hard taking a talk-on to a single compound in the Green Zone, simply because for some time they couldn't see it. They eventually acquired it only because the mortar rounds had lit a small fire in one corner of it. Mastiff wanted an airburst 300 yards from his position but because it was such a vague target he wanted a mark first. He explained that the choppers were getting closer, so the Harrier pilots needed to get on with it. He was very conscious of the danger-close nature of it all and wanted Type One control.

'I tipped in for the mark,' Bernard said, 'and banged out flares all the way down the dive, but then I had to abort the attack because the JTAC couldn't see me. As I reset, Mastiff told us they were going to have to pull back in their vehicles, because they were taking too much incoming fire for the QRF to land there.

'I tipped in for the second attack and emptied the flare bucket down in the dive. This time Mastiff saw me and cleared me in hot, but as I pressed the pickle button I saw another compound with an even smaller fire in some trees way short of the intended target. Sure enough, Mastiff said they went long – we'd first identified the wrong compound. Then I called tally on the right target, but at that moment the QRF arrived on the scene. They weren't on our frequency, so we couldn't de-conflict the engagement and the boys on the ground had to withdraw. We provided top cover for their withdrawal, but by that time we were approaching bingo fuel.'

You can set your own 'bingo' – low-level – fuel at a higher figure than the minimum, which we did all the time, because when you reached that state you could then decide whether to stay on task or go. But the aircraft has its own sets of warnings, and when the fuel level gets really low these will come on and stay on.

The warning appears in two stages: steady and then flashing when fuel is critically low. When both lights come on steadily, it means you're down to about 750lb each side, which is enough for about 100 miles of flight. Double flashing bingo lights mean 250lb a side. At the best possible burn rate, and with about 50lb a side always unusable, that equates to about eight minutes of flying time left. At a high power setting, for example in the climb, that reduces to maybe three or four minutes, and this means a landing is impossible because you can't get the aircraft down from high level in that time and land safely.

'Then Fenners and Gandalf arrived as Devil Five Seven and Five Eight to provide RIP,' Bernard continued. This pair who provided 'Relief in Place' for their two fellow pilots were Rob Fenwick, a Royal Marine major and one of only three RM Harrier pilots, and Lieutenant Nathan Gray, known as Nath when he wasn't Gandalf.

Bernard and Mouldy stayed a bit longer to talk them on to Mastiff and get them visual with the helos, and then started a bingo recovery to Kandahar. They'd planned to leave and get back with 1,200lb of fuel, not 1,600, as they were on a TIC, but the talk-on with Fenners had taken a little longer than they'd hoped, and Bernard estimated he was going to get to the overhead at Kandahar with only about 1,000lb. He didn't think that would be a problem, as he was going to start his descent at twenty miles, which would bring him back up to around 1,200.

But as soon as they checked in with Trumpcard, about sixty miles from the airfield, they were asked if they could do an air-to-air refuelling for a major TIC that was in progress, because there were no other assets available. Mouldy said the only way they could attempt it would be if the tanker could meet them on the way to Kandahar, and explained that they couldn't deviate from their course.

A few minutes later Shell Nine One, a USAF Boeing KC-135 Stratotanker fitted with a Multi-Point Refuelling System, appeared in a sixty-degree turn and rolled out right in front of them. They had to sacrifice some fuel to climb the extra 1,000 feet and close the mile to the tanker. Refuelling from an MPRS is tricky at the best of times, because the drogue is close to the ends of the wings, and the chicks always get buffeted by the wingtip vortices.

'Mouldy asked me what my fuel was in clear,' Bernard said, 'and I lied a little bit about that – sorry. But he knew I had to have less fuel than him because of the attacks I'd carried out.'

'When he told me what he had,' Mouldy chimed in, 'I said he had just one chance to do this, and only if the tanker would clear him for a direct contact from one mile astern. The tanker crew agreed to this and Bernard made the plug of his life – quite outstanding. We kept on trucking towards Kandahar till I plugged in, and then the tanker started to drag us towards the Baghran Valley at the far north end of Helmand Province.'

'While we were plugged in,' Bernard said, 'Mouldy chopped to Trumpcard in the green to get the details of the TIC while I stayed on the boom frequency, and even wrote down the stuff while he was in the basket, which was pretty cool.'

'That's why he's the Senior Pilot,' I said.

While Mouldy was off frequency, the Shell crew explained that they'd been on their way home, which fortunately took them right across the Harriers' return to base track, but had been told to swing by and give the two aircraft every last drop they could spare. Bernard managed to coax an extra 1,000lb from them after they stopped flowing fuel, which brought him up to 6,000lb, pretty much in line with Mouldy.

'The moment we unplugged,' he explained, 'Mouldy told me that the ground callsign Mastiff Zero Six was in a hell of a state. They had two A-10s already on station, but the Warthogs had Winchestered themselves – they'd fired everything they had – and were remaining as the on-scene commander just waiting for our arrival. And Mastiff reckoned there were so many Taliban facing them that they were about to be overrun any minute.'

The Harriers left the tanker and steamed in there as fast as they could. They arrived above the A-10s and the American pilots started talking them on to the JTAC, Mastiff Zero Six. It turned out the troops had been conducting an advance to contact down the valley and had run into a Taliban unit later estimated at between 300 and 350 strong. The JTAC was so exhausted by the time the Harriers arrived he was pretty much unable to speak at all except to clear them in hot.

All the talk-on, de-confliction and target marking was performed by an FAC(A) – forward air controller (airborne) – qualified A-10 pilot with the callsign Hawg, with final clearance from the Mastiff Zero Six. Also on station was a Predator, and he was continuously lasing the Taliban units. It had been bloody busy out there as the Harriers held position in the overhead, listening to Hawg sort out all the information before giving him the fighter check-in and starting the talk-on.

'The first thing the A-10 pilot said was, "Hey, fellas, these guys are in a whole world of trouble down there. They're firing all kinds of arty and mortars at the Taliban, but if they stop they'll be overrun. I haven't got a clue what the max-ord or gun target lines are. Are you happy to continue?"

'Well, obviously we said we were, so he gave us a five-line and the Predator driver said he was going to lase the target for us.'

A 'five-line' is simply an abbreviated version of the standard nine-line brief given to a pilot by the FAC or JTAC.

The de-confliction plan required the Harriers to hold on one side of the river while the A-10s would hold on the other, because it might be necessary to tip in one of the Warthogs for white phosphorus marking, or get some smoke laid down by mortars on the ground.

'This was already pissing our fuel over the side by making us turn up our own arses in the overhead, and by this point I was sweating bullets,' Bernard muttered. 'This had already been my first TIC support sortie, my first engagement, and the tightest I had ever considered pushing the fuel before the pressure plug to end all plugs.

'And now there we were, once again approaching bingo

fuel, 120 miles away from Kandahar Airfield, listening to a terrified and out-of-breath JTAC screaming over the noise of belt-fed machine-gun fire as we started to attack. I didn't bugger about, just ran in and dropped the five-forty airburst on to the Predator laser spot as soon as everyone was happy for the engagement.'

Bernard set up to re-attack straight away with the operational pod of rockets, but the bingo warner was already going off in his ear. He'd reset Sangin bingo off the tanker, not realizing how far away they were, and he knew that this had to be his last attack as the fuel was now too tight to push it any more.

'Down in the dive, at the exact moment that I pickled I got four hashes on the screen and nothing happened. I let go of the WRB and mashed down on it again but got the same four hashes. But the SMS page still showed the operational pod.'

The SMS page was the interface with the stores management system, the computer that controlled weapons mode, selection and release.

'After listening to the JTAC and his predicament for thirty minutes I no longer cared about the consequences. I just wanted to get the rockets off. I tipped in again and this time everything *looked* like it should work. As I approached the release point I heard Hoggy – Lieutenant Adam Hogg – and Flatters check in as Knife Five Three and Five Four. They'd been scrambled to help out on this TIC.

'I pickled, the rockets fired and I immediately radioed the JTAC. "Mastiff Zero Six, Devil Five Five, you've got Knife Five Three flight in the overhead, and they've got the same load out as us, but we seriously need to go."'

Mastiff acknowledged. The two Harriers climbed up to 29,000 feet and Bernard worked out that he should make it back to base OK with the fuel he had but, as he levelled at twenty-nine he got double flashing bingos, and at that moment he knew there was no way he was going to be able to reach Kandahar. For some reason it seemed that the fuel level was so low that it wouldn't flow at that altitude when he pulled the power back. As long as the engine was at full power there was enough fuel tank air pressure to push it all through, but of course he couldn't stay at full power.

The Harrier's fuel tanks are pressurized by tapping a little air flow from the engine, and what Bernard was telling me suggested that he had so little fuel in them that the air pressure wasn't enough to push it through the large tanks unless the engine was running at almost full power, which of course then drank the scarce fuel faster. It was Hobson's Choice.

'I screamed like a girl to Mouldy, and started looking for somewhere to jump out as we began to descend. When I got down to 19,000 the starboard fuel light went out but the port stayed on. It eventually dawned on me that I had refuelled asymmetrically on the tanker and so all of my remaining fuel was in the right-hand set of tanks. Really, really embarrassing.'

But at that point Bernard had stopped panicking and done what he should have done in the first place. As the good book says, 'he carried out the appropriate actions in accordance with the Flight Reference Cards'. Translated into English, that just means he looked up what he was supposed to do, then did it. And as he transferred fuel into the correct tanks, at a stroke his fuel crisis was over. It didn't make him feel much better. 'It felt more like I should be filling out a Human Factors Occurrence Report,' he admitted, 'explaining that I was a fucking idiot who shouldn't be allowed up in a Cessna trainer unsupervised, far less sent into combat in a Harrier.'

Bernard and Mouldy landed back at Kandahar, shut down the two jets and drove back to Ops in silence. Which is when they stumbled across me. Probably the last person Bernard fancied confessing to.

But for all the drama on that occasion, tanking was something we got very used to carrying out. From a practical point of view, the length of our sorties depended on the number of times we were able to refuel, so a six-hour sortie would see us at the tanker twice.

If there was a lot of activity planned for the A-10s and F-15s out of Kabul, the tankers would be positioned on one of the northerly tracks. But the reality was that there was always a lot of action down to the south, in the Kandahar area, so the tankers were invariably prepared to move south, and there was almost always one we could get to if we needed to refuel in an emergency.

Night-time tanking is 'sporty', to put it mildly, and any form of tanking really concentrates the mind. It's a bit like driving a car up to the rear of a truck that's doing seventy miles an hour and getting close enough behind and to one side of it so that the car's driver can open his window, place his hand on the back of the truck and then hold it in that position for five minutes.

On the GR7 Harrier, the refuelling probe is located

above the left-hand engine intake and is normally folded flat. To refuel, we raise the probe so that it stands above the intake, and in this position the tip of it is just about visible in our peripheral vision. The tanker is a modified airliner, travelling at maybe 300 knots indicated airspeed – which is over 450mph over the ground because of the altitude we're flying at, between 20,000 and 27,000 feet – and it trails a hose behind it, on the end of which is a basket perhaps two feet in diameter.

This basket has little vanes on it to give it some aerodynamic stability and keep it straight. Our closing speed is only three or four miles an hour faster than the tanker, and the intention is to fly the probe into the centre of the basket so that it plugs in properly to the geo-lock and the fuel starts flowing. Then we hold that position for some five to seven minutes while the Harrier's tanks fill. Once we've taken on sufficient fuel, we disconnect and drop away below the tanker and return to our tasking.

Now while this may demand a little concentration in broad daylight, at night, in turbulent air, maybe a little adverse weather and doing the whole thing wearing night-vision goggles, the refuelling operation can get more interesting. In a sphincter-tightening kind of way.

I was still reflecting on what Bernard and Mouldy had told me about their sortie when, tired out, I crawled into bed that night. I was aware of a number of aircraft incidents and accidents that involved a succession of problems, insignificant in themselves, but which, taken cumulatively, had resulted in the loss of an aircraft, and in some cases the death of the pilot as well.

The story Bernard had told struck an immediate chord. *If* the talk-on at Sangin had taken any longer; *if* the Shell tanker had been empty, or too far away to carry out the refuel; *if* Bernard had made a pig's ear of plugging into the tanker; *if* he hadn't realized he'd refuelled asymmetrically, I could now have been looking at a crashed Harrier and, quite possibly, a missing or even dead pilot. Certainly if Bernard *had* ejected, and been found by the Taliban before we got a rescue chopper out to him, he would certainly have been killed, probably very painfully.

But it hadn't happened that way. And I knew Bernard, on his first combat tour, would chalk the whole episode down to experience and ironically be a better pilot for it.

We simply couldn't afford to lose a Harrier – the propaganda victory that would hand to the Taliban, who would immediately claim to have shot it down, would be overwhelming – and I certainly wasn't prepared to lose a pilot. That really would validate the doubts that had been conveyed to me about the suitability and viability of 800 NAS operating in Afghanistan.

As I drifted off I wondered if I really had done everything I could to head off problems at the pass. I tried to put the thought to one side and get to sleep.

I 2

We had received intelligence that a coalition convoy was very likely to be attacked by a suicide bomber, who was driving around the area in a VBIED, a vehicle-borne IED – a car or truck stuffed with explosives, just looking for a coalition target.

The two main routes near Kandahar were Highway One and Highway Four – the second runs down to the Pakistan border – and whenever we were flying in those areas we would always try to follow the roads fairly closely, in what we called 'highway patrol'. There's a balance to be struck between risk and effect, but we could put down a lot of noise and still remain outside the threat envelope of most missile systems.

The lifelines of the coalition forces were the roads, because the bulk of our regular supplies arrived at Kandahar by road convoy. If a group of Taliban was busy laying an IED by the side of the road, or digging in a few mines, the chances were that they'd stop and scatter if they heard an aircraft approaching.

Road convoys in Afghanistan were always escorted by heavily armed troops and armoured vehicles. With Neil Bing as my wing-man, I'd been tasked to provide top cover. From the cockpits of our two Harriers we could provide detailed surveillance of the route the convoy was having to take to get to their main internal FOB, only about a mile away – sixty seconds on a motorway, but possibly a whole lifetime in Afghanistan – on the other side of a fairly densely packed residential area, an ideal hunting ground for the Taliban.

Cruising overhead, we'd been in contact with the troops on the ground for a while and were nervous on their behalf, although there was nothing we could do to help them apart from visually checking their route through the village. The risk of collateral damage would have prevented us dropping weapons there even if they did come under attack.

What struck both of us was the very rapid speech of the men on the radio – in a tense situation, most people talk a lot faster than normal – and the sheer naked fear in their voices, fear that reflected the knowledge that their convoy was almost certainly going to become a target.

And suddenly their fears seemed to be justified. Down on the ground below us, we could see a car or a small truck, getting closer and closer to the convoy. It was driving systematically through the residential area, and it looked to us like the driver was probably carrying out a search for something. And in the circumstances it was more likely that he was looking for the coalition convoy rather than just, say, an address to deliver some goods.

'Recoil Four Seven. Heads-up. We can see a vehicle moving towards you. It's zigzagged its way through the residential area and now, as you come up through the centre of the area, it's coming in at ninety degrees down the next street on your right-hand side. Its range is about two hundred yards . . . One hundred and fifty . . . One hundred. You'll see it any second now.'

On the ground, the troops in the convoy were taking no chances. They'd spread out into defensive positions as soon as I'd started counting down the distances as the vehicle approached them, and the moment it rumbled into view they opened up with everything they had. From the air the tracer rounds were quite evident in the dark, and we could hear their .50-calibre machine-gun blatting away in the background while one of the troops talked to us on the radio. They didn't aim at the vehicle itself, because there was still a possibility that it was entirely innocent, but they laid down a wall of fire directly in front of it.

The result was exactly what they'd hoped. As bullets chewed into the ground ahead of them, the vehicle slammed to a halt, did an immediate about-turn and got the hell out of it. We never found out who the driver was, or what his intention had been. It might have been the suicide bomber, who changed his mind when he saw the firepower the patrol could muster, or perhaps it really was just a lost delivery driver or someone looking for a particular address, who would at the very least have needed to go home and change his trousers.

That was the first hurdle overcome for the convoy, but they still had a long way to go. A little further on we were steering the convoy vehicles around the edge of a village when I spotted something we couldn't identify. What I was looking at simply didn't make sense.

'It's the weirdest thing,' I radioed the troops in the leading vehicle in the convoy. 'About five hundred yards in front of your position, as you go round the next bend in the road, we can see what looks like something burning.

It's like a burning disc, and it's spinning round very quickly. I can't work out what it is.'

As soon as I passed the warning, the convoy slowed as the men on the ground tried to decide what the hell this thing could be. Risking attack from the ground, I flew lower – a lot lower – to try to identify the object and what it was being used for. The overriding fear was that it was some kind of a trap, perhaps something to attract the troops' attention while a suicide bomber attacked them from a different direction. And all the time the convoy, which simply had to keep moving, was getting closer and closer to this object, with no way to avoid passing close to it. But when I contacted the convoy again I was none the wiser.

'I've just dropped right down to low level to take a look,' I radioed, 'but it still doesn't make sense. It looks just like somebody swinging a burning tyre round on the end of a rope.'

Somebody in the convoy responded almost immediately. 'That's it, then,' they drawled, suddenly unconcerned. 'It's a burning tyre on a rope. We're good to go.'

'What?' I demanded.

'You're right. You've identified it. This is the start of the festival of Eid ul-Fitr. This must be just the locals enjoying their celebration.'

Eid ul-Fitr marked the end of Ramadan and is a major cause for celebration. What I'd picked out from the cockpit of the Harrier was a whole gang of Afghan locals setting light to tyres and swinging them round on the end of ropes. To us, not the most obvious way to mark the end of a fast, but clearly it suited them. We had known about Eid, but not that the celebrations involved such a bizarre activity.

So all the consternation, both in the air and on the ground, had been caused purely because, in a battle environment, *anything* out of the ordinary raised immediate suspicions and the safest reaction was to assume that what we were looking at was some kind of highly sophisticated and lethal trap.

It was another reminder to all of us that, just because a bloody war was being fought in the country, life for most of the locals carried on pretty much as normal. As far as they were concerned, Ramadan was over, so they could get back to their normal diet, and that was something worth celebrating. The fact that a noisy convoy of trucks full of heavily armed troops was rumbling past the mud walls of their compound was completely irrelevant to them.

And for the people in the convoy no doubt there were sighs of relief as they realized they weren't going to have to fight their way out of yet another ambush.

My satisfaction at a job well done didn't last long. Back on the ground, a handful of my pilots were waiting outside the Ops building after we landed. A couple of them walked round to the front of my Harrier and ostentatiously counted the stores bolted to the wings, and as I climbed out the bantering started.

'He must be saving them for something special.'

'Perhaps he's a Talib in disguise?'

'A bloody good disguise if he is.'

'Right, you two, knock it off,' I said. 'In case you hadn't

noticed, we're only supposed to drop bombs on legitimate targets. This time the most exciting thing we saw was a burning tyre.'

'A what?'

As we walked over to Ops I explained what we'd seen from the air and the deduction that it was part of the festivities marking the end of Ramadan.

'Hm,' said one of the pilots. 'I still think you've turned into a pacifist, or a war-dodger, boss. I mean, look at the evidence. We've had three sorties today. In the first two, both pilots cleared their wings. You take off, and it's like the Taliban simply aren't there any more. We get called to TICs – you get called to check out a burning tyre. I mean, something's not right.'

I smiled as I walked inside. I could pretend that it was all water off a duck's back, but the truth was I was getting a little fed up with the 'war-dodger' stuff. And it wasn't as if there was the slightest truth in it. It just seemed to be Sod's Law that whenever I was airborne either nothing at all happened or I was carrying the wrong weapons.

If I got airborne carrying five-forties, that day the Taliban would all be firing from inside buildings, and my wing-man's 1,000lb stores would be the weapons of choice. If I was carrying the heavier munitions, all the TICs would be in the open air, and the five-forties or CRV-7s used. And I was fairly certain that if I got airborne with both five-forties and 1,000-pounders, the Taliban would all decide to stay at home. In short, the 'war-dodger' tag was looking more and more justified, and there didn't seem to be anything I could do about it. I gave it one last roll of the dice.

'What you have to realize,' I said, 'is that everyone's got a fixed allocation of bombs they can drop, and I used up most of mine over in Iraq, during TELIC. Oh,' I added, to try to pop the youngster back in his box, 'I forgot that this is only your *first* war, isn't it? What you should do is try not to deliver too many munitions out here, so you'll still have some of your allowance left over for later.'

'No, no, I'm not buying that, boss. Let's face it, you're almost a non-swimmer.'

Ouch! That one stung. 'Non-swimmers' was what we called people or nations who contributed little or nothing to the coalition effort. And with the number of countries involved there were always going to be wildly different opinions of the value of some people's efforts. Even among those who were, indisputably, pulling their own weight.

13

The Harrier squadron was a part of a wide range of air assets based at Kandahar Airfield, but, when we arrived and took over from IV (AC) Squadron, 800 NAS was the only fixed-wing combat squadron on the base. A few months later, at Christmas 2006, we were joined by a squadron of Dutch F-16s which came down south from Kabul, and currently there are also French Mirages based at Kandahar. American AV-8Bs would sometimes drop in at the base and spend a week or so operating out of Kandahar before returning to their Wasp-class carriers holding off the coast.

One of the issues that frequently came up was the way the Americans seemed to always get the juicy tasking. That's the way it seemed and it was definitely the case when the carrier was in town. They always took the prime windows when there was likely to be any action from the Taliban.

There are two ways of looking at this. At that time the Harrier didn't have a sniper pod which would provide a video down-link to the troops on the ground. If the F-18s were around, and had that kind of equipment, why wouldn't you put them in the programme at prime times during the day and let them use it, because it would provide good interaction? So, from an operational point of view, this was a smart move. It just slightly pissed us off because we were there seven days a week, and the moment the carrier appeared, its aircraft would come in and take the juicy slots.

The Dutch detachment commander, who was a major, phoned up the CAOC and ended up speaking to a three-star USAF general about this. The Dutchman asked him why during Operation BAAZ TSUKA – the Pashto name means 'Falcon's Summit', but I strongly suspect some staff officer with too much time on his hands picked it mainly because it sounds remarkably like 'bazooka' – the F-15s had been drafted in during the heavy fighting periods.

The American general slammed him and told him that the campaign wasn't some kind of coalition love-in. He had a job of work to do, with a pre-planned operation running for two weeks, and he was bringing in the F-15s because they were the best aeroplanes for the job. This wasn't, the general said, some kind of pleasant task-sharing event I've got going on, and you'll get what you're given. And, of course, he was absolutely right.

The Dutch were flying F-16s with a laser-guided bomb and a gun and that was all. The general wanted an aircraft like the F-15, equipped with a data link, a range of weapons including a small-diameter bomb, a gun, JDAMs, GBUs, two people on board and plenty of time on station. So he pretty much told the Dutch officer to get back in his box and shut the fuck up.

Given the commitment and skill of the Dutch, it was, to say the least, an unfortunate reaction, especially as some of the nations involved in the coalition really do attract the light-hearted label of 'non-swimmers'. But even these countries that, on the face of it, didn't bring a huge amount to the party often contributed valuable niche capabilities.

Of the few countries that made a significant contribution to the air campaign, the French, like the Dutch, flew Close Air Support. If the French Navy were involved, flying from the deck of the FNS *Charles de Gaulle* steaming in the Arabian Sea, they would often fly in mixed pairs. As the RAF operated Buccaneers and Tornados during the first Gulf War, the former providing laser designation for the latter, so the French would fly Super Etendards and their new Rafales. The French Air Force also operated different types together, in their case, the Mirage F1 and the newer twin-seat Mirage 2000 delta-winged strike aircraft. Both flew out of Dunshabe in Tajikistan, meaning longer transit times than for the British Harriers at Kandahar.

You could never call the Americans non-swimmers. Quite the opposite. What really struck you was the sheer volume of ordnance they would drop in comparison to us. This was partly, I suppose, because they could. Each of their big B-1 swing-wing heavy bombers could carry the same load as the entire force of British Harriers in theatre. But the B-1 didn't have a targeting pod and often put down sticks of four or five bombs to obliterate a target. And in almost every case the job could have been done by a tactical jet like the Harrier, fitted with a targeting pod and able to place one bomb exactly where it was wanted. But there was more to it than just the relative capabilities of the aircraft. When the US wages war, protection of their own forces is less an overriding priority than an obsession. But given that they've lost some 4,000 personnel in Iraq and Afghanistan since 2001, this is a powerful argument. The sometimes overwhelming force used by US forces may raise eyebrows here, but it's understandable, legitimate and undeniably effective. In the end there's no right or wrong about it – it just boils down to a difference in approach.

We worked very effectively with the Canadians, and a number of their troops were based in an outpost some distance to the north of Kandahar, in a pretty grim FOB called Martello. It was in the back of beyond, at least a two-day drive from Kandahar, and with the kind of terrain the drive involved and the near certainty of Taliban ambushes, they might just as well have been on the moon. They were completely cut off.

They were routinely attacked, and always very aggressively, by the Taliban. Early on in the detachment one of the younger pilots from the squadron got involved in a pretty hectic firefight up there. The base was being attacked from two sides, with groups of insurgents firing both mortars and machine-guns, and this pilot did an absolutely brilliant job of identifying the very small target that was presented and engaging it with CRV-7s. His attack took out that group of Taliban – he managed to either kill them or destroy their weapons, but, whichever was the truth, the firing stopped.

Then he repeated the process, identifying the location of the second group of insurgents and detonating a five-forty airburst weapon above them. Again, it wasn't clear if he'd completely destroyed the site or killed the Taliban there, but it certainly stopped them engaging the Canadians.

After that our Harriers were there almost every night,

providing overwatch for the Canadians, identifying any Taliban mortar positions we could, and then taking them out as comprehensively as possible. And every day the Canadians thanked us for being up there, because our Harriers managed to suppress the Taliban so well that for forty-three consecutive days they didn't have to endure a single attack.

It became a routine. The pilots would make a point of always trying to fly past Martello, whether they were just leaving Kandahar or returning to the airfield – although because Martello was so far to the north we couldn't always achieve this – or were actually tasked with patrolling in that area. The noise of the aircraft was a constant reassurance to the marooned Canadian troops and a reminder to the Taliban that not only had the Harriers already done a lot of damage to them, but were still around in case they wanted to try their luck again.

Then there was the ANA. While we were at KAF, members of the Afghan National Army were being trained by the coalition troops to do the job themselves, so a lot of the time the patrols were mixed, with ANA soldiers accompanying either British or American forces to learn the techniques first-hand. But, as the ANA soldiers became more experienced, the emphasis shifted from a few of them tagging on to a patrol composed of coalition troops, to a handful of coalition advisers accompanying a patrol of ANA soldiers. It was classic on-the-job training, conducted in the environment the ANA will eventually be working in, if the Taliban ever give up, which looks unlikely.

And the ANA were as welcome to the aerial firepower provided by 800 NAS as any of the NATO members of the coalition. When the scramble rang we didn't discriminate. Dunc Mason, and Nath Gray, who was one of the younger squadron pilots, roared into the air to help out a mixed group of about a dozen ANA soldiers and the two American marines who were mentoring them.

Nath was fairly short, very slender – one of my officers described his figure as being like a racing snake – and extremely fit, having done both the Green Beret (Royal Marine Commando) and the Peak Company (Parachute Regiment) courses. When they got back to Kandahar he told me what had happened.

The patrol had been ambushed by the Taliban, which was by no means an unusual event. But in the confusion of the assault, as the coalition troops scattered to find the best defensive positions, three of the Afghans somehow got separated from the main group of soldiers, and all contact with them was lost. Of the nine ANA troops remaining, one of the Afghans was killed outright when the Taliban opened up on them, and another was badly wounded.

When Dunc and Nath arrived overhead, they got good two-way contact with one of the American marines, and once they knew that three of the ANA soldiers were missing, saw that finding them had to be their first priority. They couldn't drop weapons on the Taliban until they knew exactly where the three Afghans were – whether they were dead or alive – to avoid a blue-on-blue incident. And of course they wanted to find the three missing soldiers before the Taliban did.

The only information the patrol members could supply was that they thought the three ANA soldiers had broken away to the north. That didn't give Dunc and Nath much to go on, so they immediately began running a logical search pattern, starting from the ambush position and working their way up towards the north.

It sounds straightforward, but Nath was using a target reconnaissance pod that he hadn't had very much training in, and this was far from the easiest piece of kit to use. But, calmly and efficiently, he performed a very thorough search, following the route that he thought the escaping Afghans might possibly have taken if they were heading north. Using the pod was a bit like looking through a drinking straw, he told me. For ages all he seemed to be able to see was 'lots and lots of shit-brown sand and bits of scrubby bush, all at really high magnification'. His diligence was rewarded, though, when he finally located the three men, who had taken cover beyond a group of buildings.

Nath called the US Marine radio operator to let the patrol know where they were. The problem was there were no convenient reporting points anywhere close, so he had to describe the position as best he could. The moment he did, the marine told him, with some frustration, that they had already seen the Taliban heading that way, so it was possible that they had spotted the three ANA men. As the Americans were already advancing to that position, he asked, could the two of them try to hold off the bad guys until they got there?

But Dunc and Nath had a problem. When they swung round to begin the attack, they both saw at once that the

26. The squadron's engineers worked round the clock to keep the Harriers flying throughout the det.

27. The bomb dump.

28. The route to and from the bomb dump was well worn. Over the course of a four-month det we dropped over 100,000 lbs of ordnance.

29. 'Bombheads' – naval armourers – load a 540 lb dumb bomb on to the outboard pylon of a Harrier in the hangar at Kandahar.

30. Pre-flight briefing.

32. The safety tags are removed from a 1000 lb Paveway II laser-guided bomb before take-off.

31. The stencils sprayed on to the side of the jet give a pretty clear indication of the intensity of the operations flown by the squadron in Afghanistan. The circles to the left represent CRV-7 rockets fired. Bombs dropped are on the right.

33. Yours truly, just before climbing in to the cockpit. Wearing a g-suit and survival gear, I'm standing next to one of the 800 NAS det Harriers. To my left is a live 540 lb high-explosive bomb.

34. With the jet chained to the ground, the squadron engineers run a high-power engine test. The air fills with oily black smoke whenever the Rolls-Royce Pegasus is fired up.

35. The office – the instrument panel of the Harrier GR7. The two flat-screen displays are evident. Top centre are the radios. Top right, the engine instruments. And below the radios the attitude indicator – or artificial horizon – can be seen.

36. The view from the pilot's seat, which clearly shows the position of the Head-up Display (HUD).

37. The ridges surrounding KAF seen through the HUD with a C-130 and Mi-24 just visible in the foreground.

38. Taxiing out.

39. Filling up. A Harrier takes on fuel from an RAF TriStar tanker. Air-to-air refuelling dramatically increased the time the squadron could spend over the operating area.

40. Self-portrait.

41. We always hunted in pairs. In reality, we'd fly in a loose battle formation separated by thousands of feet. This picture was actually taken as the jets streaked past *Illustrious* as she steamed in the Indian Ocean.

42. Loaded for bear. A GR7, armed with CRV-7 rockets and bombs, *en route* to Helmand, ready to support troops on the ground. The yellow bands around the bombs indicate that they're live.

43. KAF from the air. A picture taken from about 20,000 feet, using the GR7's centreline recce pod. The base's uninviting location is pretty evident. As is the infamous 'poo pond', the circle in the bottom right corner of the airfield with the four distinct segments, representing different stages of the treatment process.

44. RAF Regiment patrols that pushed the Taliban back from the perimeter led to a significant decrease in the number of rocket attacks on KAF.

45. A 3 Commando Brigade mortar team in action. Accurate mortar fire from the RAF Regiment counter-battery teams helped tackle the threat of rocket attacks at source.

46. Here I am getting it all out of my system with a compact 'mini-me' machine gun on the KAF ranges.

47. Downtime. A few members of the squadron relax over coffee at Tim Hortons, another of the takeaway outlets flown in by the USAF. I'm the one in the middle with my hand in the doughnut bag.

48. Celebrating 2,500 flying hours with an alcohol-free 'near beer' during the otherwise dry det in Afghanistan.

Taliban were so close to the three Afghan soldiers that they couldn't use a bomb, not even a five-forty, without a high risk of killing or injuring the ANA men. So they decided instead to use CRV-7s in an attempt to scare off the Taliban. While rockets wouldn't be as accurate or do as good a job as a bomb, they were the only weapons they were carrying that they could use safely, and would inflict little collateral damage.

The Afghans were close to a cluster of buildings, probably abandoned, and Dunc and Nath could see that the Taliban were searching through the compound, clearly looking for them.

Dunc went in first. Pulling his Harrier into a tight turn, he steadied up to check his aim, then fired. He targeted a building that some of the Taliban had entered just a few seconds before. Although he knew he wasn't likely to do them or the buildings any serious damage, he figured the rockets might make them think twice about coming outside again.

As he unleashed the first salvo he was reminded just how tough the traditional mud-walled Afghan dwellings and compound walls were. High-velocity armour-piercing rounds that were capable of unzipping a tank seemed to just bounce off these solid old structures, leaving hardly more than a little dent.

Although Dunc and Nath could see the ANA patrol approaching in the distance, they knew they would take quite a while to get to the compound. In the meantime, once the Taliban spotted where three escaped ANA soldiers had taken refuge, they would slaughter them. They also knew that just two Harrier pilots were never going to be able take out all the Taliban. There were just too many, they were too spread out in too many different parts of the compound and the two of them had a limited number of rockets.

They decided to fire small salvoes – half a dozen or so CRV-7s with each attack – in repeated runs, hitting the building where they could see the Taliban hiding, and trying to keep them away from the three escapees. But it seemed unlikely that they could hold them off until the rest of the patrol caught up, and even then the ANA would be heavily outnumbered.

'Talk about a bit of luck,' Nath said afterwards. 'Just as we'd fired the last of our CRV-7s, an Apache attack chopper pitched up, and that altered the odds dramatically, because he could bring his more accurate weapons to bear. That was a hell of a relief.'

The upshot was that the three ANA soldiers made it safely to a coalition checkpoint, largely because of the cool and considered actions by the two Harrier pilots, who had kept the Taliban far enough away to allow them to make good their escape. And although the CRV-7s had exploded very close to the Afghans, the two pilots had aimed them so accurately that none of the men was injured.

14

Another day, another dollar. I turned on to the end of the runway at Kandahar, the surface shimmering in the heat and making it look almost as if the far end was under water, and pushed the throttle fully forward, releasing the brakes moments later.

The noise of the Pegasus engine rose to a shrill scream as the Harrier leapt forward, pushing me back into the seat. I concentrated on keeping the aircraft straight – though with a runway the width of Kandahar's you'd need to be *seriously* incompetent to run off the edge – and checking my instruments. I lifted off and retracted the gear, got the wheels in the well, but kept the aircraft low, watching the speed increasing and steadily reducing flap, until I approached the far end of the runway, where the huge whale-like shape of the UN Mi-24 Halo had become a familiar and comforting sight.

Only then did I pull back on the control column and point the Harrier's nose up into the sky. With the sudden change of direction the 'g' loaded up. My legs were squeezed by the air bladders as my speed jeans inflated to prevent the loss of blood pressure in my brain.

As I climbed I turned on to my pre-planned vector and continued my tactical departure. All the way up to medium level I was alternating my attention between the Harrier's instrumentation – particularly the engine-monitoring systems – and the mirrors. No coalition aircraft had ever been shot down on departure from Kandahar Airfield, as far as I knew, and I was determined not to be the first. So I watched the mirrors constantly for the telltale pinprick of smoke and flame that might indicate the launch of a SAM.

Once above 20,000 feet I relaxed, levelled at my cruising altitude and watched the airborne TACAN that showed me that my wing-man, Bernard, was closing up on me, 1,000 feet below. A couple of minutes later he called visual and we joined up as a pair.

Then we ran through our checks to make sure the Harriers' weapons systems were working properly.

I uncaged the targeting pod, designated a waypoint on the ground and pointed the pod at it. The pod locked on to the exact feature I'd selected, which proved that the aircraft systems and the pod were working in sync. I selected another point and fired the laser at it to check that system as well. We also cross-checked our equipment, so that when I fired my laser, Bernard confirmed that his systems were detecting the reflected energy.

'Recoil Four Five, Four Six, got it. Terminate the laser.'

I stopped firing my laser. Bernard turned his on and called: 'Laser fires.'

He aimed his laser at the same target I'd picked, and I set up my laser receiving system to ensure I was able to detect the reflected energy.

'Roger, happy, terminate.'

Once we'd done the mutual flare check and the radio and laser pod checks, internally I ran through my own checklist and, reaching down to the distinctive brown and white pattern of the Late Arm switch in the left-hand side of the cockpit, switched it to live. Some people have a different preference, but I like to have my Late Arm on all the time I'm airborne. I don't want to have to remember it each time I select a weapon. And I know that if I *have* just selected a weapon it probably means I'm about to drop it because I am in a war zone. And if you forget to switch your Late Arm on, you won't be able to drop it. Simple as that. And embarrassing.

So, from the moment I'm at altitude, I'm ready.

We did a final visual check to ensure that our expendable systems were working, and that we were ready for the mission, and headed off into the badlands.

Our two Harriers were, as usual, carrying a mix of weapons distributed across eleven weapons stations on the wings and fuselage. A GR7 'loaded for bear', as the Americans say, will carry about 3,000lb of ordnance usually split between four of the eight wing pylons. And on this sortie Bernard's jet was equipped with two 1,000lb Paveways – these are the GPS- and laser-guided bombs – which actually weigh about 1,300lb each with all their associated kit fitted. On other stations were two external fuel tanks and a target designation pod.

Under my wings I was carrying a pair of 540lb bombs, one set for impact and the other for airburst, plus two CRV-7 rocket pods. I also carried a big fuel tank under each wing and a targeting pod under my Harrier's belly. On top of this, briefed to fly a tactical reconnaissance and intelligence-gathering sortie, we both had reconnaissance pods slung from the centreline station.

Recce is essential in any combat. Without knowledge of where the enemy is located and what they're doing, any military force is effectively blind. So we frequently got airborne carrying camera pods and, in the absence of any activity that required our intervention, we'd be tasked with photographing a particular area where it was known or believed that the Taliban might be located. It was a low-intensity, but absolutely vital, task.

But we'd hardly got started on our briefed photographic runs before we were re-tasked.

'Recoil Four Five, Crowbar,' a distant voice crackled over the radio. 'TIC India Bravo declared.'

The controller followed this with a position, and the callsign and frequency of the unit that had requested urgent assistance.

I immediately identified the location on the map display on my left-hand TV screen, and we altered course and increased speed. At around 400 knots and heading straight towards the mountains north of Kandahar, I dialled in the frequency and called up the unit's radio operator.

'Jaguar One Five, this is Recoil Four Five.'

'Recoil Four Five, Jaguar One Five, roger. Ready for fighter check-in.' The man's voice, even over the filtering effect of the secure radio link, sounded tense with fear and apprehension.

I quickly passed him all our details and finished with our current position. 'Estimate minutes four to your overhead, request SITREP.'

'Recoil Four Five, Jaguar One Five, roger. We've just had an IED strike, one man down. There's a rescue chopper coming in but it'll be at least thirty-five to forty minutes before he gets out here.' There was a brief pause, filled with static. 'Please hurry.'

The American JTAC sounded terrified, as if he expected to be massacred by the Taliban at any moment. And when we heard the full SITREP, we realized why.

The mountains north of Kandahar were one of the principal hideouts of the Taliban in winter. They go up there to regroup and recover from the punishment they've had inflicted on them during the summer, especially August and September.

The unit we had been re-tasked to assist was a US patrol that was returning to Kandahar after what had already been an eleven-day sortie. They were only about forty miles out, but they still expected that it would take them at least two days to get back. As well as being limited to travelling about twenty miles a day by the difficult terrain, they had to clear their way through areas where contact with the Taliban was likely, so extreme caution was needed.

From the air, it was easy to see the problem. Nobody wanted to go through the choke points, because they were also the obvious sites for an ambush. Particularly dangerous were the *wadis*. They were ideal for vehicular movement because the surface was firm and fairly flat, but patrols never went down them unless it was unavoidable. Visibility from a *wadi* was severely restricted. The river bed was of course always lower than the surrounding terrain and so you couldn't see over the banks, which made them ideal spots for an ambush. Instead vehicles would always drive along the much more rugged and difficult ground along the sides of the river valleys, wherever possible avoiding the tracks made by other vehicles, just in case the Taliban had decided to position an IED on what looked like a regular route.

That was a regular tactic employed by the insurgents. If they could identify a route that was in frequent use by coalition troops, they would conceal either a mine or, typically, a pressure-plate IED, buried under the vehicle tracks or sometimes just beside them. And a *wadi* crossing was a prime location for this kind of device.

The problem facing troops was that there might only be one point where it was possible to get from one side to the other. Often the sides of the *wadi* were steep, almost vertical and completely impassable to vehicles. Patrols always had to pick a spot where both slopes were gentle enough to allow their vehicles to drive down one side and up the other. The most critical vehicles were the heavy supply trucks, often driven by locally recruited nationals, because they hadn't got the engine power or the climbing ability to tackle really difficult terrain. And so the reality was that there might only be a single location along a stretch of a mile or more of a *wadi* where a crossing was possible at all.

From the aircraft, turning hard directly over the *wadi* as we arrived on the scene and looked straight down, we could see exactly what had happened. Tracks snaked away in all directions from both sides, but they all came together at a single location, the only viable crossing point in the whole length of the *wadi*. And in the middle of the river bed was a wrecked Humvee, burning fiercely.

It looked to me as if the Americans had been sensibly cautious. Instead of simply following the other tracks straight across the *wadi*, which is where the Taliban would be most likely to have positioned an IED, the driver of the Humvee had crossed slightly to one side of the obvious crossing point, and in doing so had hit the device. Ironically, if the Humvee had simply followed the existing tracks, the vehicle would have missed it altogether.

The IED had stopped the vehicle dead, and seriously injured one of the crew members. The medevac helicopter was on its way out to pick up the wounded man and take him to the medical centre at Kandahar, but until that happened the patrol had no option but to stay in its present position. And that location was far from ideal from a defensive point of view. They were low down in the *wadi*, surrounded by high ground on all sides, and their real worry was that an IED strike was normally the precursor to an all-out attack by the Taliban. The stress and tension in the radio operator's voice showed that clearly enough – he sounded terrified.

The moment the device had detonated, the patrol spread out into battle positions as quickly as they could, but they were right in the middle of a classic Taliban killing ground and for the moment they couldn't move away from it. They were stuck down by the *wadi* crossing, unable to reposition because of their injured man, and also because they would have to blow up the Humvee to completely destroy it before they left. This was essential to ensure that none of the sensitive and classified equipment and information it contained could fall into the hands of the Taliban.

They had taken up positions on the highest ground they could find, about 500 yards from the Humvee, but because they were still down in the *wadi* they had higher ground on both sides and so only limited visibility. And every man in the patrol knew that there could be hundreds of heavily armed Taliban fighters lurking behind the river hills – mounds formed by a combination of water and wind – that surrounded them. They were expecting at any moment to come under fire from heavy machine-guns positioned on the high ground either side of them and probably to be facing hordes of Taliban attacking from concealed positions within the *wadi* itself. And, against those kinds of odds, they knew their chances of survival were slim, at best.

No wonder they were nervous.

'Four Six, Four Five. Stay at twenty and watch the outer perimeter. I'll go down and check out the rest.'

'Roger.'

I throttled back and pointed the nose of the Harrier towards the ground. The first thing we had to do was eliminate any blind spots – not difficult from the air – and then expand the safe perimeter around the troops.

Dropping down to about 7,000 feet, I began to fly a circle around the *wadi* crossing point. I trimmed the aircraft so that I could almost fly it hands off, put on the altitude hold and started checking the area below me.

I had found that just about the single most useful device in the Harrier's cockpit was the set of gyro-stabilized binoculars. These were easy to use and allowed me to survey a considerable area very quickly. They were especially valuable in a confused situation, where there were many potential targets to check. Once I'd identified a possible target I used the Harrier's targeting pod, a very high-fidelity sensor, to examine the location through the optics on the flat screen in the cockpit, and to refine the coordinates. The equipment wasn't actually designed for this task, but all of the squadron pilots had achieved considerable success with it.

Some non-aviators imagine that modern sensors have taken a lot of the skill out of identifying targets, but the reality is rather different. There's no denying that the sensors *are* highly sophisticated pieces of equipment, but for optimum and efficient employment the pilot must first locate the target, or at least its approximate position, and then slew the sensor on to it: the aircraft needs to know what it's pointing at. If the pilot can't do this, the search and acquisition of a target is still possible, but it can take a hell of a long time.

Using the wrecked Humvee as my datum point, I began an immediate visual search of the *wadi* and the surrounding area, moving steadily outwards from the patrol's position and remaining in constant radio contact with the JTAC on the ground.

Almost at once I spotted a couple of areas that I was unhappy with, where it looked to me as if insurgents could have concealed themselves and their heavy weapons.

'One Five, Four Five. Two suspect positions. First, from the Humvee, bearing one seven five, range about 900 yards. There's an outcropping with vegetation behind it. Second location. Bearing two three five, range one click. A tumble of rocks.'

'Four Five, One Five, roger. We'll check them out.'

I flew lower still, watching as the armoured Humvees headed out to check each spot, followed cautiously by heavily armed troops, and continued my detailed scan of the whole area.

'Recoil Four Five, Jaguar One Five, that's a negative

on the first location. Standing by for the second.' The voice paused for a few seconds, then spoke again. 'And the second's also negative.'

Even then, I could quite clearly hear the tension in his voice easing. The first two possible hiding places for Taliban fighters had proved to be harmless and, so far, nobody had shot at them. Was the IED strike just a freak incident?

High above me, Bernard was reporting no signs of hostile activity. From his higher vantage point he could cover a much greater area, but he could see neither vehicles nor people on the ground.

I identified another half a dozen possible ambush sites in and near the *wadi*, and relayed the coordinates to the JTAC for investigation, but in every case they found no enemy forces. Each movement outwards from the *wadi* steadily increased the perimeter around the patrol's position, and it soon became clear that there were no Taliban in the near vicinity.

As the perimeter widened, the blatant fear in the radio operator's voice lessened markedly. It was clear that the IED strike had been a one-off and that they were not about to be attacked by the Taliban.

The next problem the patrol faced was getting away from the *wadi* once the medevac chopper had picked up the wounded soldier, and again the presence of the Harriers proved to be crucial.

Beyond the *wadi* there was an Afghan village that the patrol needed to pass through, and a number of other *wadi* crossings they would have to use that also had to be checked. We had to be totally certain that there were no

Taliban or other insurgents positioning IEDs or setting up ambushes anywhere along the route the American troops were going to follow.

Bernard and I were immediately suspicious of several different activities that we could see. One of our problems was that although the politicians may describe what's happening in Afghanistan as a 'police action', a 'peace-keeping exercise' or even 'reconstruction', the reality is that at the moment it's all-out war, with allied forces battling an enemy that is ready to fight to the very end. So *any* activity by people on the ground could well be hostile in intent.

But at the same time, of course, not every Afghan is either a Talib or a Taliban supporter. Most of them are just regular citizens going about their normal daily activities. So what we saw on the ground below us was always subject to at least two different interpretations. But what we were looking at from our Harriers certainly appeared peculiar, if not suspicious.

There was a local truck – what the coalition personnel called a 'jingly truck' because they were festooned with chains that jingled as they moved – working its way along the rough road that ran close to the *wadi*. It was stopping at frequent intervals, but was getting closer and closer to the location of the IED strike.

Even more curiously, a man was riding a motorbike up and down the *wadi* and stopping beside the truck at frequent intervals. The fear was that he was some kind of a scout, checking out the *wadi* and leading the truck, which might easily have been full of Taliban warriors, towards the stranded Americans.

'Jaguar One Five, Recoil Four Five, look due south down the *wadi*. On the east side, range about three clicks, there's a truck heading towards you. He's stopping frequently, and he seems to be working with a motor-cyclist who's riding up and down in the *wadi* itself.'

'Roger that. We'll send a couple of the Humvees on ahead.'

I watched from above as two of the sand-coloured armoured vehicles eased ahead of the slow-moving column and fanned out, making widely separated targets.

But the truck and the motorcycle suddenly stopped and reversed direction, heading back towards the nearest village, well before the Humvees got anywhere near them, and we never found out what either the truck driver or the motorcyclist had been doing.

Then there was the village itself, where we saw quite a large gathering of people. This again raised our suspicions, and I passed the information down to Jaguar One Five, but this also proved to be entirely innocent.

The upshot of the incident was that the American patrol successfully exfiltrated from the area, and made it through the village without encountering any hostile forces. The injured soldier was airlifted out and survived, though he was badly injured.

That was one of my first experiences of hearing sheer naked fear in a voice on the radio. And the change to genuine relief, once we were overhead and able to reassure the troops that they weren't about to get massacred by the Taliban, and that it wasn't their last day on Earth, was very obvious.

It had actually been pretty unusual to hear the troops sounding at all rattled. These small patrols were usually the coolest guys on the block.

Most people at Kandahar Airfield – and in fact at all the coalition bases in Afghanistan – wore uniforms of one sort or another, for the unsurprising reason that they were in some branch of the military of their home country. But I noticed that everywhere there were significant numbers of men in civilian clothes, usually cultivating longer than usual hair and substantial beards; men who very rarely engaged in conversation with anyone who didn't look and dress just like them and who, for some reason, all seemed to favour North Face sports gear. They were clearly military – or ex-military – of some flavour or other and they really were *everywhere*.

When our TriStar had landed in Kabul about half a dozen of these guys stepped off it and were met by another bunch of bearded characters, bundled into a wagon and driven off into the middle of nowhere. The beards and long hair seem to be part of their attempt to blend in when they're out in the badlands, because there's no such thing as a clean-shaven Talib, though it's also fair to say that not many Taliban wear North Face sports gear.

The efforts of regular forces in Afghanistan were clearly being aided and augmented by some of these secretive, ragged-looking men. And, no doubt, as the campaign in Afghanistan continues, their help will continue to be sought.

*

Every so often, the media gets its hands on footage of similarly unconventional-looking operators going about their business.

In late November 2001, after enduring a sustained bombardment from American forces at Kunduz in northern Afghanistan, between 300 and 500 – the exact number is the subject of dispute – Al Qaeda and Taliban fighters surrendered to General Abdul Rashid Dostum of the Northern Alliance. It is still not clear whether this was a genuine surrender or a suicidal Taliban plan of attack.

Whatever the insurgents' motivation, the provisions of the Pashtunwali Code meant that the surrender was accepted at face value and, crucially, that the prisoners were not searched for weapons. This is incomprehensible to the Western military mind, but self-respect and respect for others meant that physical searching of the prisoners would be considered a serious insult. The fact that the Taliban had surrendered meant, to the Afghan mindset, that they had ceased being combatants and had, by implication if not in fact, also surrendered their weapons. And the prisoners had, at least, handed over their Kalashnikovs, RPGs and other heavy weapons. Nobody seemed to notice that virtually all of them were carrying pistols, knives and grenades hidden away in their voluminous clothing.

The prisoners were incarcerated in the huge, nineteenth-century Qala-I-Jangi fort, which Dostum was using as one of his main armouries and headquarters. Significantly, Qala-I-Jangi had until a short time previously been in Taliban hands, so many of the prisoners were very familiar with its layout.

On 25 November the prisoners revolted, killing or overpowering the guards, and quickly broke into the armoury, where they equipped themselves with assault rifles, mortars and rocket launchers.

Though heavily outnumbered by the prisoners, the Northern Alliance soldiers fought hard to contain the situation, assisted by American troops and, the film reveals, a handful of rough-looking soldiers wearing mix-and-match kit and speaking with clearly British accents who were also operating in the area. The coalition forces called in repeated air strikes, but despite the ferocity of this bombardment, the Taliban held out for seven days. In ending the siege, about fifty Northern Alliance soldiers and one American perished.

A number of countries were critical of the conduct of the siege and the use of heavy weapons – tanks and air-delivered ordnance – against the comparatively lightly armed insurgents, but it is significant that, despite their losses, the surviving Taliban refused to surrender until their only alternative was to drown.

And perhaps that single incident, more than any other, indicated the calibre of the enemy we were all facing in Afghanistan.

There has been a lot of hype and groundless speculation about what British Special Forces may or may not have been involved with in Afghanistan. A good example were the breathless reports that appeared following the first major contacts between coalition troops and the Taliban after 9/11.

In January and February 2002 the British press was

full of overheated accounts of what they were calling Operation TRENT, a search, locate and destroy mission, they said, aimed at finding Osama bin Laden and his senior Al Qaeda commanders, and that, they said, saw the SAS pursuing their targets deep into the cave systems of Tora Bora in eastern Afghanistan. It was reported that four SAS soldiers were wounded in the actions, which involved bitter close-quarters combat dubbed the 'Battle of the Caves' by the papers. Some of the SAS men were said to have tackled Al Qaeda terrorists with fighting knives or even their bare hands when they ran out of ammunition. When further details of the operation emerged, most of the papers called for the issue of medals for some of the SAS troops, some editors even suggesting that their incredible bravery fully merited the Victoria Cross.

A significant proportion of the 800 squadron's effort had been in support of exacting, small-unit operations – sometimes with significant, strategic importance. Vital to the success of the NATO mission in Afghanistan was the protection of the infrastructure. There was little more crucial in this respect than the Kajaki Dam in Helmand, which produces hydroelectric power for a large area of southern Afghanistan and provides local irrigation.

Despite all the fighting the area has seen, the dam has been kept in constant operation since its completion in 1975. Throughout 2006 the Taliban launched attack after attack on it, but not one of them was successful. They had decided that the Kajaki Dam was one of their prime targets in the region, though the thinking behind this wasn't clear. Not only must they have known that the dam's strategic importance would lead to its strenuous defence by coalition forces. They would also have guessed that if, by some miracle, they did manage to seize control of it, troops would be sent there in overwhelming numbers to wrest it back.

In any case, the structure was too massive to be destroyed by the amounts of explosive the Taliban were likely to possess, and even if they had somehow managed to do so, the immediate result would have been to deprive most of southern Afghanistan of electricity and destroy the irrigation system upon which the narrow strip of arable land in southern Helmand depended. Neither achievement would have endeared the Taliban to the Afghan tribesmen, the very people they claimed to be representing, and whose goodwill and support they ultimately needed.

There are two peaks on the ridge to the south of the dam, and during our det a small unit of Royal Marines occupied one peak and the Taliban the other, only about 500 metres apart. Each side was living in one of the old Russian observation posts that dated back to the days of the Mujahidin, the insurgents apparently underground, beneath the building. The British troops, who had put out a big dayglo orange tarp to show clearly which peak they held, were keen to flush out the Taliban from what was a very strategic position close to the dam.

It was during this stand-off that Hoggy achieved quite a feat of precision delivery of munitions. He was airborne on a routine Close Air Support sortie over the area, flying solo because his wing-man had gone unserviceable back at Kandahar and no spare aircraft was available. The JTAC told Hoggy they'd been taking a lot of mortar fire from the Taliban OP and requested that he look out for any suspected mortar baseplates.

Hoggy spent the best part of an hour overhead, staring down at the enemy position with the binoculars, as well as through his targeting pod, and there was one thing in particular that stood out to him. It was white, small, square and definitely man-made. He just couldn't tell what it was, but it was certainly something not normally seen on an Afghan ridgeline, so it wasn't a rock or a goat.

When Hoggy told the JTAC what he could see, the controller got excited and asked him if he could take it out. The snag was that the Harrier was carrying only 1,000lb bombs and, unless Hoggy's delivery was absolutely accurate, one of these would make a real mess of the target. Just to make sure there was no pressure at all, the JTAC then said the weapon must only take out the object – which he confirmed also looked like a mortar baseplate to him – and had to leave all the rest of the infrastructure intact so that the British troops could use it when they took the position.

Hoggy's other problem was that the two ridges looked identical through the targeting pod, so he did a couple of dry runs to make sure he'd correctly identified the enemy position and not the friendly one. As if that wasn't enough, the pod was useless at discriminating between the two ridges, and it had been dodgy in tracking and kept losing the target. He ended up having to do the tracking manually on to this tiny target.

As he ran in for the third time he dropped the weapon.

It went smack on to the target and left everything else intact, so everyone was happy.

About a week later we heard that a small British force had successfully taken the Taliban position and now owned the whole ridgeline.

Not all these operations went entirely to plan, though. Just days after the episode with the wrecked American Humvee, I was back in the air supporting another small team of US soldiers.

15

I pulled back on the throttle as I headed east back to Kandahar. As the RPM dropped I scanned the cockpit instruments, my eyes ranging, almost unconsciously, over displays recording temperatures or pressures, fuel and electrical systems. No cause for alarm. And as I descended I looked down from the Harrier's big glass cockpit. As always, it amazed me just how spectacularly beautiful Afghanistan is from the air, even if that beauty is rather harder to discern on the ground. It's a country that runs the gamut of both terrain and climate, from the highest to the lowest extremes of both.

Immediately to the south of the airfield is the Red Desert, which, when the sun is rising or setting, is blood-red. From the air, in certain lighting conditions, it looks like a crimson sea – quite extraordinary. In the desert there are sharp and craggy rock features – almost aggressive in their appearance – surrounding the very few small clumps of habitation.

The Helmand River runs down the Kandahar Valley, flanked on each side by a strip of productive arable land that follows the valley all the way down and within which stand most of the district's dwellings. Scattered around the edge of this area are large numbers of circular holes, almost like bomb craters, but in fact these holes have been caused by a much less dramatic force than high explosive. They're actually a sequence of unsuccessful drill holes made by the Afghans as they searched for water.

As you fly north the terrain gets even more spectacular with mountains rising from the plains to ever-increasing heights as they ascend towards the Hindu Kush, the formation that extends well out beyond Afghanistan and up into the Himalayas, rising to 25,000 feet, and all the way down to Kandahar in the south. It then runs even further south towards Pakistan and west to the Iranian border of the Red Desert. Just south of Kandahar Airfield there is a sheer cut-off of this geological feature. This is marked by the range of unmistakable red sand dunes that run as far as the eye can see, before the land rises up to form the mountains that extend all the way down to Pakistan.

The difference between the mountains and the lowlands – which are actually quite high as the desert there is at some 3,000 feet until it starts to descend towards the border with Pakistan – is stark, especially in the winter. At that time of year the mountains are covered in snow and the temperature on the peaks is well below zero Celsius even during the day, but it will still be very hot in the high desert, with virtually no rainfall.

The landscape was extreme and spectacular, especially when the sun caught it towards the evening. Further north, from the Kandahar area and the Panjwayi Valley into the Helmand Valley and River, the land rose quite quickly into steep-sided north–south valleys and then further into the high mountain area, where the Taliban usually retreated in the winter to regroup. It was inhospitable yet impressive, especially in the winter, when snow covered the mountain tops.

The country is arid, apart from a brief period in the spring when some rain falls, and almost everything lives around the rivers, especially in the Helmand and Panjwayi valleys. In each valley the narrow fertile area extends for between two and five miles either side of the main rivers, and virtually everything that grows in the country grows there, a bright ribbon of green that stretches all the way down to the Pakistan border.

Yet, as vivid as the country seemed from altitude, it wasn't always entirely clear what was happening on the ground. One of the problems in providing top cover for a patrol is the difficulty of interpreting activity on the ground from a height of certainly several hundred and perhaps several thousand feet. In a hostile environment pilots have to weigh the potential danger from surface-to-air missiles and other weapons against the requirement to observe the ground, and sometimes this didn't quite work out as planned.

On one sortie we were out in the Naw Zad area, following the progress of a British patrol that had been attacked by the Taliban every single day that it had been out. Not surprisingly, the troops were staggeringly nervous because of what had been happening to them.

We knew their exact route and were following it and doing our best to scan the terrain ahead of them. In Naw Zad itself I suddenly spotted a huge group of people moving around on the edge of one particular street, a location that I knew the patrol had to pass close to. I reacted immediately.

'Stand by! Stay there!' I radioed. 'There's a whole mass of people right round the next corner.'

This produced real drama on the ground. The patrol scattered, fully convinced that they were going to get massacred, and took up defensive positions immediately.

Above them, I descended slightly to get a better view and continued describing what I could see, the location of the mob and anything else that would help the troops below get a handle on the situation.

Then the radio operator asked me: 'Is this near Green Seven?'

I double-checked the coordinates on my map and replied immediately: 'Yes, it's exactly on Green Seven.'

'Good,' said the patrol member, the tension instantly vanishing from his voice. 'Right, I should have told you. Every Thursday they hold a market here. That's what you're looking at. That's the Naw Zad Thursday Market.'

But it wasn't often that things on the ground turned out to be *better* than expected. Too often the opposite was true. And as I changed frequencies on my return to base there was a shock reminder of just how grim things could get. I was more or less overhead Kandahar when suddenly I saw the flash of a huge explosion in the centre of the city, as far as I could tell somewhere near one of the mosques. A huge, ugly cloud of dust and smoke rose high above the sandy-brown walls and dark shadows of the city's familiar streets. Naturally I reported it by radio, but I was surprised when I landed after my sortie that nobody at Kandahar Airfield seemed to have heard anything about it.

I had to wait for the CNN headlines the following day to find out what had happened. It turned out that what I'd seen from the air was a suicide car bomb attack on a coalition convoy that left eight civilians and a soldier dead. Two other soldiers had been wounded – one of them later died of his injuries – along with a number of Afghan civilians.

It hadn't been a good Friday the 13th.

That suicide bombing, and the IED strike a short time earlier, suggested that the war in Afghanistan might be taking a dangerous new turn. In the early part of the conflict most of the contacts between coalition forces and the Taliban were straight firefights. When the insurgents used IEDs they were normally just a means to an end – a way of stopping a coalition patrol in a location that the Taliban had chosen as an ambush – but the insurgents would then normally attempt to engage the coalition troops with small arms.

In Iraq the situation was entirely different. There IEDs had become increasingly sophisticated primary weapons, detonated by remote control, often using either mobile phones or a keyless entry system taken from a car. The Iraqi bomb-makers frequently included anti-handling devices and booby-traps as further refinements, but the important point was that the IED essentially stood alone. Once it had detonated there was no gang of gunmen waiting in the wings to try to massacre anyone left alive afterwards.

I was beginning to wonder if the techniques that had been honed and perfected in Iraq were being exported to

Afghanistan and, if so, what effect that would have on the way the coalition troops conducted their campaign.

Fighting the Taliban is difficult. Battling an enemy that has no fear of death and whose warriors will never surrender is perhaps the hardest task any armed force can ever face, because almost literally the only military solution is to kill them all. Nothing less than that will achieve the short-term objective on the battlefield, though clearly a long-term solution will require some kind of negotiated political settlement.

The Taliban and Al Qaeda share at least two common short-term objectives. They want the opium trade to continue, because that generates huge amounts of income for both factions, and neither want the rule of law – unless it's the Taliban's interpretation of the Koran – to be applied in Afghanistan because that would prevent them from setting up terrorist training camps in the country. For both organizations an Afghanistan at peace, and with a strong government that properly regulates life within its borders, is the worst possible outcome. They can only flourish in chaos.

Apart from actual conflict with the Taliban, the other major difficulty facing the coalition forces is that of obtaining good intelligence about the organization. The Taliban have proved to be almost impossible to infiltrate, and any information that is passed on by paid informers and others is often suspect or simply wrong.

This has resulted in a rather different approach to the problem. Instead of trying to actively identify and engage the Taliban – though of course this does still happen – ISAF is making a determined effort to wage a genuine 'hearts and minds' campaign on the ground, and by most accounts it seems to be working.

The Army and Marine officers who are tasked with talking to the village elders – the local leaders of the community – and working in the villages and compounds, have to be all things to all men. They have to be politicians, counsellors, fighting men, engineers and diplomats, all at the same time. They have to show strength, because they represent the forces of the coalition, but at the same time be subservient because they are talking to the local chief. They have to have a very clear idea of what they're trying to achieve and know exactly what they can do and offer to get it. In many ways it's much more difficult than simply flying around in a jet aircraft dropping bombs, and is a thankless and most unglamorous task.

Whenever an electricity generator is installed in a village or a hospital, whenever the coalition forces bring proper medical attention to the occupants of a compound, or repair a piece of broken machinery, it's a small victory over the Taliban, which is, of course, why the insurgents make such strenuous efforts to destroy or disable any such facilities that the coalition troops do manage to install or get working.

But each new generator, or water pump, or happy patient improved the flow of intelligence. And, in the end, our success was dependent on the quality of our intel. We were fortunate that the Harrier det was particularly well served. One of the reasons was that our Ground Liaison Officer, Captain Mick Trafford, the

Harrier Force's first-ever Royal Marine GLO, had proved outstanding.

In the years before British forces became seriously engaged in combat there was a tendency for this kind of exchange posting to feature second- or third-tier officers. This was simply because the Army appointer, say, faced with a requirement to send a captain or major to work with the RAF, would deliberately not choose a rising star on the grounds that the Army should hang on to its best men.

But when the Royal Marines were required to second an officer to the Harrier detachment in Afghanistan, their appointer rightly decided that we needed the best man he could find.

The moment Mick Trafford arrived in theatre, even before he relieved the existing GLO, he picked up his rifle and his Bergen and disappeared. He joined up with some of his colleagues from 3 Commando Brigade and went off on foot patrols with them to places like Lashkar Gah, which were the hotspots of Taliban activity.

He came back with an incredibly detailed assessment of the situation on the ground – the real 'ground truth' – and then gave us all a hugely vivid and accurate presentation on exactly what was going on with the troops on the ground, about what they were doing and how they were having to do it.

Mick was a very fit ex-ranker who'd then taken a commission, but you could tell from the way he talked where his heart lay.

'Right,' he said, when we were all assembled in Ops, and his first sentence set the tone for the whole briefing.

'First day out with the Green Death, we went out for a yomp over at Lashkar Gah, found the Taliban and gave them the good news.

'Now, these boys are right on the front line, however you slice it,' he went on. 'They're doing patrols that might last twelve or fourteen days, deep into bandit country. They've got the most basic rations – the dreaded MRE, Meals Ready to Eat, and some of those are really bloody awful – they often can't have brews because they're too close to the enemy, so they're drinking lukewarm water. They grab sleep where and when they can, and the whole time they're out there they're living with the knowledge that they could take a Taliban bullet at any moment.'

He paused and glanced around the room.

'And the biggest problem you lot have got is coping with the stink from Poo Pond!'

Mick's presentation was, for most of us, a real eye-opener, and some of the things he described literally made my hair stand on end as he set the scene. For the first time he made us properly appreciate the reality of what the troops were going through on a daily basis. He really did put everything into context.

At the end of the briefing one of the pilots asked about the danger of being hit by a Stinger.

'Right,' Mick said. 'Well, it's not quite as simple as you might think. You need to understand something about the dynamics of the situation on the ground with regard to these weapons.'

In the 1980s the CIA supplied at least 500 and, according to some reports, possibly as many as 2,000 Stinger missiles – the correct designation is the FIM-92 and it was initially manufactured in America by Raytheon Missile Systems – to the Mujahidin guerrillas who were fighting against the Russian military in Afghanistan.

After the Russians withdrew in 1989, the Americans initiated a $50-million programme to buy back the remaining Stingers, and at the time it was assessed that there could be as many as 300 remaining in the hands of the Mujahidin. Quite a lot were recovered, but it was known that some found their way into other countries that have been linked to the supply of arms and ammunition to the Taliban. In short, numerous missiles are still unaccounted for, and almost certainly a lot of these are hidden away somewhere in Afghanistan. The Afghans have always been well armed as a nation, and it's likely that many of the nationals who had Stingers decided to hang on to them, just in case.

'Now,' Mick said, 'it's quite possible that the Taliban possess a bunch of Stingers, but there's rather more to the equation than that. First of all, they're now so old that the batteries needed by the launcher to function are probably knackered.

'Second, they're not that easy to use, even for people with a military background. Without proper training, even experienced soldiers struggle to make the things work. If that's true of the best NATO armies have to offer, how good do you reckon the Taliban would be at firing them?

'Then there's target acquisition. The Stinger's envelope is pretty tight, and my guess is that before a Talib realized there was a Harrier in the area and powered up his Stinger, you'd be long gone.'

Mick glanced around the room. 'Oddly enough,' he

said, 'there's another good reason why you're not likely to find one of these missiles up your jacksie, and it's all to do with street cred. Just about everybody in Afghanistan owns a Kalashnikov or something similar, but a Stinger's a special weapon, expensive and powerful; that means the man who owns it is something special in his community. Thing is, he'll have that status right up to the moment he fires it, when he'll be left with a short length of *very* expensive drainpipe and a few electronics. In short, it's cool to own a Stinger, but if a Talib uses it he doesn't own one any more. He's just another raghead with a Kalashnikov.'

That was a typical 'Green Death' assessment of the situation, though Mick was right, and it was good to have him working with us. But it only made us even more aware of the very real dangers faced by the Royal Marines on the ground out to the west of Kandahar.

And Wedge and Flatters soon saw exactly what the Marines were facing.

16

Wedge began flying operational sorties in Afghanistan less than a week after joining 800 Squadron as a medium-level combat-ready only pilot. That meant he'd done the training course but hadn't had time to do the full combat-ready work-up, which normally takes a pilot about six months. We needed him in theatre so quickly that he'd done an abbreviated course to get him ready for medium-level combat in Afghanistan.

That day he got airborne as Mamba Four Three flight, with Flatters flying the bomber jet and Wedge in the rocket jet, in support of Windmill Six Nine – a Dutch JTAC – in the vicinity of Tarin Kowt.

The weather was pretty shitty at Kandahar and they step-climbed up through solid cloud. Immediately after contacting Trumpcard at the top of the climb they were redirected to support a TIC at Naw Zad in support of Widow Eight Four, a British JTAC, and both pilots noticed heavy icing on the intakes as they vectored west, still in thick cloud. Mamba Four One flight had already been supporting the patrol, but had been forced to break off when they ran short of fuel.

When Wedge came up on the JTAC tactical frequency they realized that the British patrol was in real trouble.

'Mamba Four One fired rockets,' Widow Eight Four reported, his voice high and tense with fear, 'but we're still taking heavy fire, really heavy fire. They've got mortars and machine-guns and we're pinned down here.'

Over the radio Wedge could hear the crump of mortars landing, and the louder, repetitive sounds of the Royal Marines returning fire with .50-cal machine-guns.

'There's a big group of these bastards right in the middle of the town, hidden in a small tree-line,' Widow Eight Four reported. 'They're your target.'

'We dropped down over the desert to the south of the town, where it was almost level, in an attempt to get VMC,' Wedge told me afterwards, explaining his search for clear air and a view of the ground. 'I was checking my position on the moving map as we edged down below safety altitude, still in solid cloud. Watching the radalt like a hawk, I went a bit lower. I was confident that our GPS position was accurate and that there was flat ground ahead.'

This was against all peacetime safety rules but when there were guys on the ground yelling for help, all my pilots knew there really weren't any other options. They simply *had* to get down there.

'I knew that the previous aircraft – Four One flight – had managed to get down below the weather. They'd told me it was closing in before they left, but logically I knew it couldn't have got that much worse.'

At about 1,500 feet Wedge began to get glimpses of murky brown desert below him. At about 1,000 feet he broke cloud and found himself at low level over the desert in driving rain. He met up with Flatters and they established an orbit about ten miles south of Naw Zad while the JTAC passed them the target details.

'Mamba Four Three, Widow Eight Four, we'll take a five-forty airburst.'

'Negative, Eight Four. At this altitude none of our weapons will have time to arm before they hit the ground. The only options we can offer are either CRV-7s or one of the GPS-guided Enhanced Paveway II bombs from height, but for that we'll need a *really* accurate target position.'

'OK, that's understood. My coordinates aren't accurate enough for the bomb, so I'll take the rockets.'

Naturally, the JTAC didn't want 1,000lb of high explosive going off in an urban area, quite possibly close to friendly forces.

'Roger,' Wedge replied, and prepared himself for the attack.

He ran in from the south of the town, accelerating up to the attack speed of 450 knots – rockets are delivered when the aircraft is moving much more quickly than is needed to release a bomb. As the ground rose towards the town the cloud base dropped. Flatters had been trying to keep in battle formation with Wedge, but kept losing sight of his aircraft in the rain, so sensibly elected to get out of the way and climbed up into the cloud to await developments.

A few miles from the target Wedge eased up to the cloud base to try to acquire the target.

'The designation diamond was right in the middle of a built-up area,' he explained, 'but I couldn't see the tree-line that concealed the Taliban. Widow Eight Four cleared me hot for the attack, but all I could see through the sight were nondescript compounds, so I pulled off the target without firing because I couldn't positively identify the area.

'Then, just as I was recovering from the aborted attack, I suddenly caught a glimpse of the tree-line flashing past under my wing. The weather had closed in – I reckoned I had no more than about two clicks' visibility – and I then found myself stuck at low level right over the town. My original route in seemed impassable.'

Naw Zad is surrounded by hills, the peaks of which were in the cloud, and Wedge was in a sort of bowl where he could see the ground. He knew that if he climbed up, he doubted if he would ever get back into the area to attack again.

'I pulled the jet round the corner at full power with the hills uncomfortably close, and Widow Eight Four called that he could mark the target with smoke.

'I yelled, "Fire it now!" and pulled the Harrier round for a re-attack.

'I tipped into the target area, but again all I could see were murky buildings through the rain. Then the smoke round suddenly bloomed right in front of me and I identified the tree-line just in time. I fired the operational pod from the cloud base at 900 feet, a little inside the minimum prescribed range.'

The exhausts of the nineteen rockets blazed brightly in the darkness as they raced towards the target. Wedge pulled up and dropped the wing to see the debris from the rounds impacting around the tree-line. The JTAC called a direct hit, but the enemy continued to press their attack. Once again Wedge set up for the attack, this time with the six-round training pod in ripple mode Q6M1.

This stood for quantity and multiple, and meant six rockets, fired once.

Wedge was very conscious of the fact that he was now on his third low-level orbit over the town and that, historically, aircraft don't normally come out of re-attacks very well.

'The Marines fired smoke again to mark the target, and I ran in and fired the rest of the CRV-7s.'

Then, with no usable weapons left, he rapidly pulled up into the sanctuary of the cloud. As he levelled off and put the altitude hold on he realized that he was physically shaking. He composed himself, and heard Flatters being called in for a potential attack with his GPS bomb. Then a relieved Widow Eight Four stated that the rockets had had the desired effect and that any remaining enemy had withdrawn and broken contact, so the Enhanced Paveway attack would not be needed.

At that stage Wedge thought the excitement was over. But after charging around at low level for that long he realized he was quite low on fuel. Flatters, too, was short of fuel. They contacted base but were told that the weather at Kandahar had deteriorated, and this meant they didn't have enough fuel to shoot an approach and still have fuel in hand for a diversion to an alternative field. And if Kandahar was clamped that safety margin wasn't optional.

As the nearest tanker was over 100 miles away, they were immediately diverted to Bagram Airbase in the north-east of Afghanistan. They just had enough fuel to cover the 280-mile journey there on a VFR profile. As they transited, the cloud began to break over central

Afghanistan to reveal magnificent snow-covered mountains, and Wedge couldn't help but think how good the skiing would be there if circumstances were different.

Disappointingly, the clear air didn't last all the way and they re-entered cloud as they got close to the airfield. It turned out that Bagram was also operating radar recoveries, which they barely had enough fuel to cope with. The two pilots declared a fuel emergency and were quickly vectored in by the American controllers.

'With my lower fuel state,' Wedge said, 'because of the time I'd spent prosecuting the attacks at low level, I went in for the approach first. I even delayed dropping the undercarriage in an effort to save fuel. It was bloody hairy. As I approached the minimum descent height I still couldn't see the airfield, but there was nothing for it but to continue, as neither of us had enough fuel left to go anywhere else.'

Clearly it hadn't occurred to the controllers to turn on the airfield lights and Wedge was concentrating so hard on finding the runway that it didn't occur to him to ask.

'Then I saw a bright flashing X, and took this to be the disused runway light, but I aimed for it anyway, because by that stage I was going to land on the first runway or taxiway I saw, disused or not. Or even a road if I couldn't find anything else.'

The flashing X thankfully led him to the airfield, and he saw the correct runway late, which put him high on the glidepath.

'Because of that, I landed long, and had to go into a full PNB stop to slow the Harrier down.'

'PNB' means 'power nozzle braking', or rotating the

vectored thrust nozzles fully forward to slow down the aircraft.

Wedge crossed the raised cable at forty knots – which the aircraft definitely wasn't cleared for with a recce pod fitted – and finally came to a stop. He cleared the runway and quickly told Flatters what to look for so that he was able to make a much better approach.

'Once we'd both landed and taxied clear, I shut down my aircraft and opened the canopy. That let in the cold, wet air. It felt great and I sat there calming down for a good few minutes before climbing out of the aeroplane. On the wet tarmac Flatters and I shook hands solemnly. During that sortie I'd used up all of my counter-measures down at low level, and I suppose I had the privilege of being one of the few pilots who could claim they'd done low-level CAS for real, and that when only medium-level combat ready qualified!'

Flatters was the formation leader, so he left the dispersal and went to A-10 Ops to sort things out. That left Wedge to do the turnarounds on both jets in the pissing rain. He was soaked to the skin and hasn't let Flatters forget it. Needless to say, both men slept very soundly in their beds that night after refuelling and flying back to Kandahar.

The following day Wedge was still on a bit of a high after the rocket attacks, but what had taken place was still a real concern to me. Not what Wedge and Flatters had done – they'd shown cool heads and presence of mind – but this was a really close shave. If we'd had nine lives to start with, I reckoned we were probably now down to our last three or four. And with the pace of operations we faced, the odds were that we'd get through them pretty quickly too.

The tempo remained relentless. We were dropping ordnance every day, and the squadron's tiredness was beginning to reveal itself in the lines on people's faces and the occasional flash of anger.

The near-constant flying also placed a huge strain on our maintainers and engineers – the people who had the awesome responsibility of getting the Harriers ready for every sortie – and who up to now had miraculously achieved almost 100 per cent availability.

Because we were on the front line at Kandahar, we were very well supported, with all the spares we needed, so our serviceability rate was exceptionally high. This was helped by the fact that the maintainers were a captive audience, just like being on a ship. Instead of working eight hours, they worked twelve-hour shifts, and teams were available twenty-four hours a day, so we had very good service.

The squadron arrived there at the end of the summer and stayed through most of the winter. Most of the time it was cold, with very unpleasant conditions outside and, although each aircraft lived in its little rubberized hangar, these structures weren't particularly well heated. Two of them were known as Cobb hangars and the others were really just sand shelters – old-style metal frames with a tarpaulin roof, and we couldn't close the fronts of those.

If a jet did break, for whatever reason, the engineers generally got it fixed pretty quickly. Most maintenance problems were caused not by any inherent failures in the system, but simply because of the tempo of operations. Surge periods were always more tense because we needed more aeroplanes available at any one time, but usually the flying programme allowed us to take aeroplanes away for routine maintenance. Surge days didn't allow that, however.

The Harriers are cleared for 720 flying hours between major maintenance schedules, and you consume around 60 hours per aircraft per month, so every ten months or so an aircraft would have to come out of Afghanistan and fly back to the UK before going into the big maintenance cycle there, so we planned on each aircraft being in theatre for ten months at a time.

Aircraft that came out from the UK took time to bed in, and we never knew exactly why that was. Every aircraft had its own little quirks, and they certainly had their own personalities.

It was slightly disconcerting that when aircraft number 13 came out it was an absolute bag of nails. Nothing on it seemed to function as it should: the radios didn't work properly, the expendable system didn't work, the stores management system kept failing, and it took weeks to get that jet functioning reliably. Some jets just seem to enjoy testing people's patience.

We inherited aircraft number 61 when we arrived, and its navigation system had failed so many times that the IV (AC) Squadron pilots had come to expect that whenever it got airborne the nav system was going to fall over during the sortie. This is a fundamental part of the aircraft and is an important part of the weapon-aiming system as well, so it was potentially a very serious fault.

When our maintainers got out there, they fixed it permanently within two days. It was just a classic case of a fresh set of eyes looking at the problem from a new angle. 'Have you tried this?' they said. Nobody had, so they replaced that component and the system gave no more trouble.

Without exception our engineers had a genuine pride in getting the aircraft ready in time and maintaining a high serviceability rate. They took a very proprietorial view of 'their' Harriers, and would frequently admonish us not to break them.

Around the aircraft, the plane captains – the individuals who were responsible for the before-flight servicing of the aircraft – would walk round the Harrier with us as we were doing our external pre-flight checks. And they were always desperate to find out what our sortie consisted of, where we were going and what we were programmed to do when we got there. And when we returned to the dispersal all the engineers usually turned out, especially if we'd expended some or all of our ordnance. Then they all wanted to know what we'd done, how we'd done it and what the effects of the weapons had been on the ground and, obviously, on the Taliban.

But with most of the pilots in the squadron delivering bombs against the Taliban almost daily, I still wasn't getting my fair share. I couldn't remember the last time I'd felt my Harrier lurch as a bomb left the wing. The most I normally managed to do was fire off a few CRV-7s.

I just never quite seemed to be in the right place at the

right time. The 'war-dodger' epithet was now happily being applied to me by almost everyone in the squadron, as far as I could tell. It was time I did something to vent my frustration, and Mick Trafford, of all people, came up with a temporary solution.

Mick had good contacts with some of the no-name, no-rank, no-razor outfits on the base, and in early November this resulted in a session of firing some weird and wonderful weapons on the range at Kandahar.

Our hosts were late in arriving, as usual – that seems to be almost traditional where their sort are concerned. Apparently they were often late for their ops as well. Eventually a Toyota Hilux turned up and three scruffy bearded blokes – real hairy oddballs – hopped out. Their clothes were dirty, possibly even slept in, their long hair uncombed, and they didn't look as if they'd been anywhere near a shower for weeks.

In short, they looked like the kind of people you'd expect to see standing on a street corner somewhere and dealing drugs, instead of the highly skilled products of the most intensive specialist military training courses yet devised. And one of their tasks in Afghanistan was trying to *stop* the flow of opium out of the country, so their appearance really was deceptive but, I knew, necessary for the covert operations they were involved in out in the badlands.

In the back of the Toyota were three big haversacks. These they hauled out, opened them up and emptied out whole piles of weapons, all covered in crap and corruption, on to the ground. One of the bearded wonders dragged them over to the firing point, laid each weapon on its side so that the bolt was open and facing upwards, then took a big drum of oil and poured some into the action of each one. That, apparently, was the 'cleaning phase' completed.

'Come on, then, get on with it,' another beardie instructed, dropping piles of appropriate ammunition beside each weapon, and so we all hunkered down and started firing. I had one of the machine-guns, dripping with oil, and I noticed immediately that one in five of the rounds in the ammunition belt was tracer, which I was fairly sure we shouldn't be using on the Kandahar small-arms range. But I wasn't prepared to argue the toss with dangerous-looking operators, just in case he decided to kill me with his bare hands, so I just started firing. That wasn't such a good idea as the moment the first round fired I was sprayed with hot oil from the action, and each subsequent round showered me again. But what the hell. It was bloody good.

As the British contingent at Kandahar looked forward to commemorating Remembrance Day, I couldn't help but be struck by how the anti-drugs effort being waged by the coalition was about to become a little confusing. To many Afghans at least. The irony certainly wasn't lost on me.

On the one hand, the US were flying choppers full of soldiers into the badlands to try to locate the Afghan poppy fields and destroy them. At the same time the ISAF forces were doing their best to persuade the Afghans not to continue cultivating the crop, explaining that it was an evil thing to do.

On the other hand, the British were shipping boxes of artificial poppies out to the country every November for Remembrance Day.

During the morning of 11 November I put it to Colonel Taylor and the one-star officer at Kandahar Airfield: 'Don't you think there's a certain amount of irony in the way that the Americans are doing their best to cut down the Afghan poppy crops, and telling the farmers that growing them is illegal, a bad thing to do. And then, once a year, all the Brits appear wearing fake poppies on their jackets?'

'Possibly, I suppose.' Taylor sounded undecided. 'But of course they won't know the significance of the date.'

No, I thought, and nor would they care. All the Afghans would be aware of was that the foreign soldiers who had established a major presence in their country were forbidding them to grow about the only cash crop the poor soil would sustain and then, on one particular day of the year, a whole bunch of them appeared wearing a copy of that same flower. They probably wouldn't even think it was ironic. They'd just assume that the British were taking the piss, and that's not necessarily an impression I personally thought the coalition forces should be fostering.

But this seemed to be lost on the colonel.

'You're right,' he said. 'It might seem a bit odd to the locals, I suppose, but there's nothing we can do about it, Orchard. It *is* our Remembrance Day.'

What followed didn't have quite the solemnity normally associated with the ceremony at the Cenotaph. Trying to get a bunch of soldiers to sing in tune – or indeed to sing at all – was amazingly difficult. I saw far more people miming than singing, and those who did try to join in only occasionally seemed to be singing the same verse of the same song as the majority. It was like being at a church service with a *really* reluctant congregation. With all due respect to the Fallen, it was bloody awful.

Later that evening, sitting in the air-conditioned cool of the Ops building, I mulled over the threat posed by poppies to a successful outcome in Afghanistan. The whole question of the poppy crop and opium production is complex. Many Afghan farmers had grown poppies for decades. The poppies grew well in the area, were easy to farm and attracted a good price. For them it was an ideal crop.

The 'hearts and minds' aspect of the Afghan campaign was the bedrock upon which success or failure in the country ultimately rested, and ruining the livelihood of the farmers – who made up the bulk of the country's population – by simply destroying the poppy crops would clearly be non-productive.

The other side of the coin was the absolute determination of the Afghan government to stamp out the trade in illegal drugs.

Some have argued that the best option might be to legalize and regulate poppy production. The idea is that farmers continue to grow their poppies, then sell to pharmaceutical companies for the manufacture of opium-based prescription drugs, for which there is a continuing worldwide demand. On the face of it, it seems ideal, but Afghanistan's a country that seems to confound easy solutions. And at such a relatively early stage in the war-ravaged country's reconstruction, it's hopelessly unrealistic to imagine that a workable legal infrastructure could yet be set up and managed.

So a multi-pronged approach remained the only way forward for the foreseeable future. Along with education, incentives for regional governors to reduce cultivation and support for farmers trying to grow alternative crops and targeting traffickers, the cat-and-mouse game of 'hunt the poppy' on the plains of Afghanistan will continue unabated. The scale of the task was immense and while progress was being made at many levels, poppy production was still going up. It seemed clear that gaining the upper hand wasn't going to happen overnight.

'Boss!' I was called out of my reverie. 'We've got company.'

I walked outside to see a motley bunch of troops clustered around one of the Harriers and chatting to a couple of the pilots. As I walked across to join them, I could see immediately that they weren't British or American, and when I got closer I realized they were Canadians. We quite often received visitors at the det, but usually we knew in advance who was coming and what they wanted to see. Very few people just turned up on spec.

'Can I help you?' I asked on reaching the group.

'No, thanks. You already have.' A somewhat enigmatic reply, but a few seconds later the officer qualified it and immediately we all knew exactly what he was talking about. 'We're from FOB Martello,' he explained. 'We've just been relieved out there, and it's mainly thanks to you guys that we're here now.'

Martello was the remote firebase where we'd beaten off a serious Taliban attack against the garrison, the men standing in front of us. We'd used CRV-7s and five-forty airburst bombs, and since then we'd made a point of overflying the place whenever we could, just to remind the insurgents that we could do it all again if we needed to.

'We just wanted to drop by and say thanks in person, and to shake your hands. If you guys hadn't been on the ball when we had that first attack, we don't reckon any of us would have survived the day. We were that close to being overrun.'

It was a humbling moment for me and the rest of the officers to meet a group of people who had spent a long time inside a firebase – a place that we had only seen from the air – in very unpleasant conditions. And to realize that a major reason they were still alive and had survived the experience was that we were flying the Harriers around and had delivered some pretty aggressive violence to the enemy.

For us it had just been a part of the job, another attack by the Taliban that we'd managed to foil, but for the guys on the ground, the Canadians surrounded by dozens of square miles of Taliban-occupied territory, it was a life or death situation. And their gratitude for our efforts – and the fact that they'd detoured via Kandahar to track us down and shake our hands – meant a hell of a lot to us.

However bizarre the combination of frantic and deadly action we experienced in the air and the comparative peace of Kandahar Airfield, this incident again hammered home the vital importance to the troops on the ground of our getting the job done.

And, at last, I was about to properly play my part.

17

'Recoil Four Three, this is Crowbar. TIC India Bravo declared. Stand by for position.'

'Crowbar, Recoil Four Three, roger.'

I felt the familiar surge of adrenalin as I hauled the Harrier round into a hard turn to open out on a new heading, and started looking ahead towards the mountains. But we'd barely begun tracking towards the TIC when Crowbar updated us, and it wasn't good news.

'Recoil Four Three, Crowbar. Expedite. We've lost radio contact with Victor Two Seven.'

Bernard and I were already travelling pretty much flat out, at well over 500 knots, but I gave the throttle a firm push forward.

'Crowbar, Four Three. We're at full chat now. Request SITREP.'

If the patrol had suddenly stopped talking to Crowbar, the C2 controller at Camp Bastion, it could just mean that their radio had broken or been hit by a Taliban bullet. Or it could mean that they'd been overrun and were all dead or wounded. So we needed as much information as possible before we reached the location of the TIC.

'Four Three, Crowbar. We don't know a lot. The patrol was moving through a high mountain pass when they came under fire from a large group of Taliban from one side of the pass, and they're pinned down in the location

I gave you. That's all we have. Oh, and there's no JTAC or FAC in the patrol.'

'Roger.'

That complicated the situation even more, because it meant that none of the people on the ground – at the other end of the radio link – had been trained to control aircraft. They were just a bunch of soldiers carrying a VHF set.

To make matters worse, as Crowbar had already reported, now there was no radio link at all because we couldn't raise any of the patrol members.

'Victor Two Seven, this is Recoil Four Three. Request SITREP.'

Total silence. There was no response to this or to any of my subsequent calls as we ran in towards the mountains.

Moments later I pulled back the throttle as we reached the location of the ambush and dragged the Harrier round into a hard left-hand turn. The 'g' increased, pushing me back into the ejection seat as reassuring pressure from the g-suit tightened around my lower body. With the jet standing on its port wing, I looked out to my left, staring straight down at the ground about 10,000 feet below me.

The terrain comprised a ridgeline with a mountain on either side, another ridgeline and then a col through which the pass descended down the valley on one side of the mountain before continuing to the nearest town. From what Crowbar had reported, the patrol had been near the top of the second ridgeline when a large group of Taliban opened up on them with RPGs, heavy machine-guns and assault rifles in a classic ambush situation.

'I can see their vehicles,' I radioed to Bernard, as I dipped lower, trying to assess the situation. 'Right at the top of the second ridge.'

Just then I saw a couple of explosions on the ground below. They looked like RPGs going off, which might be good news.

'Two explosions,' Bernard said, before I could press my transmit button. 'If the bad guys are still firing, the good guys must still be shooting back.'

'Agreed. I'm going a bit lower, see if I can work out where they are.'

I dropped the Harrier closer to the ground and flew a quick, tight circuit round the top of the ridgeline where I could see the patrol's stationary vehicles. Then I pulled up, grabbing height to keep me clear of any of the enemy's weapons.

'Their vehicles have stopped,' I told Bernard, 'and I can see that the troops have scattered. Most of them seem to be pinned down behind the trucks.'

Without two-way radio contact, we had no way of knowing either exactly where the enemy forces were or, just as important, where all the patrol members were. The last thing any soldier or pilot wants is to be involved in a blue-on-blue incident, and there was a clear danger of that happening if we released any of our weapons without being fully aware of the exact locations of all the coalition troops on the ground below us. Yet we had to do something – those troops were taking a hell of a beating, and the only people who could do anything to stop it were the two of us. But there was still no response to any of our radio calls.

Then I had an idea.

'Four Four, Four Three. We can't

unless we get two-way with these guys

close to the Taliban. Your cab's bette

mine for this, so I suggest you just put

At the very least it'll deafen the bastard

'Four Four, copied.'

Without radio contact, the only thin

do was try to show the Taliban attack

serious about ending their ambush, and

do that was by putting on a low-level sho

one of our aircraft very, very close to the

Bernard ran out about ten miles an

back over where we thought the insurge

his Harrier low and fast. It wouldn't d

the Taliban, except to momentarily d

because they didn't usually see the aircra

impressive shock value. But they'd get a

stores underneath the aircraft and gue

move would be to release a weapon at t

make them back off, though the Taliban

cated fighters that the prospect of ins

might well have no effect on their action

Going down to about 100 feet, Ber

power over the ridgeline, then pulled u

about all we could do until we establish

with the patrol.

'I see two groups of Taliban,' he radi

his Harrier into a full-power climb. 'Th

the other side of the ridgeline. It's a goo

ambush.'

I agree, but we still don't know how close the patrol
Break, break. Victor Two Seven, Recoil Four Three,
io check.'
If we'd known the friendly troops were a safe distance
ay, we could have put a 1,000lb bomb on the other
e of the mountain, where we'd both seen some of the
liban firing positions, but lacking communication with
: patrol, and especially being unable to talk to a JTAC,
it was far too risky. So Bernard and I continued flying
ound the top of the ridgeline, close enough so that the
liban could clearly see and hear us, and I kept trying to
se the patrol.
'Victor Two Seven, Recoil Four Three.'
And then, finally, they answered.
'Recoil Four – er – Four Three, this is Victor Two
ven.'
'Victor Two Seven, request SITREP. We can see two
oups of Taliban behind the ridgeline. What is your
:ation?'
The information was bitty, but within a couple of
nutes we'd established that the patrol was much too
ose to the insurgents for us to safely drop a bomb. But
it wasn't all we were carrying.
'Four Four, Four Three. I'll take them with rockets.'
'Roger.'
We swung round, in loose battle formation, me leading
d Bernard on my left and some distance back, and again
aded towards the ridgeline at high speed. As we ran in
eached forward to the right hand flat screen to select
: CRV-7 rockets. A salvo of ten, five from each pod.
rhaps the Taliban thought we were just going to do

another low pass – or maybe they just didn't care – but they held their positions, firing everything they had at the patrol opposite.

For the delivery of rockets, the attack run is much more aggressive. I accelerated to over 400 knots, maybe 420 or 430, and rolled into a twenty to thirty-degree dive. Then, a little over two miles from the target, I checked the 'death dot' in the HUD. Projecting on to the glass screen ahead of me, the HUD gave me speed, height, track and so on. I just had to put the dot on the target and keep it there. And press the WRB to fire the weapons. (Or, as Neil Bing would say: 'You put the thing on the thing and press the thing.')

The CRV-7s were unguided but very fast – about Mach 5 – and very accurate. The term death dot was not an idle one. There was so little dispersion that the effect of a salvo of CRV-7 rockets was quite devastating.

I pressed the pickle button and watched as the unguided missiles streaked off towards the ridgeline, leaving yellow-white trails as they ripple-fired. I eased the aircraft round in a turn as the rockets screamed into the area where I'd seen the shadowy figures of the Taliban. The ground around them suddenly blossomed with a succession of explosions as the 4.5 kg warheads detonated, soundless to me in the cockpit as I turned away – but catastrophic where they impacted the ground at five times the speed of sound.

'Recoil Four Three, this is Victor Two Seven. Nice shooting. That's stopped the machine-guns.'

A couple of minutes later it was clear that the rest of the enemy were retreating, just firing a few sporadic rounds from their assault rifles as they scrambled away from the ridge and into cover.

But our job wasn't over. The troops still had to get off the ridgeline and continue their patrol, so we provided overwatch as they got back in their vehicles and continued down the track. We overflew the route they were going to follow and checked that there were no Taliban anywhere along it, and then returned to Kandahar once they were safely clear of danger.

That was one of those situations where you can go from complete calm to the possibility of having to make high-end decisions without the benefit of knowing the full picture. In this case it was clear that the situation was so dangerous that, even without speaking to the patrol members, we believed the risk to their lives was real and imminent. If we'd been unable to talk to them we would probably have had to engage the enemy anyway, and make a decision we would have to live with for the rest of our lives. Fortunately, once we did establish two-way communications we were able to carry out a surgical strike and there were no serious casualties in the patrol.

And at last I had managed to deliver *some* ordnance, though I was very much aware that both my five-forties were still hanging under my wings, so I knew I would get some more flak from the boys when I landed.

As Bernard and I headed back towards Kandahar I thought about the problems we'd faced in bailing out the ambushed patrol.

In combat these days almost all of the responsibility is placed on the man in the cockpit. He needs to know the

Rules of Engagement intimately, and has to understand the laws of armed conflict, in particular those relating to proportionality. He has to ensure that any action he decides to take is both legitimate and in proportion to the threat. For example, dropping a 540lb bomb on a single Talib armed with a Kalashnikov is clearly *not* proportional. But if there were twenty or so insurgents armed with RPGs and heavy machine-guns pinning down a coalition patrol, using that weapon probably *would* be considered a suitable response.

It's quite a responsibility to place on young pilots, most of whom were experiencing combat for the first time. In Afghanistan the combat rules were intended to ensure that the loss of life – to coalition troops, *and* the Taliban and their supporters – was minimized. Obviously, once a firefight was in progress, pilots and soldiers would respond to their attackers with whatever force seemed appropriate.

It was a much more difficult decision to make once the firing had stopped. The question then was: 'Does that person or group of people still pose any direct threat?' Because the mere fact that they'd stopped shooting might only mean they were relocating to a better – and more dangerous for the coalition troops – position. They would of course still be there, and still have their weapons. One of the most difficult decisions any combatant has to make is whether or not it's legitimate to release a weapon on a target that isn't firing at that precise moment. The Rules of Engagement were supposed to help the decision-making process and ensure that only legitimate targets were prosecuted by coalition forces.

A further difficulty was that when we were in the air we almost never had to decide whether or not to actually carry out an attack. That was the job of the commander on the ground, for the simple reason that we lacked the fidelity of information that the ground commander possessed. Normally when we were overhead an incident we were just reacting to the orders we'd received over the radio.

The advent of precision-guided munitions has added a new dimension to the ground-attack discipline, as have the very different yields available. Today it's possible to deliver a genuine surgical strike by selecting a weapon of precisely the right yield and placing it exactly where it's needed. That minimizes the possible collateral damage but maximizes the effectiveness of the weapon. And it also gives us the ability to drop bombs closer to our own troops than earlier generations of pilots would ever have dared to.

Even so, there were a number of occasions during the detachment when our pilots didn't drop their weapons because of fears of collateral damage to the troops on the ground.

The Taliban weren't slow to figure this out for themselves and began to take up positions in which they knew they were safe from a 'fast air' attack. Usually they either dug themselves into a compound where we knew there were a number of civilians, especially women and children, or they fired from a mosque. There was also a third option: getting in danger close to coalition troops themselves.

For just a few weeks the situation in Afghanistan – at least from our perspective in the squadron – seemed to quieten down a little. This was towards the time when the British Army's 16 Air Assault Brigade were approaching the end of their time in theatre.

My wing-man and I had been tasked with carrying out a surveillance routine colloquially known as the 'Pattern of Life'. I was flying with Adam Hogg, a tall, slim youngster with a slightly large nose and longish, fair hair that always looked a bit scruffy. He would have missed it if I'd stopped asking him when he was going to get his hair cut. But Hoggy was an exceptional pilot, even if, whenever he was outside the aircraft, he was invariably plugged into his iPod.

Our two aircraft were above Musa Qala, flying off-set egg shapes. One end of the 'egg' was based on the town or other point of interest, and while the aircraft was overhead we would be running our surveillance routines using various onboard sensors, the binoculars, targeting pod or whatever was appropriate. On the outbound leg we would reset our equipment and get ready for the next run, and at the same time talk to 16 Air Assault Brigade's FAC. There was nobody else on the circuit, and we were using a secure radio, so we could speak freely.

'How's it been for you?' I asked, knowing that the brigade had been in theatre for about three months and had to be somewhat shell-shocked by the whole thing. 'How's your war been?'

But the reply from the FAC, who I knew was a young corporal, surprised me.

'It's fine. It's been good. We've had quite a lot of action.'

'Any particular dodgy moments?' I asked. 'Because it's looked pretty busy on the news.'

'Yeah,' the corporal replied. 'It's been quite dicey. We've almost been overrun several times. But the delivery of air ordnance has been brilliant – we've been able to put it exactly where we needed it. Right up close and personal sometimes.'

'How close?' I asked. 'Four or five hundred yards?'

'Oh no,' his voice crackled back over the radio. 'I delivered a 2,000lb bomb from an American aircraft in the compound one down from us.'

'Bloody hell,' I muttered. As I overflew the compound where the FAC was based, I looked down and saw the crater the weapon had left. I quickly calculated the distance and worked out that it was only about 230 yards away from his location.

'Christ,' I said. 'Didn't that sting?'

'We've got really big thick walls here,' he laughed. 'When the aircraft started its attack run we just got down behind the wall and covered our ears. But it did crack the roof of the house, though, the platoon house. I couldn't hear that well afterwards, but I turned the radio up and after a while the ringing stopped and we just carried on.'

As I started the outbound run I thought about the plight of the men on the ground, and was grateful – not for the first time – that I was fighting this war from the cockpit of a jet aircraft. The men of 16 Air Assault Brigade had been in theatre for about three months, and shortly before my conversation with the FAC they'd had *forty-three* days of continuous daily contact with the Taliban. They had been exchanging fire with the insurgents every day for a month and a half, in a period that had seen the highest tempo of sustained military operations since the

Korean War. No other units had taken that level of continuous barrage, of exchanges of fire and daily contact with the enemy. And yet this young corporal was so matter-of-fact about delivering massive weapons so close to his position.

There is a military codeword – 'Broken Arrow' – which simply means 'direct all fire on my position' (it can also mean the accidental detonation of a nuclear weapon, but the meaning is usually clear from the context). What this corporal was doing was essentially just that, tweaked slightly, simply because he had to. He was bringing down high-yield bombs – in fact the highest-power weapons available in theatre at that time – within a couple of hundred yards of his own position. And he had to do this, had to risk the collateral damage and possible injuries to his own comrades, because the Taliban knew that getting as close as possible to the coalition troops significantly reduced the chances that they would face air-delivered ordnance. So in any contact they always tried to get as close as they possibly could, as quickly as possible.

Extreme situations call for extreme responses, and in the case of 16 Air Assault Brigade, that meant dropping weapons at a distance that was well inside the normal safety range. The simple fact was that, if they hadn't, the Taliban would have overrun their positions. And nobody was in the slightest doubt about what would have happened to the coalition troops then. It wouldn't have been pretty.

18

Back on the ground, I shut down the Harrier and slid back the canopy. As always, the heat hit me like a hammer as I took off my helmet and climbed out. I signed in the aircraft in the F700 maintenance logbook, removed the rest of my survival gear and did the sortie debrief with Hoggy. Then I headed off in search of caffeine.

A few minutes later I was sitting by myself at the Tim Hortons just as the sun was starting to go down behind Three Mile Mountain. Drinking fresh coffee and eating a freshly baked muffin that was still warm, I mulled things over. In front of me, a hockey game was being played on a small pitch that the Canadians had built for their own recreation.

As I watched citizens of forty countries all based at Kandahar go about their business, I considered the squadron's performance to date. The squadron was getting tired now, for sure, but we *were* still performing exactly as we should. We'd not dropped the ball. The det was doing its job, because we knew we were saving the lives of coalition soldiers every time we responded to a TIC or were launched on a GCAS scramble. And we'd suffered no casualties. But, much to my annoyance, I couldn't shake the distinct feeling that we were to some extent just rearranging deckchairs on the *Titanic*.

Fighting the Taliban never brought a sense of lasting

success. Even if coalition forces managed to completely eliminate the Taliban from a particular area or village, this had no long-term effect. The moment the troops began to withdraw – as they always had to because they aren't in Afghanistan in sufficient numbers to hold the territory they gain in the way that an occupying army would do, and this is not, in any case, their reason for being there – the Taliban would begin moving back in.

The enemy of the coalition forces in Afghanistan comprised three main groups. There were the Taliban themselves and the groups that were associated with them, the two most evident being Al Qaeda and the HIG. The latter was the Hezb-es-Islami Gulbuddin, which was founded in 1977 by a man named Gulbuddin Hekmatyar, and is now the larger of the two sections of the country's Hezbi Islami Party. Like the Taliban and Al Qaeda, the HIG was regarded as a terrorist organization by the coalition. And there were multiple other smaller groups of insurgents – at least twenty in all – with allegiances to one or more of these. But as far as we and the troops on the ground were concerned, they were all a part of the 'Taliban regime'.

In practice these distinctions meant little, as none of the three groups wore a uniform or displayed any other means of ready identification, though many of the Taliban tended to wear a black *shalwar-kameez* – an outfit comprising a long shirt and wide trousers – and black *lungi* turbans. The Taliban also all wore beards for religious reasons, but even this wasn't particularly useful in a country where few men shaved. And the fact that an individual might be carrying a Kalashnikov was irrelevant because almost every adult male in Afghanistan owned a weapon of some kind. But if that Afghan aimed and fired the weapon at coalition troops, this would be a fairly reliable indicator of his intentions and affiliation.

There was also the 'smoke and mirrors' aspect of the situation. Fighting the Taliban is not like fighting any other enemy. Coalition troops have no idea, no way of telling, if a handful of Afghan men standing beside a compound are just a group of poppy farmers discussing the price of raw opium, or Taliban fighters concealing a heavy machine-gun and a cache of assault rifles that they'll open up with the moment they spot an opportunity. And a man who's a farmer today might decide he's a Talib tomorrow, or vice versa. The Taliban are in a constant state of flux, with volunteers constantly joining their ranks as others leave. It's impossible to quantify the number or disposition of enemy forces, and it's almost certain that even the Taliban leaders have no real idea of the number of men they have under their command.

The Afghanistan border is extremely porous, and it's been estimated that there could be as many as three million people still in Pakistan who were displaced by the 1980s conflict. The Taliban have a fairly successful recruiting operation running there, based on a heady mix of religion, money and drugs. There is a potentially un-limited supply of new recruits, drawn from the pool of displaced Afghans in Pakistan, from the villages and compounds within Afghanistan itself and, increasingly, from dedicated radical Muslims in all the countries of the world.

This was emphasized after the siege of Qala-I-Jangi in

49. The view from the cockpit at 30,000 feet. Dominating the picture is the refuelling probe on the engine intake.

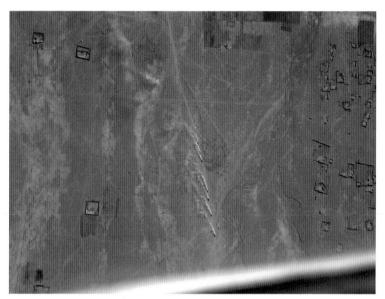

50. The view from above. The difficulties of being sure about the situation on the ground from the air are evident. Through the cockpit glass as the Harrier banks to the left, a column of vehicles can be seen kicking up dust. But who they are and what they're doing, without further information, is anyone's guess.

51. This picture graphically demonstrates how hard it is to identify a target from the air based on directions from the ground. If we're told the enemy are holed up in the compound to the west of the road we have to ask which one. And hold our fire until we're sure we've found them.

52. There are groups of people on either side of the bridge. Is it a firefight or a Sunday market? Further evidence of how hard it was to be sure of the situation on the ground.

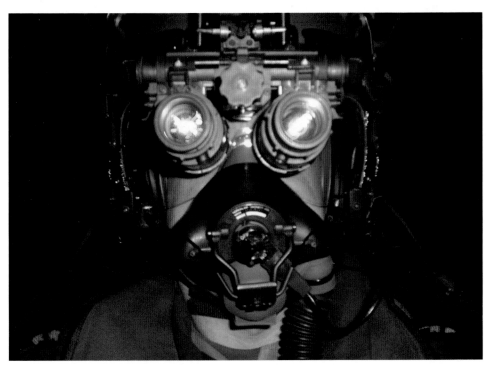

53. Cyborg – the cumbersome sets of Night Vision Goggles gave their wearer an outlandish appearance. But without them, flying close air support at night was significantly more challenging.

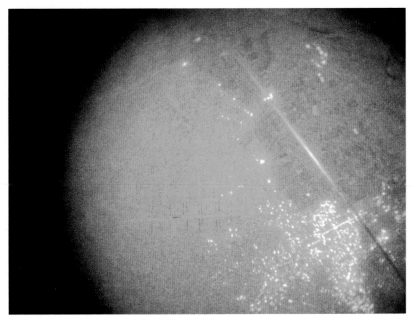

54. The view through the NVGs. Interpreting what you were seeing took some getting used to.

55. Santa's got a brand new sleigh. The Taliban didn't rest for Christmas, but that didn't mean we couldn't try to enjoy a little festive spirit.

56. When the scramble bell rings, the alert crews drop whatever they're doing and run to the jets.

57. On alert. A Harrier, armed, pre-flighted and ready to go, sits on the hangar, waiting for the scramble bell to ring. The pilot's Mae West lifejacket and helmet hang in the foreground.

58. Scramble. A GR7 gets airborne on another GCAS mission.

59. Wingman. A great portrait of one of the Harriers. The stencils on the side of the cockpit show it's been well-used.

60. Flares fired from the Harrier's belly were our best defence against the threat from heat-seeking surface-to-air missiles.

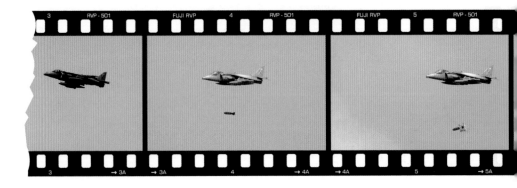

61. Carrying a fairly standard load-out of bombs, CRV-7 rockets, drop tanks, and recce and targeting pods under the fuselage, a GR7 breaks right, high over the mountains.

62. A job well done. I spoke to the squadron on our last day in Afghanistan to acknowledge the success of the det. During our four months at KAF, we were forced to fly our Harriers at a tempo not previously seen in Afghanistan. I was proud of every single one of my people.

63. Something to remember us by.

November 2001, when one of the few surviving Taliban was found to be an American citizen named John Walker Lindh. He had converted to Islam and then travelled to Afghanistan to become an active member of the Taliban. When his identity was revealed he became known as the 'American Taliban' and was sent back to the United States and there charged with treason.

And I was keenly aware that the Russians – the world's second-largest superpower, with an enormous and sophisticated military machine at its disposal, fighting the natives of one of the world's poorest countries who were largely armed with simple assault rifles – had tried taking on the Afghans and they'd been comprehensively beaten. Bearing that in mind, what could we hope to achieve with a handful of Harriers and a few bombs and rockets?

It begged the question: what plan was ISAF actually running? There was no air campaign in the traditional sense of the expression, simply because the air assets were being used to contain an insurgency, not conduct a conventional battle. There was no 'if we get to this point here then we've won'. Nothing like that.

Instead most of the operations conducted by the coalition troops were reactive – they would mount a patrol somewhere in the badlands, get ambushed by the Taliban and call in air support to eliminate their attackers. Or intelligence might be received suggesting that a compound or area was being used as a Taliban safe house, and an operation would be mounted to attack it to kill or capture the insurgents.

The reality of the campaign in Afghanistan is that the

coalition forces will never be able to bomb, blast and shoot the Taliban into submission. Arguably, each time a Harrier drops a bomb that kills a group of Taliban, or members of a foot patrol manage to shoot a Talib, the coalition forces have failed. There's no point in killing the Taliban except for reasons of pure self-preservation – to save your own life or the life of an ally – and certainly no point in a long-term strategy, to use that word in its loosest possible sense, of engaging in conflict with the Taliban. The fact is that there are far more Taliban, either already fighting the coalition, or able to be recruited as willing volunteers, than we have weapons to destroy them.

The best that the coalition forces can do in Afghanistan is to create an area that is free of the Taliban and provide the nation with sufficient breathing space to devise and set up a political solution that it can live with. And our job, as a military force, was to give the Afghans, and the country's own security forces, primarily the Afghan National Army and the Afghan National Police, the opportunity to take the fight to the Taliban.

Sometimes the Afghan people themselves do manage to assert themselves, and the Musa Qala ceasefire was a good example. In the summer of 2006 much of Musa Qala lay in ruins. The town had been the scene of fierce and continuous fighting for months and it was, in reality, held by the Taliban.

At the start of that summer the coalition forces in Musa Qala comprised Somme Platoon of the Royal Irish Regiment and the 1st Danish Light Reconnaissance Squadron, known as the Griffins, but in August the Danes pulled out, taking with them their Eagle light armoured vehicles and, more importantly, their .50-cal machine-guns. They were replaced by Barossa Platoon of the Royal Irish Regiment and a Headquarters Company formed from 3 Para personnel. This amalgamation nicknamed themselves 'Easy Company' as they were the battle group's fifth company and so took the letter 'E' as their designator.

These troops occupied a compound roughly 100 yards square – known as a platoon house – right in the centre of the town, but they were, in every sense, under siege. The base was hemmed in on all sides by narrow streets and buildings that offered excellent shelter for the Taliban, and they were being attacked not just every day, but some days almost every hour. The insurgents fired everything they could at and over the walls of the compound: rockets, mortars, RPGs, recoilless rifles, Kalashnikovs and sniper rifles. The observation post on the main building was hit so many times the British troops nicknamed it 'the Alamo'. The Royal Irish and 3 Para men replied with assault rifles and machine-guns, but mainly mortars, firing over 850 mortar rounds during their brief tenure of Musa Qala.

The philosophy behind the platoon house concept was that the base would allow coalition troops to quickly establish control over the town or location by mounting aggressive patrols to flush out the insurgents and establishing good relations with the local community.

That didn't work at Musa Qala – which the troops quickly decided was the worst platoon house in Helmand and nicknamed 'Camp Shit Hole' – simply because there *was* no local community. Almost the only Afghans lurking in the alleyways and buildings were heavily armed Taliban. Patrolling outside the walls of the compound was out of the question because there was no coherent evacuation plan for casualties, and the troops had both limited supplies of ammunition and nothing like enough men to make it work. Even getting resupplies of ammunition and other stores was fraught with danger, because almost everything had to come in by helicopter, and simply securing a landing site normally meant a full-on firefight with the Taliban, who had soon recognized how dependent the coalition troops were on these supply runs.

The reality of Musa Qala was that the coalition troops were held captive in their compound, rarely able to venture outside, and were achieving nothing except inflicting losses on the Taliban as the insurgents launched their regular attacks. It was an untenable situation and everybody on the ground knew it, but for political reasons it had been decided that a continued coalition presence in Musa Qala was essential.

For the troops inside the compound it was a stalemate, but salvation appeared from an unlikely, and completely unexpected, direction.

The Afghan authorities were approached by a group of the village elders from Musa Qala. For the town's inhabitants the continual fighting had been disastrous. Dozens of Afghan civilians had been killed, many homes and shops were nothing more than burnt-out shells and almost everyone who was able to leave had fled elsewhere. And there was, they had realized, little prospect of this state of affairs changing.

The village elders' proposal was simple: the Taliban

and the coalition forces were to stop fighting each other and both leave the area. The people of Musa Qala would take back their town and try to rebuild it.

On 13 September 2006 a *shura*, a conference or meeting, was held in the desert outside Musa Qala, and attended by both the Taliban and the local military leaders. There an agreement was reached: the coalition forces would withdraw and the Taliban were to leave the village alone.

The ceasefire held for about five months, and then the Taliban moved back in. They killed Haji Shah Agha, the village elder who had formulated the withdrawal plan, and regained control of the town. What a fucking mess, I thought. But in the ultimately depressing story of the Musa Qala ceasefire, I had to believe there was a glimmer of hope. It was a tantalizing glimpse, nothing more, but a glimpse nonetheless of what might be achieved.

I finished my coffee and climbed wearily back into the 4x4 to return to the accommodation area.

When I walked round the corner, one of my pilots was talking – or perhaps arguing – with an officer I hadn't seen before, right in front of the gazebo. At some point one of the groups of Americans based at Kandahar had built a wooden deck outside the entrance to one of the accommodation blocks used by the squadron. These were all Nissen-hut-type structures, and they'd erected decking and a gazebo and put sheeting over the top of it to create a pleasant – by Afghanistan standards – sitting area shaded from the sun.

'What's going on?' I asked.

'I think I'll let this muppet tell you himself.' With that,

the 800 pilot turned and vanished inside the building. I met the other man's gaze.

'I'm a health and safety officer,' he said, 'and that awning has got to go.'

'I'm sorry. What?'

'That awning, sir. It's a health and safety hazard.'

'In what way, exactly, is it a hazard?'

'It's potentially blocking a fire lane.'

'No it isn't,' I pointed out. 'We're inside the blast walls. You can't get any vehicles in here unless you demolish the blast walls first.'

'Then there's the danger that bits of it could fall off and land on somebody's head and injure them.'

For a few seconds I just looked at him.

Forget that we were standing in an airfield in the middle of Afghanistan. Forget the potentially daily attacks by mortars and heavy machine-guns and 107mm rockets. Forget the fact that the surrounding area was considered so dangerous that people were forbidden to leave the base unless their duties absolutely required it, and even then they had to be heavily armed and part of a group, also heavily armed. Forget the fact that if everything went wrong and the Taliban somehow managed to overrun the airfield they would – and this is *not* a figure of speech – skin everyone alive. Forget all that. As far as this idiot was concerned, the most dangerous hazard on the entire airfield appeared to be a solidly constructed gazebo with sheeting on top of it, inside the blast walls.

'Were you anywhere near the rocket attack last night?' I asked.

'No, sir, I wasn't. I was over on the other side of the airfield.'

'Well,' I said, 'I was here, sitting in a bomb shelter and listening to the sound of warheads exploding on the ground all around me. Don't you think being hit by a rocket is possibly more of a health and safety hazard than the chance of a piece of wood falling off this and giving somebody a mild headache?'

'No, sir. In my opinion this is a health and safety hazard.'

'Yesterday I landed after a sortie where I dropped a bomb and probably killed ten or twenty people,' I continued. 'I'm flying a high-workload single-engine aircraft in one of the most hostile and unforgiving environments in the world. This base is under almost constant bombardment from an enemy that would happily kill us all, and you're seriously trying to tell me that this gazebo is more dangerous than any of that?'

'Not necessarily *more* dangerous, but in my opinion it *is* a hazard, yes, so I'm instructing you to take it down.'

'I hope you won't mind me saying this, but you do realize that you're completely fucking mad, don't you?'

The slight smile on the officer's face vanished instantly, and he buggered off to waste somebody else's time with another mind-bogglingly stupid request.

That was one of the problems with Kandahar, and with anywhere in the military, in fact. There are rules, rules about almost everything, from the speed you could drive to the structure of a building, and always, it seemed, there were small-minded idiots employed specifically to ensure that those rules – no matter how stupid, pointless or quite simply nonsensical – were obeyed. It was bollocks, frankly. And we were about to be reminded that there were far more immediate threats to our health and well-being than the remote possibility of a piece of wood falling off an awning.

19

I was in Ops getting ready for a sortie when word reached us that the UN Halo had gone down.

The Mil Mi-24 is the biggest, heaviest and most powerful chopper so far manufactured. It's been built in Russia since 1983 by the Rostov and Kazan manufacturing enterprises. Powered by two Lotarev D-136 turboshaft engines mounted above the cabin, it's the only helicopter with an eight-bladed main rotor, and is designed to carry up to twenty tons of cargo – a similar load to that of the C-130 Hercules transport aircraft. It's an enormous machine and, since we had arrived in theatre, the Halo had been operating from the far end of the airfield.

The Kandahar Halo was all-white with large 'UN' markings painted on the side, and we assumed it was being operated by the United Nations for some unspecified purposes. You could almost set your watch by it. Every morning at around 7.30 it would fire up its engines, engage the massive rotors and lift off majestically. It would do a left-hand turn and head off up into the mountains, almost creating a partial eclipse of the sun as it overflew the airfield, and presumably do whatever UN-type things it was supposed to do. Despite its size, it was reasonably quiet for a helicopter, and it seemed quite odd that something so huge could make so little noise and be so graceful, though it was still difficult to miss. About ninety minutes later it would reappear and settle back on the hard standing.

The launch and return of the Halo, and its permanent presence at Kandahar, became a part of the daily routine. In daylight the huge helicopter was a landmark at the western side of the airfield, the opposite end from where the Harrier det was quartered. By night it was, if anything, even more visible to us, because to launch in an easterly direction we had to taxi our aircraft all the way to the western end of the runway, before turning the aircraft through 180 degrees for take-off.

Because the airfield had almost no lighting installed – or at least very little that was ever switched on – we used night-vision goggles and the infrared targeting system fitted to the aircraft to find our way safely to the end of the runway. All the way down the taxiway we would be able to see the Halo on our screens, getting bigger and bigger as we approached it. For some reason, it was strangely comforting to see it parked on the airfield.

And now it had gone down. Maybe a missile, or a lucky shot from an RPG launcher, mechanical failure or even what's called CFIT, or controlled flight into terrain – simply meaning that the pilot flew the aircraft into the ground. Whatever the cause, the Halo had gone and, if nothing else, it was a stark reminder to us all that flying *any* aircraft in Afghanistan was inherently dangerous. If the Taliban didn't get you, there were plenty of natural hazards out there waiting to pounce.

Soon after hearing the news that the big UN chopper had been lost, I was in my Harrier, bouncing down the taxiway towards the end of the runway where the helicopter would normally be parked, and saw with something of a shock that it wasn't there. A wave of sadness rolled over me at the sudden realization that it had gone for good – it's one thing to be told a fact and to understand it, but there's a kind of visceral shock when you actually see, or in this case don't see, the visual confirmation of that fact. Though I had known none of the crew of the Halo, I knew they were fighting on the same side as us, playing a crucial part in the war against the Taliban, and I still felt as if I'd lost a friend. And, tragic as its loss was, I still felt we were lucky there hadn't been greater losses among the ISAF forces since we'd arrived in theatre. We were definitely running through our nine lives.

The postscript to the story is that a day later a virtually identical replacement aircraft arrived, and the 'UN' sorties carried on exactly as before.

Its quick replacement underscored the fact that the war in Afghanistan is very much a war of logistics, as well as seeing some of the fiercest fighting in recent military history.

The country produces virtually nothing except opium, and that meant external supply chains were essential to keep the coalition forces properly equipped and provisioned. Although a lot of the heavier equipment was shipped to the region by sea, Afghanistan is landlocked, so everything had to reach its final destination either by air or road, and both routes had their problems.

Road convoys carrying supplies routed down to Kandahar and Kabul through Pakistan, and were a frequent target for the Taliban, who knew very well just how fragile that lifeline was for the coalition forces. Despite being heavily guarded by troops, these convoys were often attacked while they were out in the wilds. But it was resupply by air on which ongoing operations at Kandahar depended. And the sheer variety of nationalities, aircraft types and operating procedures involved always created an atmosphere of barely contained chaos.

Air transport was an attractive alternative to road convoys, and almost anyone who owned an aircraft capable of carrying a reasonable load, and who was prepared to sign a contract, could find work in Afghanistan.

Perhaps predictably, a lot of the aircraft used were of Russian origin, and their countries of registration wildly varied. There were large numbers of cargo planes, mainly old Antonov and Ilyushin aircraft, from the former Soviet-bloc breakaway states like Azerbaijan and Kazakhstan, ageing Hercules from tiny companies based in South Africa, and a host of others. Kandahar Airfield was stuffed full of the things, like a Wild West town on a new frontier.

The cowboy attitude extended to the aircraft, which were almost all filthy and battered and, in the case of the Russian planes, visibly sagging as well. Maintenance probably wasn't high on their list of priorities, and every time one of them took off it belched thick black smoke from the engines as it staggered into the air. Nobody who had a choice would be likely to want to climb into any one of them.

The international language of aviation is English, and all pilots are *supposed* to have a sufficient command of it to allow them to communicate properly and to clearly understand ATC instructions and information.

In Afghanistan that rule didn't seem to be too rigorously enforced.

So what we had were dozens of pilots flying in and out of Kandahar who were not really able to speak English. On top of that, they were probably not brilliantly trained. The aircraft they were flying were not competently maintained, equipped with very basic gear and usually very heavily laden. It's not surprising that these guys were an absolute law unto themselves and a danger to everything else in the air, birds included.

The harsh reality of this was demonstrated to me one afternoon at Kandahar. I was sitting on the runway, with Tim Flatman in the Harrier next to me, waiting for an American aircraft to disappear so that we could take off, when I noticed a dot in the sky that seemed to be getting bigger.

'Is that aeroplane coming straight at us?' I asked Flatters.

'Isn't that the one that's just departed?'

'No,' I said. 'That's way over there to the right.'

I switched boxes to use tower frequency and called the local, or tower, controller. 'Tower, Recoil Four One. Is there an aeroplane coming straight at us on the reciprocal?'

'Stand by.' There was a pause of maybe five seconds, and then the controller was back on the radio, his voice noticeably higher and more excited. 'Affirmative, Four One, affirmative. Clear the runway immediately.'

As we complied with this mandatory instruction, the American air traffic controller (ATCO) tried to clarify the situation.

'We think that's an inbound UN flight, and that the pilot's misunderstood which runway we're operating from. The approach controller told him to land on your runway, but he's supposed to be ten miles behind you, which means you'd be long gone before he touched down. But now he's actually coming from the other direction. We've tried about a dozen times to contact him, on Guard as well, but he's just not responding.'

'Guard' is the military emergency frequency of 243.0 megahertz.

We watched with a kind of cautious fascination as the big transport aircraft approached the airfield. Eventually, at very short range, it turned right, did a monstrously wide circuit and eventually landed on the correct runway, in the correct direction, and taxied in to the dispersal.

The pilot got an absolute bollocking on the radio from the American ATCO, which wasn't particularly professional, though both of us could understand his frustration. But these guys are a law unto themselves, and they just go off and do their own thing. Most of the time you have no clue what they're planning to do next, but they do it anyway. I saw a couple of them on the base. They were like something out of *Air America* – two weird blokes who looked as though they had just walked away from a nuclear disaster. Tatty, dishevelled and clearly knackered. These two pilots stumbled out of their aircraft and headed straight for one of the cafés on the base for some strong coffee to get themselves going again.

Realistically, as we'd seen the incoming aircraft while we were still on the runway waiting for take-off clearance, if we *had* got airborne we would have been easily able to avoid it. But it wouldn't have been an ideal departure, because the incoming aircraft would have been in a piece of the sky we would be trying to pass through. And we certainly wouldn't have had the freedom to carry out the tactical departures that we'd briefed and planned.

Our only other option would have been to abort the take-off on the runway, and that would have been the least favourable course of action, purely because of our full fuel tanks and the heavy weight of ordnance we were carrying.

The moment we were cleared to take off, I poured on the coals and accelerated down the runway. I was keen to get the Harrier into the sky where it belonged, and where I felt I could exert a little more control over my own destiny.

By the end of December everyone was beginning to think about home, and particularly about not being home for Christmas. This wasn't a surprise, of course – we'd known the dates of the detachment well before we left Cottes-more – but the pervious three months had stretched us and we were all physically tired, as well as tired of living in one another's pockets.

At an airfield in the UK, squadron personnel would work their shift and then go back to their married quarters or rented accommodation or whatever, and that provided a clear break from their work environment. At Kandahar that simply wasn't possible. We couldn't leave the airfield, and we were living and working together in much the same way as we would be on a ship, but without even the possibility of a port visit to break the routine.

So it was perhaps inevitable that occasionally frustrations and irritations surfaced, and some of the banter between personnel took on a bit of an edge. It was nothing serious, but it served to emphasize the problems that could arise when a large number of people are cooped up together, and especially in a hostile environment like Afghanistan.

And ever since Neil Bing had first taken the bait when Dunc Mason remarked on the need for a few RAF pilots who knew their way around the Harrier, the two of them had been at it hammer and tongs. As well as being one of our few RAF pilots, Dunc was also our only former Red Arrow, much to the disgust of Bing Bong, who thought the 'cream of the Royal Air Force' were a bunch of posers.

With the battle ensign hoisted high over Kandahar, Dunc had put up with it all in a good-humoured fashion, but just before Christmas he decided it was time to get his own back.

He telephoned a friend who was serving on the Red Arrows squadron and asked him to send an enormous 'goody bag' of publicity material out to Kandahar. When it arrived we decided to decorate the crew room with it, but there was so much stuff – posters, stickers, badges, pens, mugs and all the rest – that there was hardly a vertical or horizontal surface that wasn't covered with some kind of Red Arrows publicity material.

Bing Bong was scheduled for night-flying, so Dunc took the opportunity to 'decorate' his locker and all of his flying gear while he'd been resting during the day. When Bing Bong appeared in the crew room that night, his face was a picture. But he never mentioned the Red Arrows again.

With Christmas on the horizon when the squadron deployed, I'd thought forward and tried to get ahead of the game by taking a whole load of decorations with me when we flew out to theatre. Unfortunately, almost everyone else in the squadron had had the same idea, but because the unit had deployed to a war zone, everybody – including me, I'm sorry to say – had all bought the cheapest, most garish crap they could find. We'd all thought the same thing: we were going to have to leave whatever we bought out in Afghanistan, so we decided we'd just nip down to the pound shop or its equivalent and spend about a fiver.

The result was that the accommodation ended up looking like the worst Christmas grotto any of us had ever seen, full of bobbing Santas, horrible flashing lights and the tackiest of decorations. Apparently, it's unlucky to have more than one Christmas tree in the same building. We had eight of them positioned all around the Ops room.

Our efforts to make sure that being stuck in the middle of the GAFA, or Great Afghan Fuck All, as it was affectionately known, wouldn't disrupt Christmas didn't stop with the decorations.

The Royal Navy has always been good at organizing charity events, and just because the squadron was out in the wilds of Afghanistan didn't seem any reason why they shouldn't do something. Back at RAF Cottesmore a charity walk around Rutland Water had been organized, and the squadron decided to do a charity run around the Ops area on the same day and at the same time as the event at Cottesmore. The difference was that we made our event a relay race and between us ran the equivalent of the distance from Kandahar to Kabul and back – just over 600 miles.

As a follow-on from the charity run held on Christmas Eve, the squadron engineers decided that they, too, were going to raise some money for charity. But, being engineers, they weren't prepared to just don running gear and cover a mile or two. Instead they each pulled on a Santa hat, trainers and one sock, attached by an elastic band that ran round their waist, and into which they inserted their 'tackle'.

They ran round the whole base raising money, and finished off doing press-ups on the ground outside the Tim Hortons, a location chosen deliberately because of the large number of females who worked there. Their antics were clearly much appreciated by a very vocal audience, and the money rained down on them. They raised an awful lot of cash and lifted spirits all around the airfield, though I couldn't help but wonder what the Afghans made of it all: *They got rid of the Taliban – for this?*

I'd decided right from the start that the Kandahar det was going to be 'dry', because I didn't relish the idea of people carrying loaded weapons and working on aircraft with alcohol inside them, and we didn't even relax the rule for Christmas. Fortunately, nobody seemed to mind. And the chefs in the DIFACs did their best to cheer us up with some traditional Christmas fare – we even got some turkey with all the trimmings.

But, we discovered, turkey with all the trimmings has exactly the same effect on your waistline in Afghanistan as it does back home. As Wedge learnt to his cost. Just after Christmas he was flying over Naw Zad on a very dull and boring sortie when the following conversation took place between him and Widow 84 on the ground:

Wedge: 'So, how was Christmas out here for you?'

Widow 84: 'Not too bad – I even got some real turkey to eat! How about you?'

Wedge: 'It was good, but I had no time for Christmas dinner, sadly. Not that that's a bad thing. I could do with losing a bit of weight.'

Widow 84: 'Are you the one they call Wedge?'

'I didn't,' he said to me as he pulled off his g-suit after the flight, 'quite know what to say to that, but obviously I'm now renowned as some kind of a lard-arse throughout the Regional Command.'

And throughout all the festivities, the GCAS alert system remained firmly in place. The Taliban's attacks and ambushes on coalition forces continued exactly as they always had done.

20

The new year began the same way that the old one had ended, with long periods waiting for the GCAS scramble bell to ring, then a race to the latest TIC. The pace of operations offered no let up. Every day, no matter how tired we were, we got airborne to storm in and give it everything. Flying a Harrier is extremely demanding at the best of times – it's not the easiest of aircraft to handle even in peacetime – but when you add the constant pressure of flying in a very active war zone, it's not surprising that some of the pilots were showing clear signs of fatigue. And when people are tired that's when they start to make mistakes – mistakes none of us could afford to make.

But there was very little I could do about it. I was determined we would meet the tasking – that was why we were there in theatre – so about all I could do was keep my eyes open for any tell-tale warning signs and try to make sure that the aircrew and maintainers got as much rest as possible.

Early in January I was sitting with Nath Gray in one of the coffee houses on the airfield. With less than a month of the det to run, we were talking about home. We chatted enthusiastically about the things we most looked forward to enjoying again. And then the bleepers went off. Our routine was now well established. When a scramble was called, as on-alert pilots we simply stopped what we were doing and got ourselves to the aircraft and into the air as quickly as possible.

As always, the adrenalin started to flow as we leapt up and ran across to our scramble vehicle. You never knew what was waiting for you at the other end.

I leapt into the passenger side and slammed the door closed as Nath started the engine and shifted the gearbox into first. I switched on the flashing red light to show we were on our way to a scramble, and Nath really put his foot down, powering away towards the Harrier dispersal as fast as he could. We kept our speed down – this had nothing to do with the maximum speed allowed on the base, but was simply a limit we imposed on ourselves – but still we were travelling at well over the base limit.

'What the hell,' I muttered, as we drove past one intersection.

A traffic cop – a Smokey, the Americans called them – was standing there in the road, waving his arms frantically in an effort to get us to stop.

Nath did what any reasonable person would have done in the circumstances – he swerved to avoid him, but otherwise completely ignored him.

I turned round in my seat to look behind, and wasn't entirely surprised to see that the cop had now climbed into his car and was chasing after us, headlights blazing, roof lights flashing away and the siren now just audible.

'Don't look now,' I said to Nath, 'but we've picked up a tail.'

Nath glanced in his mirror to confirm what I'd seen.

'Do you want me to stop?' he asked.

'Absolutely not,' I snapped. 'We're responding to a scramble. It takes precedence over that idiot. Keep going.'

At the Harrier dispersal we pulled up, jumped out of the SsangYong and ran over to our aircraft. As I climbed into mine and started getting strapped in, the policeman hauled his car to a halt at the edge of the dispersal and ran towards us. He was actually trying to catch Nath and stop him getting into his aircraft. Fortunately, one of our ground engineers saw what he was doing and managed to grab him, and I could clearly hear the exchange that followed.

'What the bloody hell do you think you're doing?' the engineer asked, as he dragged the policeman to a halt.

'That guy's evading arrest,' the cop spluttered. 'That's a felony.'

'Don't be so fucking stupid. He's scrambling.'

'But he's not allowed to speed on the base. I'm giving him a ticket.'

'No, you're not, you stupid little man. Get real. If you stand there much longer, he'll start the aeroplane and just run you over. Get a grip and get the hell out of the way.'

As we started the Harriers and taxied away, the last thing I saw through the canopy glass was a couple of the ground engineers dragging the struggling cop away from the dispersal. The image was captured in the flashing red lights of the Harrier's anti-collision beacons. Minutes later we were climbing away from Kandahar into darkening skies.

On the ground behind us they had to take him inside

one of the buildings before finally managing to pacify him. And even then the officious fool left a written warning to 'the pilot of the British Harrier' for Nath to find on his return.

21

'Screw them' was Dunc Mason's view of the rules so crudely enforced by the Military Police. Especially after dark. And so Dunc drove the big 4x4 across the airfield as he always did: paying no attention to the speed limit whatsoever. The rest of us – the night team – gripped our seats and feigned a lack of concern. Dunc was convinced that, sooner or later, as we drove along the perimeter road less than 500 yards from the GAFA outside, we were going to be attacked by a suicide bomber or hit by an IED somewhere along there. He was more than slightly paranoid about it, but his argument was difficult to refute because that *was* the logical place for an attack. He pulled up outside the DIFAC, killed the lights and switched off the engine.

'There's no way I'm sticking to the speed limit along there.' Dunc grinned as we went inside for 'Midnight Eggs'.

Because the night team of pilots, engineers and bomb-heads was much smaller than the day team, we were much more tightly knit. We did everything together, irrespective of rank, and that included Midnight Eggs.

We arrived at the DIFAC en masse. Behind the counter a tiny Japanese lady of about sixty-five or seventy – the 'egg chef' – stood at a big, flat, fast-order griddle, a spatula in each hand, just waiting.

'An omelette with everything, please,' I said, then watched, mesmerized, as she vanished in a blur of action, arms and spatulas flying in all directions. It looked less like cooking than a display of some obscure Japanese martial art, but at the end of it a large, fluffy omelette duly appeared.

'Weddy,' she announced proudly. Her presence begged the question: what the hell was an elderly Japanese woman doing cooking eggs in a war zone in the middle of Afghanistan in the early hours of the morning, every morning?

Dunc and I sat down with the rest of the team and tucked in greedily. But not that greedily. We'd been followed in by a group of over-muscled Americans.

'Seven eggs scrambled,' requested the first of them.

Christ alive! Not two, or three, but *seven*. I genuinely began to wonder if these guys ever managed to go to the loo. Forget muscle-bound, these bodybuilders were just egg-bound – walking mountains of protein and cholesterol. But they fitted in perfectly. The whole place had a surreal feel in the middle of the night – like some weird roadhouse bar, or the famous Cantina from *Star Wars*. We finished our eggs, talked and studied the night-dwellers, as we called them.

These guys were contractors who worked on the base. Some of the day staff were weird enough, but the specimens that emerged from the woodwork after the sun had gone down were in a completely different league – almost Neanderthal. In fact we doubted if some of them *dared* venture out in the sunshine. It was a shame the same couldn't be said for the Taliban. We stacked our plates and jumped in the 4x4 and held tight as Dunc stood on the throttle and pointed in the general direction of the Ops building.

After briefing the sortie Dunc and I pulled on a layer of thermals underneath our flying gear. Nights in Afghanistan are absolutely freezing, and the last thing we wanted was to be stuck shivering on some mountainside after ejection (although baking on a mountainside during the day didn't strike me as lot more fun).

Then we each collected a set of NVGs and a hand-held laser pointer. About the size of a big pen and strapped to your finger, the laser had a range of three or four miles. By pointing it at a target on the ground you directed a beam on to it that could be clearly seen by your wing-man through his NVGs. He then knew exactly what you were looking at without having to rely on a verbal description via the radio. The laser pointer was simple and *extremely* effective. And, it has to be said, pretty cool too.

We pulled on our survival kit, grabbed our helmets and goggles and walked out towards the waiting jets.

Night-flying emphasized just how dangerous the skies over Afghanistan really were. As we flew over the Graveyard, the area where the Canadian troops had come under heavy fire, we could see the tracer, mortar flashes, flares and other stuff flying around. By day all that was almost invisible.

Illumination flares were used everywhere in Afghanistan as a matter of routine, so virtually every night the clear skies over the country were ablaze with lights and flares, like a constant fireworks display. Every night was like 5 November. From our cockpits we could easily see which towns and locations were busy, just because of the flares and tracer flying around. We were able to use our vantage point to identify exactly where the action was taking place, almost like watching a constant newsreel.

As we climbed to the north-west we saw, either in blue through the night-vision goggles or in white with our peripheral vision, a sequence of little stars shooting upwards from the ground as yet another cluster of illumination flares was fired and part of another town or area of countryside was briefly illuminated in the distance. The flares had a one-minute burn time, but occasionally we would notice that the troops using them wouldn't get the burst height quite right. If it was too high, the flares wouldn't light the target properly, but if they set them too low, they were still burning when they hit the ground. For all the violence revealed by the flash and burn below us, there was still something almost magical about it.

But the other side of the coin is that night-flying can give a pilot a false sense of security simply because it's dark. You can start to feel that you're in a kind of cocoon. There's the reassuring roar of the Pegasus engine behind you, and you're surrounded by the lights from the switches and controls and the two TV sets. You can hear your own breathing, and the only intrusion from the outside world is whatever's being said on the RT, the calls from your wing-man or the C_2 controlling authority. You've no real spatial awareness and you're totally dependent on your instruments and on ground control.

That might sound like nonsense, but the reality is that by day we can see the ground below us, clouds and so on, and we have a good sense of motion and dynamics. But at night, although the aircraft is travelling at exactly the same speed and performing precisely the same manoeuvres, there's much less sensation of motion in the cockpit. Somehow everything seems to calm down.

The slightly hypnotic tranquillity didn't last long. The radio crackled into life, directing us to Naw Zad in the north of Helmand. Royal Marines there were engaged in heavy exchanges with Taliban firing mortars from positions hidden in the woods outside the city limits. We selected our target and positively identified the enemy. Then Dunc brought their contribution to the war in Afghanistan to an abrupt end with a single laser-guided bomb. The British FOB was off the hook for another night. Job done – and with a minimum of drama. But something wasn't right.

There's an old expression in the military, 'There are old pilots and there are bold pilots, but there are no old, bold pilots.' In other words, pilots who take risks don't normally survive to make old bones. As well as competence in the cockpit and caution in their actions, the other thing that many pilots seem to possess is a kind of sixth sense, an extra-sensory perception that kicks in on those few occasions when things are about to turn to rat shit.

That night, as Duncan's laser-guided bomb detonated precisely on target, I suddenly felt the hairs on the back of my neck start to rise. I checked my instruments again – I'd been checking them regularly as a part of my normal cockpit drills – but all the indications were still normal. At night pilots have to rely completely on their instruments, simply because they usually have no visual cues outside the cockpit to let them know what their aircraft is doing.

That night the aircraft seemed to be handling properly. I could see my wing-man clearly, and there was no threat from the insurgents on the ground as far as I knew. I almost felt that I was being watched, that there was someone behind me. It was a ridiculous idea in the circumstances, yet I began to feel very uncomfortable.

My aircraft was at 20,000 feet, with Duncan 1,000 feet below. The firefight had been properly notified, so there should have been no other coalition aircraft anywhere near the area. But I still felt that something was wrong, a kind of horrible prickling sensation that simply wouldn't go away. I carried out a rapid scan all around my aircraft, starting with the right rear. When I'd finished it I looked up and to my left.

And, to my absolute astonishment, through my night-vision goggles I could see about half the wingspan of a Predator UAV.

My heart rate bolted, and for a long, horrible second I was caught for breath.

Then I acted. I pushed the Harrier into a steep dive to avoid the Predator and transmitted an immediate instruction to my wing-man.

'Four Eight, Four Seven. Descend 1,000 to one eight zero immediate. There's a Predator at my level.'

Dunc, thank God, was on the ball. 'Roger that. In the drop.'

An unmanned aerial vehicle isn't that big, and if I could see a half-wingspan through the limited vision afforded by a set of NVGs, it had to be pretty bloody close. Too bloody close for safety, certainly.

But that wasn't the end of the incident. All we knew was that we were sharing the airspace above Naw Zad with a UAV. The problem was that we had no idea if the Predator was in transit through the area, climbing or descending or what. And, though the Harrier is a much larger vehicle than the Predator, a mid-air collision with it would certainly ruin any pilot's day, and especially mine.

I contacted the C2 guy who was controlling us – predictably, control out in Afghanistan was fairly loose. It was primarily procedural with some limited radar coverage as the aircraft got further north, towards Kabul.

'Crowbar, Recoil Four Seven. Is there a Predator in my vicinity?'

'Recoil Four Seven, stand by.'

After a short pause the controller replied: 'That's affirmative. There is a Predator in the area, but it's twenty miles to the east of you.'

'Negative,' I said, 'it's right here. I just missed it by a whisker.'

One of the main problems in trying to de-conflict UAV activity from aircraft operations is that – as unlikely as it sounds – the Predators are not controlled locally, but from Nellis Air Force base, just outside Las Vegas in Nevada, USA. A further problem is that because the ISAF forces are fighting a war, where and how the coalition aircraft will be deployed can change literally at a moment's notice in response to a TIC call.

Having UAVs working in the same area as fighter and ground-attack aircraft is potentially a recipe for disaster, but realistically all the controllers can do is ensure that everybody in the air, or controlling aerial vehicles, is aware of what other activity is known about. And then everybody needs to keep a sharp lookout. On this occasion that had been enough.

As I turned my Harrier away from the TIC to head south-east for the transit back to Kandahar, I felt that yet another of my nine lives had been used up that night.

22

If my luck in the air – rarely dropping weapons and nearly having a mid-air collision with a Predator – wasn't improving, the same couldn't be said for the rest of the squadron. After about three and a half months in theatre most of the guys were going from strength to strength, and some of 800's younger pilots, in particular, were fast becoming hardened combat veterans.

It had already been a busy day when the GCAS scramble bell rang again. Hoggy and Flatters were the on-alert crews and got themselves airborne within about fifteen minutes of the call.

As soon as they were at altitude they checked in with Crowbar and were given vectors to a major TIC way up north in support of some Americans who were in hard contact with a big gang of Taliban.

On the ground it was clear that the Taliban had chosen the ambush spot carefully. They were properly dug in and had zeroed in on the American patrol pretty well, pouring a non-stop barrage of rounds at them. There wasn't anything the Americans could do to stop them: they were outnumbered and outgunned.

'Mastiff Zero Two, this is Knife Five One.'

'Five One, Zero Two, we're taking heavy incoming fire. RPGs and machine-guns. You've fucking got to sort this.'

That wasn't exactly the response Hoggy had been expecting, but it was already evident that the situation on the ground was chaotic in the extreme, and they were going to have to work at it if they were to get any sensible answers from the JTAC. At first Hoggy thought he was talking to a woman, because Mastiff's voice was so high-pitched and nervous. It took him a few minutes to work out that the JTAC was actually a terrified Hispanic guy.

'We're pinned down behind the trucks. We can't move. Jesus! We just took another RPG, did you see that?'

'Zero Two, Five One, confirm the enemy and your positions.'

Hoggy wasn't prepared to drop anything until he knew exactly where both sets of combatants were located.

'We're behind the fucking trucks – can't you see us? We're fucking pinned down.' At that moment Hoggy and Flatters both heard a crashing explosion through the radio. 'Fuck. That landed twenty feet away. Clear hot! Clear hot!'

But Hoggy's problem was that he couldn't go in hot until he was certain that his weapons wouldn't land anywhere near the American troops, and getting confirmation of that out of the JTAC was looking less and less likely. He guessed that the JTAC was huddled behind his vehicle, like the rest of the patrol members, just trying to stay alive, let alone talk aeroplanes on to any targets. But at the same time Hoggy couldn't just fly around over the TIC while the coalition forces were cut to bits by the Taliban's RPGs.

Then a different American voice called him on the radio.

'Knife Five One, this is Ghost Three Four.'

'Go ahead.'

'Five One, Three Four is a Predator at 17,000 feet. I have a good lock on the hostile positions, and I can lase them for you.'

'Understood. Confirm there's adequate separation between the hostiles and the friendlies?'

'Confirmed. A minimum of 600 yards.'

'Good enough,' Hoggy replied. He was carrying the heavy weapons, the 1,000lb stores, which were too big for collateral damage reasons. 'Flatters, use the five-forty airburst.'

'Roger that.'

Flatters left orbit over the TIC and opened out to the west.

'Zero Two, Five One. We're dropping a five-forty airburst. Two minutes.'

'Clear hot, clear hot. Jesus Christ, that was close!' And over the radio there was the sound of another loud explosion, followed by the steady blatting of a heavy machine-gun.

It was clear that the JTAC wasn't going to be much help to the Harrier pilots until they'd done something to reduce the amount of incoming fire.

Hoggy set himself up in a wagon-wheel over the wooded area that the Predator pilot had identified as the Taliban position, and waited for Flatters to start his inbound run.

'Five One, Five Two. One minute.'

'Roger. Laser fires.' Hoggy aimed his pod at the spot the Predator's laser was illuminating, and fired his own.

'Five Two, good spot,' Flatters said. 'In hot.'

'Clear hot, clear hot,' the JTAC shouted again, the unmistakable sounds of battle raging all around him.

'Released,' Flatters reported, pulling up from the dive as the bomb dropped off his wing.

Hoggy watched the tree-line carefully, and suddenly saw the detonation of the weapon, a soundless explosion of violence far below him.

'Zero Two, Five One, request SITREP.'

'This is Zero Two. Jesus, that helped. They're still firing, but a hell of a lot less. You wanna do that again?'

Flatters was already running outbound, preparing his second five-forty.

'Roger, Zero Two. We'll repeat the performance.'

Again Flatters ran in, and again Hoggy fired his laser at the wooded area. The second bomb was set to explode on impact, and tore a massive hole in the undergrowth when it detonated. And that's when the firing stopped.

'Knife Five One, Zero Two. That's stopped them. Thank you, sir.' The JTAC's voice, Hoggy noted, now sounded almost normal.

'Knife Five One, Ghost Three Four. I'm detecting a whole bunch of bad guys running from the tree-line towards a compound in back. They could just be regrouping. You wanna take them as well?'

'Three Four, Five Two, that's affirmative.' Flatters broke out of orbit again, selected his CRV-7s and dived down, flames bursting out from under the wings of his Harrier as he ripple-fired a couple of salvoes.

'Knife Five One, Ghost Three Four. Earlier in the

engagement I saw several groups of Taliban moving towards that compound. It's the group of buildings bearing approximately one three five from the ambush site. It might be worth taking a look at it. But I have to go now. Thank you for all your help. I know the guys on the ground appreciate what you did.'

'All part of the service,' Hoggy replied. 'Thanks for identifying the target for us.'

'Five One, Mastiff Zero Two, thanks, guys. That building the Predator driver eyeballed – we saw some of the bad guys heading that way ourselves, and our pre-mission intel brief identified two buildings in that compound as known Taliban safe houses.'

The JTAC passed the Harriers the grid position, and Hoggy tried to identify exactly which building he was talking about, but that was very difficult because his rocket targeting pod uncaged in dead ground among a number of individual buildings.

'Zero Two, Five One. I'm not happy with this. I still don't have a proper identification of the target.'

'Copied. We've just started taking fire from those buildings.'

'Mastiff Zero Two, Knife Five One, this is Bone Two Six.'

'Bone' was an American B-1 bomber callsign.

'Bone Two Six, Zero Two, go ahead.'

'This is Bone Two Six. We're up at two nine zero, well above you guys. We've copied the grid and we're tally with the target.'

'Two Six, Knife Five One. Confirm you're happy with the target coordinates?'

'That's affirmative.'

'Roger. Break. Mastiff Zero Two, if Bone's happy to drop, we'll clear out of his way, because we still don't have a lock.'

'Roger, Knife Five One.'

The JTAC and the B-1 crew carried out the usual pre-attack exchange of information while the two Harriers moved a safe distance from the target. Finally both parties were happy with the target's coordinates, and the JTAC authorized the attack run.

'Bone Two Six, Mastiff Zero Two. Call wings level with direction.'

While the B-1 set up for his attack run, Hoggy 'bat and balled' with the JTAC and Flatters, to try to establish which were the target buildings, and by the time the B-1 ran in Hoggy was happy with the first target and had his pod wrapped around it.

Then the B-1 dropped, but the weapon landed in the dead ground about two hundred metres from the building. Close, but no coconut.

'Mastiff Zero Two, Knife Five One. I'm happy we've now got a good lock on the target. Do you want us to have a go?'

'Five One, Zero Two, affirmative. We're now taking heavy fire from that compound.'

The JTAC's Battle Damage Assessment, or BDA, of the B-1's drop confirmed that Hoggy *was* looking at the right target.

Three minutes later Hoggy ran in and dropped a 1,000lb weapon directly on to the first building the JTAC had identified to him, and five minutes after that he landed his second bomb on the other building. Both were direct hits, and all firing from the compound stopped.

We didn't often get to share the same airspace as the Americans, but in January it seemed to be happening more and more often. Sometimes it highlighted the differences between us – not least, of course, in the sheer weight of firepower the USAF could bring to bear with an aircraft like the B-1 if the situation demanded it. But I was continually struck by the care with which both nations went about their business. We spent far more time and effort trying to ensure that we avoided killing people and causing unnecessary collateral damage than we did trying to blow them apart.

And one exceptional piece of flying demonstrated this rather well.

23

I was chatting in Ops with some of the squadron maintainers when Lieutenants 'Buzz' Jacobs and Ted Williamson, two of the most junior pilots in the squadron, bowled in.

Whenever I could I'd attend the mission debrief just in case there were any issues that needed to be resolved, and I always liked to know exactly what had happened on each sortie. And this one, we already knew, had involved some kind of an action: even if we hadn't known GCAS had diverted them during the sortie, the two empty wing stations on one of the Harriers said it all.

When these two young officers walked in they were clearly pumped up about something – you could see it in their faces – and the tale they told left us in no doubt why. They pulled off their gear, made coffee and sat down.

'Come on, then,' I said. 'Don't keep us in suspense any longer. What happened?'

Jacobs took a sip of his drink, and started to explain.

'Standard patrol, right, around the Naw Zad area, and we were just mooching along, looking for trouble, but everything seemed fairly quiet. Then we got a call from GCAS to go along and help out this Yank patrol near Sangin.'

From his description it was clear that this small American team had been caught in quite a clever trap by the Taliban. They were pinned down and taking heavy machine-gun and small-arms fire from two different locations, and they already had one man injured.

'When we reached the coordinates we could see it was all really pretty confused. We got good two-way comms with one of the guys on the ground, and you could tell from his voice he was pretty stressed. We could hear through the radio link that he was taking heavy fire – there were a couple of heavy machine-guns blatting away down there.'

'And we weren't the only assets in the air, either,' Williamson added. 'We'd been told there was a Predator flying about. That was being piloted from the States as usual, but he was on our frequency and trying to pinpoint the exact location of the Taliban attackers. And as well as the UAV, there was a British Apache attack chopper there as well, trying to do the same thing.'

'It was total bloody chaos, boss,' Jacobs said. 'Five speaking units all on the same frequency, one getting the shit kicked out of him by the Taliban machine-guns while the other four of us tried to work out just where the insurgents were holed up so we could take them out. Plus we were trying keep out of the way of the UAV and the Apache. It was really fierce, really confused, and this guy on the ground was getting more and more alarmed.'

As he described the incident I began to appreciate the problems they'd faced. The multiple speaking units, all on the same radio frequency, had generated continuous, urgent and pretty chaotic radio talk, but through it all the voice of the man on the ground was getting increasingly stressed and frightened. And his message was quite clear: if somebody didn't shut down the Taliban's heavy machine-guns, the patrol was going to get ripped apart. It was as simple as that.

'Anyway,' Jacobs continued, 'we finally worked out where the Taliban were firing from. It was a typical walled compound, and at least one of the heavy machine-guns was in the building at one end of it. My Harrier had the 1,000-pounders, and we reckoned those were the most appropriate weapons. We positively identified the target, briefed the UAV pilot and the Apache about our intentions so they could get the hell out of our way, and told the guy on the ground to get his head down. I selected the PGM, aimed the laser at the target building and we started the attack run.'

The procedure was simple enough. The pilot ensures he has a positive identification of the target, aims his laser designator at it and then releases his Precision Guided Munition, which is guided by the laser. The laser energy bounces off the target, and all the way through the bomb's flight the pilot steers the weapon by using his tracking ability to maintain the laser's lock on the target.

'I had a good lock, weapon release was fine, and the bomb hit right on the money. Straight in through the roof, a big bang inside the building and, as far as I could see, no damage outside it, or no significant collateral damage anyway. And it worked, because the American radio operator called us up immediately. He said that the machine-gun had stopped firing, but then the other one started up again, from the far end of the compound, and they were taking heavy small-arms fire as well from the same location. And they'd seen a bunch of men running towards that end of the compound as well, so it looked as if we'd only done half the job and the patrol was still pinned down.

'That wasn't a problem, as far as I could see. We all knew where the first weapon had landed – the hole in the roof of the building was difficult to miss – so I just confirmed with this guy that they were taking heavy fire from the opposite end of the same compound. That positively identified the target. The Rules of Engagement were satisfied, as far as I was concerned, so I broadcast that I'd drop another weapon – another 1,000-pounder – on the new target. Then Ted had to break off because he was close to bingo fuel.'

'Yes,' Williamson confirmed, 'but the tanker wasn't that far away, so I detached and punched up to it. I knew Buzz could handle the second attack run. I was only really a spectator on this one.'

'Anyway, Ted hauled his Harrier up into a climb and I swung round in a circle for another attack run. I put the laser on the target, selected the second weapon and started the run-in. I confirmed I had a good laser lock, dropped the weapon and started to turn away as usual.'

Jacobs felt and heard the normal sequence of responses following weapon release. The aircraft shuddered as the bomb fell away, and almost immediately the radalt warning went off because it fixed on the falling bomb. He heard a tone, a beep as the weapon detached, and then the higher-pitched beep beep beep from the radalt – the normal sequence of sounds that told him the bomb had separated from the aeroplane.

The weapon was on its way down. Its flight time was about twenty-five seconds from the moment of release to the moment of impact, because of the range to the target and height of the aircraft. Turning his Harrier away from the target was standard procedure, a safety precaution, so that he was paralleling the path of the weapon, but obviously Jacobs kept the laser designator locked on to the target as the bomb fell.

'Then the Apache pilot made a call that changed everything,' he said. 'He radioed that he'd just seen a woman and three children running away from the compound, right where the bomb was heading.

'The mathematics were easy. There was no way those four civilians were going to be able to outrun the bomb. Unless I did something, they were going to die – by my hand. It's all right to talk about accidental deaths, Rules of Engagement and collateral damage, but it's a hell of a lot different when you're sitting in the cockpit of a Harrier, and you know that a woman and three kids are about to be blown to pieces because of something you've done.'

And then it was a countdown.

Fifteen seconds to impact.

'Immediately I asked the Apache pilot to confirm what he'd just said.'

Twelve seconds.

'He replied: "Confirmed. One woman and three children running from the compound."'

Ten seconds.

'Nothing I could do was going to stop the weapon exploding – that wasn't in any doubt – and the only option I had left was to try to miss the innocent civilians. "Where can I put the bomb?" I asked.'

Eight seconds.

253

'"North. Put it to the north," the Apache pilot instructed.

'I knew it was going to be bloody close. I reached down to the laser designator and started slewing it. I watched as the laser spot tracked slowly across the roof of the compound.'

Six seconds.

'In the first couple of seconds I'd only managed to move it a few feet, and there was a long way to go to the edge of the roof and the boundary wall, so I slowly increased the rate I was moving it, and just hoped the weapon was still locked on.'

The way Jacobs told it made it sound easy, but the reality was that he'd had to use an incredibly delicate touch. If he tried to move the laser designator too fast, the bomb would lose contact with the reflected laser energy and just carry on its original course. But if he moved it too slowly, the weapon would detonate inside the compound and, in either case, the explosion would probably kill the woman and children.

Four seconds.

'The laser spot was still on the roof, but getting closer to the edge. I'd been guessing the bomb's flight time, and hoping like hell I'd underestimated it. I increased the rate of movement of the spot as much as I dared, slewing it closer to the edge of the roof and the outside of the compound.'

Two seconds.

'I got the laser spot to the edge of the roof and dragged it just over the edge of the compound, got it over the wall. And about half a second later the bomb exploded in the open field just to the north – I'd actually overestimated the flight time by about one second. There was a hell of a bang, but it was just outside the compound and I hoped the walls would have shielded the four civilians from the blast.

'The moment it went off, I called the Apache pilot again, because he was low and close enough to see what had happened and I wasn't. "Don't tell me that they're all dead," I said.

'"Negative, negative," he replied. "They're alive. They stopped when it exploded, but they're running again now. Running south, away from the compound."'

'Bloody hell,' I said. I'd been on the edge of my seat just hearing him recount it. But I was delighted. It was an excellent example of clear thinking, sheer professionalism and amazingly close coordination between the airmen involved. The moment the crew of the Apache identified the problem, they told the Harrier pilot, who was the only one who could do anything about it. Lieutenant Jacobs had immediately asked the only question that mattered: where should he divert the bomb to save the woman and children? And with eight seconds to spare, he calmly altered the weapon's trajectory just enough to achieve his objective. It was, by any criteria, an extraordinary piece of flying.

And now there were just days to go before we handed over to 1 (F) Squadron RAF and headed for home. We'd ridden our luck – I didn't like to think about those occasions when my pilots had landed their aircraft on fumes, or had pulled off amazing feats of airmanship in supporting the guys on the ground – and we'd been tested.

Provided nothing went wrong now, I knew we could climb aboard the trooping flight back to Brize Norton with our heads held high. But as the days and hours counted down, the possibility of some kind of sting in the tail loomed ever larger in my imagining.

But if, as a squadron, 800 NAS had delivered in spades, my own contribution still seemed to have fallen rather short of what I'd hoped for.

I'd helped shepherd a patrol past some Afghans burning tyres. I'd flown my Harrier, bristling with weapons, and provided top cover for a bustling market-place. And when I was one of a pair of aircraft that actually got involved in a shooting incident, I always seemed to be carrying the wrong weapons for the job.

The final straw came was when I was just about to take over the GCAS ground alert from the other guys. I was actually *signing out* my aeroplane when the scramble bell went. Before the other pilot and I could get outside to the pan and climb into the Harriers, the two pilots that we were relieving climbed into the cockpits and fired up the engines, leaving us nothing to do but wave goodbye.

They went off and delivered a whole bunch of ordnance on various targets and our subsequent period of ground alert, predictably enough, was completely free of any action at all.

After that the amount of flak I had to endure was enormous. 'Oh, so you just dawdled out to your aircraft? I suppose you just ambled down to the takeover so that you didn't have to go out and do the GCAS?'

I should have been able to ignore it completely, but as

I started getting kitted up for my last — and in fact the squadron's last — flight in theatre, I couldn't help but hope I might be able to drop something. If nothing else, it might shut the rest of them up before we climbed on to the Hercules to start the journey home.

In the end, it all came down to that last sortie.

24

Briefed, kitted up, the aircraft signed out and ready for the off, I walked across to the Harrier to start my checks.

I looked inside the engine intakes, checked the glass dome that shields the front of the laser spot tracker, and the little puffer jets that stabilised the Harrier in the hover, then moved on to the weapons hanging under the wings.

These included laser-guided bombs, and I checked that they were securely mounted, that the control fins were working, that the laser head wasn't broken and that the correct laser code had been entered. Each bomb had a specific code that was linked to the frequency of the laser designator on the aircraft carrying it. Without a code the weapon could follow *any* laser beam it acquired, with potentially catastrophic results. So we had a specific bomb code issued, which was entered on every weapon. Perhaps the most important check was to ensure that the tail arming vane, which spins to physically arm the bomb, wasn't spinning and in fact *couldn't* spin. It needed to remain locked in place until released when the bomb separates from the aircraft.

The CRV-7 rocket pods were easier to check, because they're just closed pods fitted with a frangible nose-cone that stays in place until the rockets are fired.

At the back of the aircraft I checked that the expendables – the very comprehensive suite of self-defence flares

– were properly seated at the bottom of the fuselage, and also in the rail mounting on the undercarriage that fitted flush with the bottom of the wing.

Knowing this was my last sortie this time round made me more focused than ever on getting everything right. Once in the cockpit I completed all my pre-start checks. I selected my navigation equipment, which had been aligning, put it into navigation mode to avoid losing all that information, and then checked all the other switches and controls.

Then I was ready to start the engine. I closed the canopy as a form of protection, looked at the guy outside and signalled to him that I was ready to start. Normally, this is the familiar 'wind-up' signal but, because the aircraft was still connected to external power, instead I gave him an 'unplug' signal which instructed him to disconnect the external power from the aircraft.

The maintainer walked to the back of the aircraft, removed the external power cable and replaced the cover on the fuselage. Then he made a final check around the aircraft that everything was correct, and looked at me. He gave me the signal to start the engine by putting his hand over his head and waving his fingers.

I reached across to the engine start panel on the right-hand side. There's a small silver vertical knob there, no more than about an inch in height. I lifted this up and pushed it forward, and a magnetic hold-on relay locked it into place. That automatically started the engine sequence.

Behind my head was a small gas-turbine generator whose sole purpose in life at that point is to start the engine, and almost immediately I could hear it spooling up. Once it fired up, it started a clutching mechanism that began turning the main engine, and spooled up the engine to a point where it was spinning sufficiently fast that I could start adding fuel by easing the throttle forward.

The igniters had been clicking away in the background all the time. The atomized fuel being sprayed into the engine ignited, and the Pegasus began to accelerate to a self-sustaining speed.

At that point the little starter engine behind my head stopped and shut itself down automatically. It took about twenty seconds from initiation of the start sequence to the main engine becoming self-sustaining. All the power came back online as the generators started running, and I began working my way through a whole sequence of after-start checks. Around the jet, heat pouring out of the big Pegasus engine's four nozzles rippled in the air. The aircraft was coming to life.

On the TV screen I brought up the Built In Test pages, which warned of any automatically selected systems and, more importantly, if they had failed or not. Then I did the Auto BIT check. This is a single soft key that forces most systems to go down and then go into an automatic self-test mode. This includes radios, the laser spot tracker, IFF, FLIR (Forward-Looking Infrared) and other electronic systems.

These tests take up to about three minutes. While they were being carried out I made a sequence of checks on the automatic stabilization system, which caused the controls to move on their own. The flaps moved to their pre-set positions, and once I'd completed that I switched back to the BIT page to see if it indicated any faults that needed rectifying. If necessary, the jet's computer systems allowed me to go in deeper and try to fix any problems, but none had been picked up. Time to make the 'go/no go' decision. Was the aircraft fit to go flying? No snags. The mission was on.

I did a force check-in using the back radio: 'Recoil Four Five, check.'

'Recoil Four Six,' Dunc Mason responded, and then listened as I contacted our Ops section. I pressed the RT button and said: 'Spitfire, Recoil Four Five. Any words?'

That call to our local command structure requested the final release for the mission, asking whether or not they had any last-minute instructions for us. The Ops people might have some advance warning of a TIC or other incident somewhere, through the chat window system.

In the Ops room one of the computers was linked to a facility, almost like a chatroom, that included networked links to personnel all over the theatre, displayed in a mosaic of windows. This allowed the people at Crowbar – the Command and Control authority based at Camp Bastion, who were effectively the tactical air traffic controllers – Spitfire and everywhere else in the system all the way up to the CAOC staff in Al Udeid Airbase in Qatar, to see the war unfolding in front of them as it related to different parts of the operational area. Staff could zoom in any window and see details of a developing incident. It was a very flexible and extremely useful system.

This time there was nothing known, because Spitfire just said: 'Negative. You're clear to push.'

'Push' simply meant 'push away from my frequency

and listen out on the new frequency', and in this case we'd switch to air traffic.

Kandahar is, in theory at least, a civilian airfield, and civilian procedures apply, including getting Air Traffic Information Service information before calling air traffic control for taxi clearance, so that's what we did. We both dialled the ATIS frequency and copied the current information, then switched to ATC.

'Recoil, push stud one.'

Once we'd switched I called the controller.

'Kandahar Ground, Recoil Four Five. Flight of two Harriers. Request taxi with Delta.'

That meant we'd copied the current ATIS information – in this case information Delta – and the controller acknowledged.

'Recoil Four Five clear to taxi. Enter runway zero five at Delta Two.'

Entering the runway at an intermediate point like this was quite common, because the taxiway was often stuffed full of helicopters, particularly in the evening and over-night, and C-17s were always manoeuvring around the airfield. The furthest end of the runway was known as Echo, so in this case we'd enter the runway at Delta Two, taxi all the way down to Echo, then turn round there and take off.

Finally I passed the controller our outbound headings and departure sectors – there were eight sectors around Kandahar – for our tactical departure. These were always decided by the pilots, and when two aircraft were getting airborne one after the other, the second one would always take a different sector, as a precaution against any insurgents spotting one aircraft leaving and trying to hit the second with a missile if it followed the same course.

I also passed the controller the height we intended to climb to.

'Recoil Four Five, roger. No ATC restrictions in place, circuit clear, and no light civilian traffic in the vicinity.'

'Light civilian traffic' meant Predator and Reaper UAVs, which were undeniably light but hardly 'civilian' in the normal sense of the word. And, after the other night's near-miss, I was particularly aware of the dangers posed by crowded skies. From where I was sitting, no light civilian traffic, I thought, was good news.

Then, pushing forward with my left hand, I increased the throttle setting, released the brakes and began the long taxi from the dispersal to the active runway. On the way out I checked that my pistol was snug in its holster – I hoped I'd never have to use it, but having it was a comfort – and glanced over at that old wreck of a hangar for what would be the last time on this detachment.

We were taking off on the easterly runway, so we had a long way to go – a couple of miles – to reach the take-off position, and it was a journey that always had the potential to turn into a Demolition Derby. C-130s would suddenly back out of their dispersals and parking slots; Russian aircraft doing God knows what and, probably, talking to nobody, would appear in front of us; fire engines, force protection vehicles, road sweepers, and trucks and vans of every type would be driving all over the place and speeding up and down the taxiways. Helicopters would appear, air-taxiing to and from their parking areas, and we really had to watch those, because some of the bigger ones, like the Chinook and the Halo, created a massive downwash from their rotors and could easily blow huge amounts of FOD around, which the cavernous intakes of the Harrier's Pegasus engine would be only too pleased to ingest, with expensive and disastrous results.

There were working parties all over the place, usually composed of Indians or Pakistanis, but sometimes including local nationals, building things, fixing things, pouring concrete, repairing lights, moving stuff and carrying out a host of other tasks. And, of course, none of them had much prior experience of working on a busy airfield, and they could – and frequently would – do completely unexpected things as we passed close to them. So just taxiing a Harrier the two miles or so to the end of the runway for take-off could be quite an exciting adventure in its own right. The chaos that surrounded us somehow reminded me of the movie *Airplane!*

C-130s were probably the worst, because to get one moving backwards it had to get up a fair speed, and that meant it would simply shoot out of its dispersal. And that was what happened at that precise moment as I steered the Harrier cautiously down the taxiway. The C-130 appeared at speed right in front of me and, to make matters worse, the dispatcher, who was at the rear door of the aircraft checking for obstacles, was looking the other way, down the taxiway and not up it.

I braked to a halt immediately, checked that Dunc behind me had also stopped, and just waited. When the dispatcher finally remembered that the taxiway extended in both directions and turned round, he did a classic double-take. The look on his face was almost comical, and I could see his mouth opening and closing as he immediately shouted, 'Stop, stop, stop' on the intercom to the pilot. The C-130 did just that – and lost all momentum. To get going again the pilot had to run the engines up to high power, pumping out black smoke and blowing debris in all directions.

To add to the workload, during the taxi we had numerous after-start checks to do on things like the brakes and steering and other systems. And at that stage we also switched on our self-defence suites.

Once we were visible from the control tower, the Ground Controller handed us over to the Local Controller.

'Recoil Four Five, clear to Tower.'

'Roger.'

'Kandahar Tower, Recoil Four Five. Flight of two ready for departure.'

We were always relieved to get to the end of the runway, because then the only people likely to cause us problems were the Taliban, and it was a lot easier to avoid their weapons in the air than reversing C-130s at high speed on the ground.

As we approached the end of the runway Dunc and I checked that we had both done everything we needed to do inside our cockpits, then did our normal pre-take-off checks.

I reached up to the top-left side of the cockpit towards the Master Armaments Safety Switch. I switched it on when I reached the runway and was sure that the forward-firing CRV-7 pods were pointing in a safe direction. And it stayed on for the rest of the sortie.

'Recoil Four Five, Tower. Clear take-off, wind zero four five at ten, gusting fifteen. Contact Departures.'

'Roger, Tower. Recoil Four Five is rolling.'

I pushed the throttle lever fully forward with my left hand and watched the numbers changing on the air speed indicator as the Harrier picked up speed. As the jet accelerated down the runway – we never took off as a pair, always one after the other – I switched to Departures and called, 'Recoil Four Five is rolling.' That would be the cue for the departure controller to watch for my Harrier appearing on his radar and to check my IFF code.

Off the runway, I selected gear up, hearing it lock shut beneath me. Then I held the jet low and flat as the airspeed wound up rapidly. I eased back on the control column and moved it to the right. The aircraft powered rapidly away from the ground, carving into a climbing turn as I steered it towards my tactical departure sector, and to the safety afforded by height. Ready to go to war.

But, far from delivering some ordnance on this, my final flight in theatre, it looked as if I was going to be disappointed yet again. For about an hour we stooged around, looking at the view and waiting for something – anything – to happen.

And then, at last, we got the divert call from Crowbar to go and bail out the combined ANA and American patrol that had been ambushed by the Taliban near the river. *Finally*, I thought, as I pushed the throttle forward. Dunc and I rolled the two Harriers on to the new heading and accelerated towards the firefight.

We did the fighter check-in, arrived overhead and

assessed the situation. We identified the friendlies and the position of the Taliban insurgents. The JTAC selected the five-forty airburst, Dunc's laser illuminated the target and I was about to start the outbound run.

And that was when the bloody Mi-24 Halo clattered past right in front of me and cocked everything up.

2 5

The huge white shape of the Russian-made chopper disappeared underneath the Harrier's nose. *Fuck it.* I hauled off, levelled the wings and headed outbound, then pulled the Harrier through a hard, one-eighty turn and started the inbound run again.

I looked at the target area ahead and checked the image on the cockpit's flat screen. The UN helicopter was now clear of the area, and Dunc's laser was properly illuminating the target. This time we'd deliver the good news. I began my run-in. But then, as I settled on the bomb run, it became clear from the HUD that all was not well. *Shit.* I seemed to have a malfunction – I couldn't get the right sighting up. And now, as I streamed impotently in over the hill, attack number two was a bust. I'd gone dry on the attack. This wasn't going well.

'Going round again,' I managed through gritted teeth, cursing to myself. 'I can't select the weapon.'

I pulled back and rolled away. I started again from the beginning, checking everything. Then I realized the problem: finger trouble. Distracted at the crucial moment by the helicopter looming ahead of me – instead of *selecting* the weapon, I'd inadvertently *deselected* it by pressing the wrong button on the throttle. Both the control column and the throttle are peppered with switches and controls.

And as I'd pulled away to avoid a mid-air collision I'd got the wrong one.

I'd lost my firing solution and could only go round again. My thoughts turned to the troops on the ground. For me there was a point of professional pride involved in getting things right – every pilot likes to get his weapons away first time, every time – but for them, pinned down by enemy assault rifles, it was potentially life or death.

I ran a couple of miles out down to the south, and checked and double-checked that I'd got the switches right.

'Jaguar Zero One, Recoil Four Five. Sixty seconds.'

'Four Five, Zero One. Call wings level with direction.'

'Zero One, Four Five. Wings level, from the south. In hot.'

'Recoil Four Five, Jaguar Zero One. Clear hot.'

And that committed me to the attack. I pressed the red button on the control column to authorize weapon release, and I continued flying the azimuth line displayed in green on the HUD in front of me, towards the ballistic release point. And, at the moment when the computer calculated the bomb was most likely to hit the target, it separated from the pylon under the wing with a jolt that resonated throughout the airframe, and fell away from the aircraft.

This time there were no hitches. The high-explosive five-forty dropped from beneath the Harrier's sloping wing and flew true and accurately. Seconds later it exploded directly overhead the target. As the shockwave spread out at the speed of sound, the fireball sucked in the air from the surrounding sky.

'Excellent, Recoil Four Five – direct hit,' the USAF JTAC reported on the front radio, 'but we're still taking small-arms fire from the front end of the tree-line. We'll take the second five-forty.'

'Roger.'

They wanted more.

I tried to assess the situation from the air. Just because a strike has been requested by troops on the ground, it doesn't necessarily mean that it can be justified. That was a decision only I could make. This one was a no-brainer. Continuing attacks on the isolated NATO patrol gave us no choice. We had to go in again with a second weapon. So I rolled the wings and swung round in another hard turn. I pulled back on the stick, maintaining altitude with a light touch of the rudder. And as I banked through the turn I began meticulously rechecking my weapon switches.

I ran in over the trees for the fourth time that afternoon, checked that the target was still illuminated by the laser, and released the weapon. The second bomb left the wing hard-point and I hauled off to ensure the soft-skinned Harrier was well clear of the blast as quickly as possible. Attacking aircraft have been brought down by shrapnel and debris from their own bombs more often than you'd imagine.

And that's when it all started going wrong.

Through my dark visor I saw a sudden flash behind and below me in my peripheral vision, and at that instant I heard Dunc's urgent voice on the back radio.

'Flares, flares, flares!' he shouted. 'We're being shot at!'

The moment I heard my wing-man's call I reacted at

once, taking immediate evasive action to pull the aircraft out of danger. I jammed the throttle lever fully forwards. At the top right of the instrument panel the RPM gauge spun like the wheels of a fruit machine as the engine wound up to full power. Climbing away as quickly as possible, I reached down to my left and the flare override switch and began manually pumping out self-defence flares, designed to seduce heat-seeking ground-to-air missiles like the Stinger away from their target. And that was the first oddity, because the automatic flare dispensing system, which *should* have been triggered by the approach of the missile, clearly wasn't working. I was being shot at, and their failure to fire automatically, I thought instantly, could easily have cost me my life.

As burning flares streamed out of the belly of the jet like fireworks, I was shaking my head in disbelief. Not only was it the last Harrier sortie of the day but the last for anyone in the squadron before we handed over to 1 (F) Squadron RAF. And it looked as if there was a good chance that the CO was going to be shot down in the last few minutes of his time in Afghanistan.

It was all, I thought, very unfair. I'd gone through a prolonged dry patch, a period of about two weeks when I'd returned to our dispersal at Kandahar Airfield without expending a single weapon. They'd ribbed me before, of course, but immediately before my final sortie several of my pilots had told me they guessed I would just drop my weapons anyway, even in an open field somewhere, just to save the embarrassment of having to return to base with the usual bunch of bombs still bolted under my wings.

As I powered up and away from the scene, flares firing in my wake, these thoughts ran through my mind with startling clarity.

'You've just got to be shitting me . . .' I muttered.

I checked in my mirrors and then looked back over my shoulder, trying to spot a second missile. With my luck, I had to assume there would be another one. And there, quite a way below me but still high above the ground, I could see a huge black cloud where something big had exploded. But what I couldn't see was any sign of where my bomb had detonated, only the aftermath of what appeared to be a mid-air explosion. Whatever had exploded, it had clearly been a large warhead, much bigger than the relatively small charge fitted to shoulder-launched missiles like the Stinger or the Russian SA-7 Grail or the more modern SA-14 Gremlin weapons. It looked more like the detonation of a turret-mounted or vehicle-deployed surface-to-air missile, a heavy weapon, but that really didn't make sense. I certainly hadn't seen any intelligence to suggest that the Taliban possessed any weapons like that, though this wasn't a particularly reassuring thought as I stared at the explosion's aftermath.

Oh, shit, I thought as I checked the GR7's handling and scanned the instruments, SAMs are all I need, but at least I haven't been hit. Yet.

Then the FAC on the ground called me again. 'The bomb exploded,' he said, 'right above our heads.'

And with a wave of relief I suddenly guessed at once what had *actually* happened. The five-forty I'd dropped had fragmented, detonating prematurely just a few seconds after it had left my Harrier. When a Close Air

Support aircraft drops a bomb, the pilot turns away for a very good reason: to get the aircraft well away from the weapon's trajectory so that if there's any kind of a misfire or premature detonation the explosion won't damage the aircraft.

As soon as a bomb drops off the wing pylon, stabilizing wings pop out of the tail. At the same time the arming process begins. The fuse is a spinning vane on the end of the tail that is turned by the airflow. As a safety measure the bomb can't arm itself until the vane has spun through ten revolutions. This delay allows the aircraft that dropped the bomb to be clear of the blast when the thing goes off. At least, that's the theory.

In my head I went through the sequence of events, trying to establish what had nearly brought me down. It looked as if the delayed fusing had worked correctly and only armed the bomb once it was clear of my wing, but then the proximity fuse had malfunctioned and transmitted a false pulse, just as though it was close to the ground. That bomb was designed to explode as an airburst and so the moment the weapon armed itself it went off, probably just a few hundred feet below me – a tiny fraction of what constituted a safe distance from the blast.

So it hadn't been a missile, just a malfunctioning bomb. This also explained why the aircraft's automatic self-defence systems hadn't been activated: they were smarter than I was. They knew no missile had approached the Harrier, that there was no threat, and so they hadn't started dispensing flares.

All the same, I knew I'd been lucky. The premature detonation could have killed me just as effectively as a

Stinger. There have been Fleet Air Arm pilots who've watched in horror as friends have been blown out of the sky by bombs detonating prematurely. I'd definitely been lucky. Being brought down by my own bombs would have been just as bad as getting shot down on my last sortie. In truth, it would have been worse, because I would effectively have shot *myself* down. The ultimate result would have been the same – only with added shame and embarrassment.

So what had started out as a very sedate mission had done the classic one-eighty, and in a heartbeat. I'd almost had a mid-air collision with the UN helicopter; I'd screwed up my switches on the first attack run; then I'd successfully launched the first weapon which had done exactly what I'd intended – it had killed most of the people I'd needed to kill, removing the threat to the patrol on the ground. Immediately afterwards both Dunc and I had thought we were being engaged by missiles, and then we'd realized that it was a premature detonation, which was almost as dangerous. And, finally, the explosion could easily have done some damage to the troops the Harriers were supposed to be protecting, because the bomb had gone off almost immediately above the joint ANA and American patrol.

'Right,' I said, and pressed the transmit button. 'Recoil Four Six, Four Five. I've had enough of this. We're done here. Let's go home.'

On the ground, the firing had now stopped completely, and the patrol members were able to do a Battle Damage Assessment. They did a body count and reported the result to us as we departed the area to the east.

'Your BDA is six KIA,' the FAC stated. A somewhat cold shorthand for 'Killed in Action', but sentiment and sensitivity aren't big in Afghanistan, or in any other war zone. And the fact is, if those six Taliban had stayed at home and not opened up on the patrol with a heavy machine-gun, they would still have been alive.

The patrol had reported they had been attacked by a seven-strong group of insurgents, so the firing that occurred after the first weapon had exploded was probably a last defiant gesture by the seventh man, before he decided to head for home so he could fight another day.

'Kandahar, this is Recoil Four Five flight on recovery.'

'Recoil Four Five, runway zero five. No circuit traffic. Call visual.'

'Four Five is visual.'

'Roger. Land. Wind zero three zero, light and variable.'

We ran in over the airfield high and fast, then descended rapidly, turning hard to bleed off height as quickly as possible – a typical tactical approach and landing. The nervous phase was always when we neared the runway, because we always had to fly through the same bit of sky on final approach. An easy target.

Flaps down, losing height, approaching the runway threshold, then the bump and a squeal from the tyres as the aircraft landed on the tarmac. And because we'd landed on the north-east runway, we were able to roll all the way down to the Harrier dispersal at the far end and didn't have to face the hazards of the taxiways.

In the dispersal I shut down the engine, rotated the lever to make the ejection seat safe and unplugged everything. For a few minutes I just sat there, eyes closed, and for the first time in four months I was able to totally relax. With that flight, 800 Naval Air Squadron had completed the detachment, without a single loss or serious injury, and we'd achieved everything we set out to do. Then I roused myself and climbed out.

Leading Air Engineering Technician Dobinson was looking critically at the bare pylons under the GR7's wings. Dobbo basically ran all the squadron weapons. He was one of the most experienced weapons technicians in the Navy, and had done every single deployment to date because men of his experience and capability were in such short supply. He nodded his shaven head in approval.

'I see you broke your duck, then, boss,' he said.

'You could say that,' I replied. 'I bloody nearly broke a lot of things today,' I added as I walked away.

26

That was my last sortie on my last day in theatre. Before I got airborne on that final sortie I just wanted to hold it together and not do anything stupid, which in view of what happened in the air proved somewhat optimistic. Yet for all that did go wrong on that final flight, it hadn't distracted me from the most important thought of all. And that was that I was in the air to do exactly the same thing as I'd been doing for the last four months: to try to save the lives of the good guys on the ground and, in doing so, take the lives of the enemy they faced.

It's too easy to remain quite detached from the reality. There's a big difference between stabbing someone with a bayonet – when you can see their face and their body and you're close enough to touch them, see their pain and see their blood – and dropping a bomb on them. When you deliver a weapon you are so focused on the process of delivering it you don't think for a moment about what effect it will have. You are totally concentrating on getting the job done and, even after the event, I would argue that you're still relatively detached. I think most of my fellow Harrier pilots would agree that it's possible to maintain that distance all the way through.

The BDA that told us half a dozen Taliban had been killed – did that bother me? The only honest answer is no. I didn't think about them as individuals. I didn't think about their families. I didn't think about any of it.

All I thought about was that those people were on one side of a river firing their weapons at coalition troops on the other side, and my job was to stop them doing that. They were combatants, we were combatants, and this time we won and they lost. Next time the result might be different.

There seems to be a perception among people who know little about the conflict in Afghanistan that the Taliban are just a bunch of religious nutters wearing outdoor pyjamas and black turbans, waving copies of the Koran and carrying Kalashnikovs.

Some, of course, will be. And none seem to have any apparent fear of death. They just don't give up. Even if, after a terrific pounding from air-delivered weapons or artillery, a single Talib was left alive in a compound with the means to fight on, he surely would. Fortunately, I'm sure that the key to success in Afghamistan lies not with the Taliban, but with the rest of the country's civilian population.

The way to defeat the Taliban as a movement is not to kill them, but to demonstrate to the majority of Afghanistan's people that their quality of life will be better without them around. Only when that situation occurs will the Taliban begin to find that they have no recruits, and no safe havens, and then the battle against this particular form of radical Islam will be won.

So why are the coalition forces in Afghanistan at all? And are we doing any good?

We are there because we were invited to send a multi-national force to the country by the Afghan government – a situation completely different from that in Iraq, where the allied troops are perceived, in some quarters, to be an invading army. The coalition is in Afghanistan by request, to help protect and rebuild the country's infrastructure and to help suppress the Taliban's constant attacks. And, yes, we *are* doing some good.

But is the present conflict winnable? It is, if by 'winnable' we mean suppressing the Taliban and keeping them suppressed for a few years. We'll never be able to eliminate them, because the movement is continually recruiting new members, and they will always be there in the wings, just waiting for an opportunity to move back into Afghanistan and try to regain control.

Ultimately that decision, too, really rests with the people of Afghanistan, because it is they who have allowed the Taliban to establish a powerful presence in their country. I would like to think that, as a result of the present campaign in Afghanistan, the Afghans might be strong enough to take a firm stance against them, but history doesn't provide much support for this view. Realistically, because much of Afghanistan is a subsistence economy with the people barely scratching out a living from the poor soil, the likelihood is that they will take the path of least resistance. Many of them are so busy trying to stay alive that they have no time to become involved in any kind of political decision. And if the Taliban appear again and offer them a choice of either supporting the move-ment or being executed – a tactic that has characterized the Taliban's 'recruitment campaigns' in the past – it's not difficult to predict what decision they, or indeed anyone else, would take.

Once the people of a village or compound join the Taliban – and it's worth saying that most Afghans are born, live their entire lives and die within about twenty miles of a single location, staying in the same village throughout – they are safe from attacks by them. But, as in any situation of this sort, there's a price to pay. The Taliban support themselves financially by taking a healthy share of the income generated by their supporters. In the days of Al Capone this was called a 'protection racket'. I've no idea what the Taliban call it, but it's exactly the same game.

There is one reality about Afghanistan that everybody acknowledges: we can never kill all the Taliban. That means that whatever the final outcome of the Afghanistan campaign, the Taliban will still be there and will still want a piece of the pie. The Afghans are going to have to live with that, and accommodate them in some – hopefully small – way if the nation is to survive.

The corollary to this reality is that, sooner or later, we will have to start talking with the Taliban, if we aren't doing so already. Peace will not be possible if all we do is bomb and shoot them. And for all the violence that's been an unavoidable feature of the campaign in Afghanistan, the priority of the British mission there remains improving the lives of the civilian population through reconstruction and aid. For that effort to take root, though, in the end a settlement is needed that will allow all Afghans, regardless of background or outlook, to live together. I can see no other realistic way forward.

From flash to bang, from inception to going out of theatre, seemed a very short period, and the squadron acquitted itself extremely well. We arrived in theatre at a time when the tempo of flying operations was at the highest ever recorded in Afghanistan. We were thrust in cold to start flying at that rate, a rate that had surged for only a month, and managed to sustain it for a further three months.

Looking back at the Afghanistan det, I knew that if it had been a steep learning curve for the whole squadron it was particularly so for the pilots. Most of them had to – for the very first time – put all their training into effect in an extremely hostile environment, delivering live weapons and killing insurgents. No matter how hard anyone trained or practised, the thought that on every sortie there was a good chance that your actions would result in the deaths of maybe dozens of human beings in a split second was sobering in the extreme. Nobody took this aspect of their mission lightly, but at the same time they realized that the squadron was at war and fighting an enemy that would give no quarter. 'Kill or be killed' sounds trite, but in Kandahar and Helmand in the first decade of the twenty-first century it is absolutely true.

In this environment I saw the personnel of 800 NAS grow up very quickly, from simple necessity. The reality of daily combat became almost routine. Nearly every day, rockets or mortars would land somewhere on Kandahar

Airfield. Running to the air-raid shelters became a part of our daily – or, just as often, nightly – existence. Repatriation ceremonies were far too common. For every single person in the squadron, the war in Afghanistan was very real.

The squadron's pilots were right on the front line. Every day we would fly another sortie to help a foot patrol under fire somewhere. We'd drop another bomb and perhaps a dozen Taliban fighters would be killed. Daily combat had become a part of our lives, an experience indelibly etched on our memories, an experience that we knew would colour our judgement and attitudes for the rest of our lives.

On 31 March 2009 the Harrier force should be finished in Afghanistan, when it's due to be replaced by a Tornado detachment. After four relentless years in theatre, the decision was made to give Joint Force Harrier a break.

There were only ever two possible replacements. The first was the new Eurofighter Typhoon, but despite an announcement in the summer of 2008 that the Typhoon FGR4 was operational in an air-to-ground role, I'd be surprised if it was yet ready to flourish in an environment like Afghanistan. As with the French Rafale, it's still relatively early days in the development of what is clearly a hugely impressive aircraft.

So the only other option was the long-serving Tornado. Like the Harrier, the Tornado, which first entered service in the early eighties, has become progressively more capable throughout its service life. RAF Tornado GR4 squadrons have been flying in support of coalition troops in Iraq since 2003. They are extremely competent and experienced operators, but the capabilities offered by the two aircraft are really very different. One was designed from the outset as a deployed CAS aircraft, the other as a low-level straight-line bomber. But the Tornado's two-man crew may be a real asset. And its internal cannon may also prove extremely useful – and was something which Harrier pilots had to manage without. But Joint Force Harrier will be a hard act to follow. And Afghanistan is an unforgiving theatre. I wish them luck – and every success.

My own personal prediction is that, following the planned three-year Tornado deployment, we'll see the Harriers sent straight back afterwards, although the jury's out on whether it will be Typhoon or Harrier. And there's certainly every probability that the Typhoons will be tasked in a higher-priority scenario, being, as it will be by then, the UK's primary multi-role aircraft. At least, that is, until the F-35 comes into service.

In the new Harrier GR9 the Fleet Air Arm is flying what is arguably the best Close Air Support platform in the world. Previously it was second only to the A-10, and now it's on a par with the famous (and bloody ugly) Warthog, because we now have the helmet-mounted cueing system. Harrier pilots can look out of the window at a target and instead of having to point a sensor at it, we can just click a button on the throttle. This enters the target we're looking at directly into the weapon system. It makes a huge difference. The speed at which Joint Force

Harrier is now able to bring weapons to bear on a target is staggering.

The aircraft is also getting an upgrade of its self-defence suite – real state-of-the-art stuff. And to be introduced before long are a data link system using Link 16 – by allowing different assets to share information, this ensures more effective cooperation – and a short-range data link for communicating with troops on the ground. From that point on, I don't believe there will be a more capable CAS platform than the Harrier anywhere in the world.

It's also worth saying that while the A-10 is an awesome piece of machinery, it does have one significant disadvantage in that it is so slow (as well as ugly). It can only travel at about 240 knots with all its gear on. That's slower than a Second World War Spitfire. At full chat the Harrier can get to the scene of the action at over 500 knots. Or, put another way, in half the time. That difference could be crucial.

On 13 January 2007 800 Naval Air Squadron returned to the UK. Since then the squadron has been back out to the theatre, leaving Britain on 1 October that year and coming home on 2 February 2008. The squadron did yet another detachment to Afghanistan at the end of July. The timing on this occasion was shifted slightly so that the squadron didn't have to spend its third successive Christmas in Kandahar.

What of the future for the Fleet Air Arm? On 9 March 2007 elements of both 800 and 801 NAS combined to form Naval Strike Wing, which in turn is one of the three squadrons that comprise Joint Force Harrier, flying the GR7 and GR9. For the next six to eight years, until the two new aircraft carriers – the CVF class, scheduled to enter service in 2014 and 2016 – are commissioned, Joint Force Harrier will represent the entirety of Royal Naval fixed-wing aviation.

But the Fleet Air Arm will soon start to expand again, with the arrival of two new 65,000-ton carriers: HMS *Queen Elizabeth* and HMS *Prince of Wales*. These will be the two biggest ships ever commissioned into the Royal Navy and three times larger than the current CVS-class ships. The Air Group they're expected to carry will include forty F-35 Joint Strike Fighter aircraft. The F-35 Lightning II is a supersonic, single-seat, single-engine, multi-role aircraft that can be configured for Close Air Support, tactical bombing and air-to-air combat. It is an awesomely capable aircraft that will take the Fleet Air Arm and the RAF, which will also operate it, well into the twenty-first century. I won't be around to fly it – I'll be behind a desk somewhere by the time it's in service – but I hope the new aircraft will be flown by men of the same calibre that I had the privilege to fly with in Afghanistan.

With this carrier and aircraft combination, the Royal Navy and Fleet Air Arm will once more have the capability of operating anywhere in the world, against any enemy in the air or on the ground, in any combat role and in any theatre. After the traumas associated with the demise of the Sea Harrier, the future of the Fleet Air Arm once again looks bright. I hope it will be said that, in the lean years, we kept the flag flying. And that, while small in number, the Navy's fixed-wing pilots, flying within Joint Force Harrier, made our own invaluable contribution to the Fleet Air Arm's proud history.

Epilogue

The sun glinted off the glossy grey wings as I pulled the
Sea Fury into a loop over the flat Somerset countryside.
I looked ahead through the blur of the propeller as I
rehearsed my display routine for the forthcoming summer
air display season. My thoughts returned to the Harrier in
Afghanistan, then back to the beautiful old machine I was
now wheeling around the sky. For all their differences,
there were also some striking similarities.

Designed in the 1940s, the magnificent Hawker Sea
Fury FB11 represented the pinnacle of piston-engined
fighter design. And it was one of the most successful and
popular aircraft ever operated by the post-war Fleet Air
Arm. It was combat-proven too. And during the Korean
War, on one of the few occasions when a piston-engined
fighter got the better of a faster and more modern jet, an
802 NAS Sea Fury shot down a MiG-15. But throughout
that conflict the Fleet Air Arm flew the Sea Fury not as a
fighter, but as a ground-attack aircraft in support of British
and UN troops on the ground.

So, although the Sea Fury and the Harrier GR7 were
separated by half a century of aeronautical development,
they carried out precisely the same role, for the same air
arm, in a distant and unexpected Asian war. And both,
bizarrely, had been designed by the same man – Sir Sydney
Camm of Hawker Siddeley. Camm died in 1966, but the

original Hawker P1127 Kestrel, the forerunner of the Harrier, was designed by him. The GR7 we'd flown in Afghanistan was recognizably the same basic aircraft.

Sir Sydney would have been staggered to discover where his design for the Kestrel would eventually lead – the Harrier GR7 and GR9 were a quantum leap into the future – but I think he would have been proud that the basic *rightness* of that first revolutionary little vertical take-off design had survived and thrived into the twenty-first century.

History, somebody once said, is the past coming in through a new door, and I knew exactly what that meant. I was in the fortunate position of being able to fly not only the Royal Navy's current Close Air Support aircraft in combat, but also, with the Royal Navy's Historic Flight, one of the last airworthy survivors of an earlier era, an outstanding aircraft, that had performed exactly the same role.

The first Naval Strike Wing detachment to Afghanistan had been a success. We had maintained the required level of serviceability; we had launched on time for all our sorties, including getting the GCAS scramble aircraft off the ground in well under the specified minimum time; and we had hit our targets accurately. We had undeniably saved the lives of a great many coalition troops of several nations. During our four months in theatre we had suffered neither casualties nor mechanical failures, and had been able to hand over the aircraft to 1 (F) Squadron RAF without excuse or caveat.

It had been a highly successful operation. And the detachment had, I believed, fully validated both 800 Naval

Air Squadron in the Close Air Support role and the Joint Force Harrier concept itself.

The rich, nostalgic thunder of the Sea Fury's engine brought me back to the task in hand. I was pushed back and down into my seat as I pulled the big old fighter out of the loop and brought her roaring down the centreline of Yeovilton's main runway. The wonderful noise of the Bristol Centaurus eighteen-cylinder radial engine echoed off the buildings and hangars as I beat past them. The last time I'd flown so low, so fast and so purposefully, I was strapped to the ejection seat of a Harrier GR7 streaking across Taliban positions in the remote battlefields of Afghanistan. Despite a sharp reduction in our front-line strength since the heyday of the Sea Fury, the Fleet Air Arm was still in the business of flying fixed-wing combat aircraft. Still doing the job.

I pulled back on the stick and pointed the blunt nose of the old warbird skyward, soaring high over the familiar tower of Ilchester church to the west of the airfield. It was good to be back home. And good to be back in the air.

Glossary

A-10 Warthog	American Close Air Support aircraft
AMRAAM (AIM-120)	Advanced Medium Range Air-to-Air Missile
ANA	Afghan National Army
ANP	Afghan National Police
Antonov An-24	Twin-turbo prop Russian transport aircraft
AOC	Air Officer Commanding
ATC	Air traffic control
ATCO	Air traffic controller
ATIS	Air Traffic Information Service
ATO	Air Tasking Order
B-1 Lancer	American four-engined heavy bomber
BDA	Battle Damage Assessment
Bingo	A pre-briefed amount of fuel that allows for a safe return to base
Blue Vixen	The Sea Harrier FA2's radar
BM-12	Russian-made unguided rockets
Boeing AH-64 Apache	Helicopter gunship operated in Afghanistan by the Americans, British and Dutch
KC-135	American aerial refuelling tanker
Brimstone	British air-launched anti-armour missile
Browning 9mm	British handgun
C-130 Hercules	Ubiquitous American-built four-turboprop transport aircraft used by air forces throughout the world including the RAF

C-17 Globemaster III	Large American four-jet transport aircraft also operated by the RAF
C2	Command and Control
Cab	Fleet Air Arm slang for aircraft
CAG	Commander Air Group
Camp Bastion	Largest British base in Afghanistan
CAOC	Combined Air Operations Centre
Casevac	Casualty evacuation
CFIT	Controlled flight into terrain
CH-47 Chinook	American-built twin-rotor transport helicopter also operated by the RAF
Chock-head	Royal Navy slang for an aircraft handler
CIA	Central Intelligence Agency
Clear hot; in hot	Cleared to drop live weapons
Click	One kilometre
CO	Commanding Officer
Crab	Royal Navy slang for the RAF
CRV-7	Canadian designed air-launched unguided missile
CVF	Future British Aircraft Carrier
CVS	British Anti-submarine Carrier
DEA	Drug Enforcement Administration
det	detachment
DIFAC	Dining facility
ECM	Electronic Counter-measures
F-15 Eagle	American twin-engined air-superiority and strike aircraft
F-16 Fighting Falcon	Single-engined American-built multi-role fighter
F-35 Lightning II	Single-engined American-designed strike fighter. Currently under development and expected to go into service with both the RAF and Royal Navy

FAC	Forward air controller
FAA	Fleet Air Arm
Fast air	Fixed-wing close-air support
FDO	Flight Deck Officer
FLIR	Forward Looking Infra-red
Flyco	Flying control – aboard an aircraft carrier
FOB	Forward Operating Base
FOD	Foreign object damage
GBU	Guided Bomb Unit
GCAS	Ground Close Air Support
GCAS 120	Ground Close Air Support on two hours notice
'g'	Unit of acceleration. One 'g' equals the force of gravity
GLO	Ground Liaison Officer
Goofer	Navy slang for spectator watching air operation aboard an aircraft carrier
GPS	Global Positioning System
Green Death	Royal Marines
Harrier	Anglo-American vertical/short take-off and landing ground attack aircraft, includes GR7, GR9 and AV-8B (flown by the US Marine Corps in Afghanistan)
HIG	Hezb-es-Islami Gulbuddin
HUD	Cockpit head-up display
Huey	Bell UH-1 utility helicopter
Humvee	High Mobility Multi-purpose Wheeled Vehicle (HMMVE) – essentially a modern day jeep used by US forces
ICOM	Intercept Communications
IED	Improvised Explosive Device
IFF	Identification Friend or Foe
Ilyushin Il-76	Russian-built four-engined jet transport aircraft

IR	Infra-red
ISAF	International Security Assistance Force
ISI	Inter-Services Intelligence. The Pakistani security service
JDAM	Joint-Attack Direct Munition. A guidance kit that converts dumb bombs into smart ones guided by inertial navigation and GPS.
JFH	Joint Force Harrier
Joint Strike Fighter	F-35 Lightning II. Currently under development for air forces around the world
JTAC	Joint Terminal Air Controller
KIA	Killed in Action
LAV	Light Armoured Vehicle
Maverick (AGM-65)	Air-launched anti-armour guided missile
MAW	Missile approach warning system
Medevac	Medical evacuation
Mi-8 Hip	Russian-made transport helicopter
Mil Mi-24 Halo	Russian-made transport helicopter. The world's biggest
Mirage 2000	French single-engined, delta-winged strike fighter
Mirage F1	French single-engined multi-role fighter
MPRS	Multi-Point Refuelling System
MRE	Meals Ready to Eat
Mud-mover	Military slang for ground-attack pilots
NAS	Naval Air Squadron
NATO	North Atlantic Treaty Organisation
Nimrod	Four-engined British anti-submarine and surveillance
NVGs	Night vision goggles
OC	Officer Commanding

OP	Observation Post
Ops	Operations
PGM	Precision Guided Munition
Pickle button	Weapons release button
MAW	Missile approach warning
PNB	Power nozzle braking
QFI	Qualified Flying Instructor
QRF	Quick Reaction Force
Radalt	Radar altimeter
Rafale	Twin-engined French land and carrier-based multi-role fighter aircraft
RIP	Relief in Place
RM	Royal Marine
RPG	Rocket-propelled grenade
RTB	Return to Base
RWR	Radar warning receiver
SA-7 Grail	Russian-made hand-held surface-to-air missile
SA-14 Gremlin	Russian-made hand-held surface-to-air missile
SAM	Surface-to-air missile
SAS	Special Air Service
SBS	Special Boat Service
Sea Harrier	British vertical/short take-off and landing carrierborne multi-role fighter aircraft
Shar	Fleet Air Arm slang for the Sea Harrier
Sidewinder (AIM-9)	Heatseeking short-range air-to-air missile
SITREP	Situation report
SMS	Stores Management System
Squinto	Squadron Intelligence Officer
Stinger	American-made handheld surface-to-air missile

Super Étendard	French single-engined carrierborne strike aircraft
TACAN	Tactical Air Navigation. Radio-based system provides range and bearing
TACP	Tactical Air Control Party
Targeting pod	Thermal Imaging and Laser Designation (TIALD) system carried on British Harrier GR7s
TIC	Troops in Contact
Tornado F3	Fighter version of the twin-engined swing-wing Tornado strike aircraft
TriStar	Three-engined wide-bodied jet transport and aerial tanker used by the RAF
Typhoon	Twin-engined multi-role fighter
UAV	Unmanned aerial vehicle
USAF	United States Air Force
VBIED	Vehicle-borne Improvised Explosive Device – or car bomb
VFR	Visual Flight Rules
VHF	Very High Frequency radio
VC10	Four-engined British aerial-tanker and transport aircraft operated by the RAF
VMC	Visual meteorogical conditions
Winchester	Out of ammunition
WRB	Weapon-release button. Also know in the Fleet Air Arm as the pickle button

HARRIER GR.7

1 Starboard all-moving tailplane
2 Tailplane composite construction
3 Tail missile warning radar
4 Missile Approach Warning radar equipment module
5 Tail pitch control air value
6 Yaw control air values
7 Tail 'bullet' fairing
8 Reaction control system air ducting
9 Rudder trim actuator
10 Rudder trim tab
11 Rudder composite construction
12 Rudder
13 Antenna
14 Fin-tip aerial fairing

49 Anti-collision light
50 Fuel tank
51 Flap hydraulic actuator
52 Flap hinge fitting
53 Nimonic fuselage heat shield
54 Main undercarriage bay doors (closed after cycling of undercarriage)
55 Flap vane composite construction
56 Flap composite construction

77 Intermediate pylon
78 Pylon attachment joint
79 Reaction control air ducting
80 Chaff/flare dispensers each side of missile pylon
81 Aileron control rod
82 Outrigger hydraulic retraction jack
83 Outrigger leg strut
84 Leg pivot fixing
85 Multi-spar wing construction
86 Leading-edge wing fence
87 Outrigger pylon
88 Missile launch rail
89 AIM-9L Sidewinder air-to-air missile
90 1000 lb (454 kg) retarded HE bomb (free-fall version, alternative)

15 Upper broad band communications antenna
16 Port tailplane
17 Graphite epoxy tailplane skin
18 Port side temperature probe
19 MAD compensator
20 Formation lighting strip
21 Fin construction
22 Fin attachment joint
23 Tailplane pivot sealing plate
24 Aerials
25 Ventral fin
26 Tail bumper
27 Lower broad band communications antenna
28 Tailplane hydraulic jack
29 Heat exchanger air exhaust
30 Aft fuselage frames
31 Rudder hydraulic actuator
32 Avionics equipment air conditioning plant
33 Avionics equipment racks
34 Heat exchanger ram air intake
35 Electrical system circuit breaker panels, port and starboard
36 Avionics equipment
37 Avionics bay access doors, port and starboard
38 Formation-keeping luminous strip
39 Ventral airbrake
40 Airbrake hydraulic jack
41 Avionics equipment racks
42 Fuselage frame and stringer construction
43 Rear fuselage fuel tank
44 Main undercarriage wheelbay
45 Wing-root fillet
46 Wing spar/fuselage attachment joint
47 Water filler cap
48 Engine fire extinguisher bottle

57 Starboard slotted flap, lowered
58 Outrigger wheel fairing
59 Outrigger leg doors
60 Starboard aileron
61 Aileron composite construction
62 Fuel jettison
63 Formation lights

64 Roll control air value
65 Wing-tip fairing
66 Starboard/forward missile warning radar antenna
67 Starboard navigation light
68 Radar warning antenna
69 540 lb (245 kg) low drag HE bomb (retarded version, alternative)
70 Outboard pylon
71 Pylon attachment joint
72 Graphite epoxy composite wing construction
73 Aileron hydraulic actuator
74 Starboard outrigger wheel
75 2.75 in (70 mm) HVAR folding fin rocket
76 Matra 155 rocket launcher (18 rockets)

91 External fuel tank, 300 US gal (250 Imp gal/1351 l)
92 Inboard pylon
93 Aft retracting mainwheels
94 Inboard pylon attachment joint
95 Rear (hot steam) swivelling exhaust nozzle
96 Position of pressure refuelling connection on port side
97 Rear nozzle bearing
98 Centre fuselage flank fuel tank
99 Hydraulic reservoir
100 Nozzle bearing cooling air duct
101 Engine exhaust divider duct

102 Wing panel centre rib
103 Centre section integral fuel tank
104 Port wing integral fuel tank
105 Flap vane
106 Port slotted flap, lowered
107 Outrigger wheel fairing
108 Port outrigger wheel
109 Torque scissor links
110 Port aileron
111 Aileron hydraulic actuator
112 Aileron/air value interconnection
113 Fuel jettison
114 Formation lights
115 Port roll control air value
116 Port/forward missile warning radar antenna

117 Port navigation light
118 Radar warning antenna
119 Reaction control air ducting
120 Vortex generators
121 Fuel pumps
122 Fuel system piping
123 Port wing leading-edge fence
124 Outboard pylon
125 BL755 cluster bombs (maximum load, seven)
126 Intermediate pylon
127 Port outrigger pylon
128 Missile launch rail
129 AIM-9L Sidewinder air-to-air missile

130 Port leading-edge root extension (LERX)
131 Inboard pylon
132 Hydraulic pumps
133 APU intake
134 Gas turbine starter/auxiliary power unit (APU)
135 Alternator cooling air exhaust
136 APU exhaust
137 Engine fuel control unit
138 Engine bay venting ram air intake
139 Rotary nozzle bearing
140 Nozzle fairing construction
141 Ammunition tank, 100 rounds
142 Cartridge case collector box
143 Ammunition feed chute
144 Fuel vent
145 Zero scarf forward (fan air) nozzle
146 Fuselage centreline pylon
147 BL755 cluster bomb
148 Ventral gun pack (two)
149 Aden 25 mm cannon
150 Engine drain mast
151 Hydraulic system ground connections
152 Forward fuselage fuel tank
153 Engine electronic control units

154 Engine accessory equipment gearbox
155 Gearbox-driven alternator
156 Rolls-Royce Pegasus II Mk 105 vectored thrust turbofan
157 Formation-keeping luminous strips
158 Engine oil tank
159 Bleed air spill duct
160 Air conditioning intake scoops
161 Cockpit air conditioning system heat exchanger
162 Engine compressor/fan face
163 Heat exchanger discharge to intake duct
164 Nose undercarriage hydraulic retraction jack
165 Intake blow-in doors

166 Engine bay venting air scoop
167 Cannon muzzle fairing
168 Lift augmentation retractable cross-dam
169 Cross-dam hydraulic jack
170 Nosewheel
171 Nosewheel forks
172 Landing/taxiing lamp
173 Retractable boarding step
174 Nosewheel doors (closed after cycling of undercarriage)
175 Nosewheel door jack
176 Boundary layer bleed air duct
177 Nose undercarriage wheelbay
178 Kick-in boarding steps
179 Cockpit rear pressure bulkhead
180 Starboard side console panel
181 Martin-Baker Mk 12 ejection seat
182 Safety harness
183 Ejection seat headrest
184 Port engine air intake
185 Probe hydraulic jack
186 Retractable in-flight refuelling probe (bolt-on pack)
187 Cockpit canopy cover
188 Miniature detonating cord (MDC) canopy breaker
189 Canopy arch frame
190 Engine throttle and nozzle angle control levers
191 Pilot's head-up display
192 Instrument panel
193 Moving map display
194 Control column
195 Central warning system panel
196 Cockpit pressure floor
197 Underfloor control runs
198 Formation lighting strips
199 Aileron trim actuator
200 Rudder pedals
201 Cockpit section composite construction
202 Instrument panel shroud
203 One-piece wrap-around windscreen panel
204 Ram air intake (cockpit fresh air)
205 Front pressure bulkhead
206 Incidence vane
207 Air data computer
208 Pitot head
209 Lower IFF aerial
210 Nose pitch control air valve
211 Pitch trim control actuator
212 Video map generator, GEC-Marconi Avionics
213 Upper IFF aerial
214 Yaw vane
215 GEC-Marconi Avionics FLIR
216 FLIR processor
217 EW transmitter
218 FLIR aperturer
219 ARBS equipment
220 EW antennae, port and starboard
221 Hughes Angle Rate Bombing Sight (ARBS)
222 ARBS glazed aperture